Craig Hoyle grew up in Invercargill wi
Exclusive Brethren. Separated fron.
attended Brethren-only schooling and worked in his family's
tyre shop. After facing interrogations and conversion therapy
for his sexuality, he was excommunicated from the Brethren
and lost his family in 2009. Today he is chief news director
for the *Sunday Star-Times*. He has worked for newsrooms
such as TV3 and RadioLive, and behind the scenes on
current affairs shows including *60 Minutes*. He lives in
Tāmaki Makaurau, Aotearoa (Auckland, New Zealand).

CRAIG HOYLE

Excommunicated

A multigenerational
story of leaving
the Exclusive Brethren

HarperCollins*Publishers*

This book is a work of non-fiction, based on the author's memories, research and family documents. The names of some people have been changed.

HarperCollins_Publishers_
Australia • Brazil • Canada • France • Germany • Holland • India
Italy • Japan • Mexico • New Zealand • Poland • Spain • Sweden
Switzerland • United Kingdom • United States of America

First published in 2023
by HarperCollins_Publishers_ (New Zealand) Limited
Unit D1, 63 Apollo Drive, Rosedale, Auckland 0632, New Zealand
harpercollins.co.nz

A catalogue record for this book is available from the National Library of New Zealand

ISBN 978 1 7755 4201 8 (paperback)
ISBN 978 1 7754 9232 0 (ebook)

Cover design: Design by Committee
Cover images courtesy of the author
Typeset in Bembo Std by Kirby Jones

Printed and bound by CPI Group (UK) Ltd, Croydon, CR0 4YY

Dedicated to Grandpa George,
who stayed true to himself despite huge costs.

PROLOGUE

GRANDMA EDITH SHOOK WITH WRENCHING SOBS AS WE stood on her doorstep. It was only the second time I'd seen her cry; the first was when she'd received news of her mother's death. This was so much worse. I knew that after this goodbye, I would never see Grandma again.

Edith had tried to keep it together when I arrived at her house that overcast Saturday afternoon. She was speaking with another Brethren woman at her doorstep, and I stood to one side as their conversation wrapped up. Grandma broke down as soon as we were alone. She wept as she said she wasn't allowed to welcome me into her neatly arranged home; she'd been told I was about to be placed in the first stage of excommunication, which meant she had to sever contact. There would be no cup of tea, no biscuits and no loving conversation at her kitchen table.

Her soft woollen cardigan and curled white hair stood out sharply through my own tears. I told her I wasn't officially excommunicated yet and begged her for one last hug. Sobbing even harder, she threw her arms around me. This was the last time we'd embrace, the last time she would speak to me without fear of retribution from the church, and the last time I would listen to her hearing aid beep because I had my head in the wrong place as we hugged.

Edith, my dad's mum, was heartbroken. She spoke of how the devil kept taking away her family: her grandfather, her parents, her husband and two of her children – and now here I was, the first grandchild she would be forced to disown. 'How could the devil be so cruel?'

But it wasn't the devil who was forcing us apart: it was the Exclusive Brethren.

On that Saturday in Invercargill, a blustery city at the southernmost end of New Zealand's South Island, I walked away from a Brethren family history that spanned seven generations and almost two centuries. I was nineteen, and life in the church was all I had ever known. Like my parents, and their parents, and their parents before them, I had been born into a system that demanded loyalty and obedience. To walk away was an act of desperation, but I knew it was the only way I could ever be true to myself.

The night before, Friday, 24 April 2009, I had come out as gay to my six younger brothers and sisters. The impact was immediate – and even more catastrophic than I'd imagined. I knew the church condemned homosexuality, and there was no future in being gay in the Brethren, but all the same I was stunned by how quickly my family turned against me. One of my sisters shut herself in her room and cried. My youngest sister, just nine, was confused about what being gay meant. My mother, trying and failing to stop the spread of information, intervened with a sharp retort: 'He doesn't love you, and that's why he's being so cruel.'

When I woke the next morning, my parents were waiting for me in the kitchen. They broke the news that my five youngest siblings had been removed from the family home and sent to stay with other Brethren households because I was a bad influence. My parents refused to say where any of them were.

Dad told me I needed to find somewhere else to live: 'You're not welcome here.' I was too shocked to process what was happening, hearing his words through a fog as my heart raced. He added that the local priests wanted to speak with me urgently, in the next fifteen minutes.

That jolted me out of my daze. I had unfinished business, and there was no way I'd be meeting with the priests so soon. I told Dad they could go stick it.

I realised I had one final chance to say goodbye to people I loved, before excommunication crashed down. For the rest of that Saturday I drove around Invercargill, gripping the steering wheel with shaky hands, as I paid visits to friends and relatives. It was as though I was about to die.

My aunt's anguished cry still rings in my ears. When I said I'd come to say goodbye, she wailed 'No!' and threw her arms around me as she burst into tears. She and my uncle then pleaded with me to change my mind, to stop being gay, to follow Brethren teachings and to think of all the kindness I'd been shown by the church. The same thing happened with all my relatives and old friends. But there was no sense in arguing over church teachings: I knew where their loyalties lay, so I took one final opportunity to show my love. Again and again, I wept as I pleaded with them to remember the good times we'd shared.

Once my farewell tour was over and the sun was setting, I agreed to the priests' demand for a meeting; I had said my goodbyes and it was time to confront them head-on. As I sat with my back to the wall in a small cluttered study at a priest's house, two middle-aged men by the window confirmed that I was to be placed in the first stage of excommunication.

I asked them what they were going to tell the congregation about me. One priest replied that the real issue at hand was 'defilement of young people'. In their eyes, telling my siblings I was gay was more of a sin than being gay itself.

Anger coursed through my veins. 'Tell them the truth,' I said. 'I'm not ashamed of being gay and I'm prepared to let everyone know, and that's why I'm being expelled.'

A priest snapped back, 'What we say is our matter and doesn't concern you!'

'Well, actually, it does concern me, because it's me you're talking about. It just goes to show that everything I've been told is true – once you're expelled from the church, the gloves come off and it's no more Mr Nice Guy from the Brethren.'

The priest snorted derisively and rolled his eyes.

'I'm sick to death of listening to your crap,' I exclaimed as I stood up, 'so please don't contact me again.' I slammed the door on my way out.

Back at my parents' home that evening, I collapsed into bed and cried. My whole body shook, and there was a dreadful pain in my chest where my heart felt as though it was being ripped apart. Months would pass before I could feel emotions again. My life as I knew it was over.

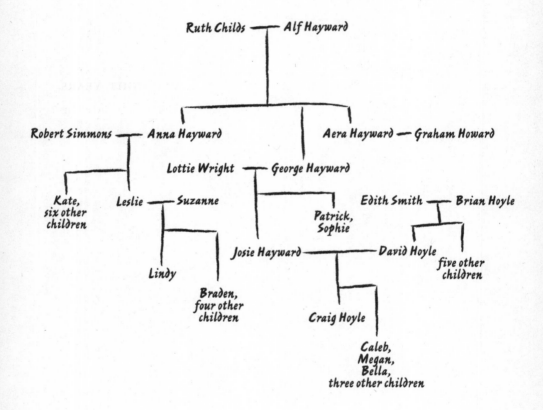

I.

DURING THE SUMMER OF 1998, WHEN I WAS EIGHT YEARS old, my five younger siblings and I clustered excitedly beside the kitchen bench as Aunty Sophie plugged a cassette player into the wall socket. It was a sunny afternoon, and we'd been racing up and down on the flying fox Dad had built for us in the backyard. We were streaked with dirt and grime – keeping us all clean was a tall order – and I scuffed my toes across the scratched linoleum as the tape clunked into place.

This was a big novelty. We weren't usually allowed to listen to music, and we didn't even own a cassette player; this one was borrowed from an older Brethren couple around the corner who used it to listen to recordings of church services. I wondered if they'd have loaned it to us if they'd known it would be used for playing music. According to Mum, just this once we could bend the rules, but it was best we didn't tell anyone.

Sophie had found the tapes in a cupboard at home in Wellington and brought them with her on this visit to Invercargill, but she hadn't told me or my siblings what was on them. All we knew was that she and Mum clearly thought they were important. To me, they were even more exciting than the flying fox. I was amazed that entire speeches and songs could be stored on thin strips of plastic film. Our lives were almost completely free of modern technology, so this was an eye-opening window to another world.

As my aunty hit 'play', the tape clicked and whirred. A hush fell over the kitchen. Then a soulful melody began, like nothing I'd ever heard. The notes of an instrument swooped through the song; Mum and Sophie explained it was a Hawaiian guitar, with a small steel bar used to pluck out the gliding sounds much loved on the islands. I closed my eyes and imagined a tropical beach with palm trees and scorched white sand. And then, an astonishing revelation: the person playing these other-worldly songs, Mum said, was her own mother – Grandma Lottie. I stared in shock.

Lottie was deeply religious, even by Brethren standards, and I couldn't fathom her being behind something so beautiful and exotic. Sophie explained that Lottie had a complicated relationship with her beloved guitar; although she loved playing it, she worried her music was coming between her and God. At one point she feared her guitar was becoming an idol and stopped playing it for years.

In the cassette recordings, she wasn't performing alone: a man whose voice I didn't recognise was playing the piano alongside her, their voices raised together in song. Her accompanist sang in a rich baritone, and their harmonies tugged at the heartstrings. A faraway look crossed my mother's face.

Our aunty warned we needed to be careful that Lottie didn't hear the recordings: 'They'll make her cry.'

*

My earliest childhood memories are a whirlwind of church.

Back then, we lived in Hamilton, an inland city on the banks of the Waikato River about a hundred kilometres south of Auckland. My dad's family, the Hoyles, had been attending Brethren meetings there for generations, since my great-grandfather purchased a family farm on land forcibly seized from the local Tainui tribe as retribution for their supposed rebellion against the Crown. A breakaway Christian sect first established in Britain and Ireland, now with around 55,000 members worldwide, the Brethren movement had been in New Zealand since the 1850s. Like my grandfather and father, I grew up knowing that attendance at Brethren meetings wasn't just expected: it was mandated. And there were a lot of them. Most nights we gathered at the main hall on Peachgrove Road, nestled between the Veterans Home and the train tracks. Freight trains roared past. Like all Brethren meeting rooms around the world, this hall had no windows because the church had banned them many years earlier to 'keep out the world'.

Every day of the week, my family trundled along to church in our grey Toyota Hiace van. When we weren't at the main Peachgrove hall, we attended communion services and prayer meetings at a smaller brick meeting room on Urlich Avenue near where we lived. Once a week there were services in Tauranga – the drive an interminable slog for a young child, winding up and over the Kaimai Range to the coastal Bay of Plenty – and occasionally we'd go even further afield to special meetings in Auckland, a centre of Brethren power in New Zealand.

The Peachgrove hall had a standard Brethren design: concentric circles of seating that rose in shallow tiers from a central front row where the elders would sit. The more important you were, the closer you sat to the inner circle – providing, of course, that you were a man. Women were relegated to the back seats, well behind even the least important men. Very young children sat with the women, and then when boys were old enough, usually around three or four, they graduated to sitting with the men. The 'sisters', as we called them, were forbidden from speaking publicly in church aside from announcing hymns, and reciting marital vows on their wedding day. The meetings were astonishingly dull, and the prayer language was archaic: thee, thou, thine. I didn't have a clue what was going on, and the expectation was that we kids would sit in silence for an hour until it was over. The only bright spot was that we were allowed to play in the yard with our friends and cousins after services had ended.

Sunday was the most demanding day of the week, with four different meetings. The communion service was at the ungodly hour of 6 am; many years earlier, a church leader in New York had moved the time from 9 am as he had a flight to catch that day, and somehow 6 am became permanent for all Sunday services across the world. Communion is the sacred Christian ritual of consuming bread and wine that represent the body and blood of Jesus Christ. We kids were expected to start drinking communion wine at a very young age. Brethren belief held that if a baby reached out when the bread and wine were passed around, they had been moved by God to ask for communion; a large chalice would be raised to their lips for them to take a sip, and their parents would celebrate. This childhood drinking sometimes came with disastrous consequences: early one Sunday morning, I was mortified when my young fingers slipped and I sloshed cheap red port wine over the person beside me.

Even by Brethren standards, my childhood churchgoing was relentless. Weekday services were mostly held in the evenings, and many young Brethren kids were kept at home by their mothers for at least a few nights a week, to catch up on sleep and take a break from the endless cycle – but not us. Dad insisted we all attend every meeting, in a rigid tradition passed down from his own father. Our family was well known for our attendance – come hell or high water, we were there, and even sickness wasn't enough to keep us away. One Saturday morning when I was three or four, I protested bitterly that I wasn't feeling well before we left for church. Dad bundled me into the van anyway. When we arrived at the Peachgrove meeting room, I vomited into a drain along the north-facing wall, deeply embarrassed as Brethren walked past with raised eyebrows. Dad didn't care; to him, there was nothing more important than going to church.

*

Outside church, we grew up in a warm familial embrace. Grandma Edith lived just down the road from us on Dermont Street, a quiet cul-de-sac in Hamilton's urban south where it was safe for kids to race their toys on the road. We knew we could wander up any time to see Edith and try our luck for chocolate biscuits, and if she wasn't home there were cousins our age living just across the road. I loved my stout-armed teddy called Honey, hand-stitched by Edith, and there was great excitement when she made a matching bear for my younger brother Caleb.

'What are you going to call him?' I asked.

Caleb jumped with joy: 'Peanut, like the sandwiches Mum makes!' Honey and peanut butter were our favourite combo, and it made perfect sense for our teddy bears to be named in their honour.

Grandma Lottie's visits from Wellington were anticipated with excitement – 'It's so good to see you, laddie,' she would always say. We had dozens of uncles and aunts – the brothers and sisters of our parents, our grandparents, and even our great-grandparents – and an overwhelming number of cousins, and family connections sprawled and twisted across cities and generations. On visits to Auckland we'd stay with Anna and Rob, my great-aunt and great-uncle on Mum's side, and a whole other circle of cousins emerged. Their grandchildren Lindy and Braden were around my age, and we played and fought in Anna and Rob's steep wooded Hillsborough backyard. On one visit there, I allowed Rob the honour of naming a stuffed toy my parents had brought home for me after attending church meetings in Australia, and Wally the Wombat joined Honey the Bear as part of my bedtime routine.

I was hazy on how all these people fitted into our lives. For more than a century the same Brethren families had intermarried – cousins were not permitted to wed, but, even so, genetic connections had crisscrossed into a complex web. Some families were my cousins three or four times over through different ancestral lines, and of the eight thousand or so Exclusive Brethren in New Zealand, more than five thousand were our direct genetic relatives. All of us, we believed, were brothers and sisters in the Lord's eyes.

A never-ending stream of Brethren passed through our roomy white weatherboard home in Dermont Street, where ruru owls hooted after dark in the gully behind this otherwise quiet backwater. My parents, David and Josie, young and full of life, kept up a tireless schedule of Brethren dinners and social events – Mum bustling in the kitchen preparing meals with the other women, while Dad was pouring drinks and holding earnest conversation with their husbands. Sometimes, if the weather allowed, we'd move outside to sit around a brazier or bonfire; young people carefully segregated to make sure the boys and girls weren't getting too close to each other. Brethren families were expected to host each other like this outside of church, but we weren't supposed to show favouritism: Mum and Dad dutifully kept a list to make sure all the local Brethren received an equal number of meal invitations to our home each year.

Mum's fun-loving humour balanced out Dad's serious religious air. Before they met, his peers had wondered whether he would ever find a wife; he'd had non-Hodgkin lymphoma at twenty and after recovering from the cancer retreated to a spiritual outlook bordering on monasticism. Then through the church he'd met Mum, a bright, bubbly, outgoing twenty-year-old, almost five years his junior, the chalk to his cheese, always laughing.

My parents, who both played piano and guitar, found common ground in their shared love of music. It was particularly an outlet for Dad, who would sit at the piano and bash out hits like Paul Simon's 'Kodachrome', his fingers, calloused from plumbing and farming, thumping out a boogie beat at Saturday night singalongs. The Brethren had a complicated relationship with music – popular songs were periodically banned, but by the time I was a child it was generally considered acceptable to learn to play them from sheet music. Brethren would pick away at songs like John Denver's 'Take Me Home, Country Roads', coming up with rhythms that were nothing like the original. But prerecorded tracks were forbidden.

One of my favourite baby pictures shows me sitting on Dad's lap as he plays the piano. Wearing blue jeans and a blue pinstripe T-shirt, he's completely absorbed as his tanned and freckled arms loop around me to the keys. I'm dribbling slightly onto a hand-stitched patchwork bib protecting a light blue jumpsuit. My deep blue eyes are opened wide with excitement, and I'm beaming from ear to ear.

But I had to grow up fast, learning from an early age that I was expected to pull my weight in the family. Birth control was forbidden, and Mum was pregnant again by the time my first tooth came in. My brother Caleb was born when I was just eleven months old, meaning Mum had to wean me early so she could start breastfeeding the newborn. Another brother and then a sister followed in quick succession, with Mum juggling four preschoolers for almost a year before I started my education at Hamilton's Melville Primary. There were more raised eyebrows at the rapid expansion of our family; the only form of acceptable contraception was abstinence, so couples who had a large number of children close together were sometimes seen as being uncontrolled. Mum was hurt when news of her fourth pregnancy was met with an eye roll by an older Brethren woman who often helped care for us: 'Pregnant again, another typical Hoyle.' When we went to town, I, the four-year-old, was expected to carry the baby while Mum hung on to the two toddlers.

Mum had a honey-coloured guitar and would sing us to sleep after we'd been tucked in. This was pretty much the only time we heard her play; she was usually too busy in the kitchen to get her guitar out at Brethren social gatherings. One of the songs she strummed was Hank Thompson's 1956 country ballad 'The Blackboard of My Heart'. The chorus mystified me when I first heard it. The singer talks about his heart as though it's a blackboard that once had 'I love you' written on it. Now his tears have washed the words away, and it's too late for him to write them there again. At the end of the song, Mum stopped to answer my questions about blackboards and explained how chalk could be dusted away. She leaned across for a reassuring hug and told me, 'The words "I love you" are written on the blackboard of my heart with permanent marker and can't ever be removed.'

*

In 1994, when I was five, our family left Hamilton as part of a nationwide redistribution of Brethren families. The mid-1990s saw a slew of church assemblies starting across New Zealand, and members were encouraged to leave the comfort of their established meetings and set out to meet a test of faith. Dad loved a good religious challenge; this sort of thing was right up his alley, and he said he'd received a message from God that he and his family were to move to Invercargill. The Southland city seemed a world away from Hamilton; New Zealand's southernmost centre, it is literally at the other end of the country, distant, cold and dreary. But this was a very 'Dad' thing to do: choose the bleakest possible path as a demonstration of loyalty to the Brethren. Invercargill, its drizzle and gloom aside, was a chance for a fresh start for a family overshadowed by the clouds of excommunication.

Our trusty Hiace van took us 1500 kilometres south, where we set about building a new life in a four-bedroom brick-and-concrete bungalow on a quiet, hedge-lined suburban crescent. Southland's rolling green pastures looked much the same as those of Waikato, albeit noticeably colder. Dad once again found work as a plumber, before going out on his own with a tyre shop.

The move was a lot for a five-year-old to take in: new friends, new house, new school. Even more daunting was the task of fitting into a different Brethren social structure. In those early days, the assembly in Invercargill existed in a state of flux. Dozens of families were thrown together from around New Zealand, united in solidarity in this distant meeting place and in many cases quietly celebrating a newfound freedom from generations of baggage in their cities of origin. Baggage has a way of following people, though, and a pecking order was quickly established – once again, my family sat somewhere near the bottom, seen as a rabble-rousing crowd of young children close in age. It was a relief when Grandma Edith arrived in Invercargill the following year with her youngest son, pressured by Dad to follow his religious convictions and making her own escape from the past.

As we kept in touch with the family we'd left behind, Aunty Anna became a regular correspondent from Auckland. I loved getting her letters and parcels. Shortly after my ninth birthday, she described the glow-worms in her backyard creek, and when I was ten, she wrote in great detail about a flying fox her youngest son was building in the backyard. Anna felt like a kindred spirit, and I soon came to trust her with my secrets.

Three more siblings arrived in Invercargill: two brothers, then a second sister born the day after I turned eleven – a late birthday present, Mum joked. Seven kids in eleven years. Mum later confided she'd kept things together until number four, after which most semblance of organisation collapsed. Her life, like that of most Brethren women, became a relentless cycle of laundry, meals, school runs and church services, and there was no space for thinking, or questioning, or taking even a moment to breathe and relax. That was never apparent to us kids, though; through a young child's eyes, Mum knew everything and could do anything. She threw all she had into making sure we were happy and loved.

When I had started school at Melville Primary back in Hamilton, I had clung to my cousin Lydia, the only other Brethren kid in my class. It was terrifying to be in a room of outsiders. The other five-year-olds didn't attend meetings with us, and I believed that meant they were a lower class of people. Brethren called them 'worldlies', children of the world. I was never allowed to invite 'worldly' kids home for playdates, and I had to reject invitations to birthday parties or after-school events. We were banned from eating and drinking with the worldlies at school; this was considered a form of fellowship and strictly forbidden under the rigid separation rules, so I spent years trudging home for food at lunchtime.

Once, as a young child, I invited a worldly classmate from up the road to play in our yard, so we could continue the games we'd started in the playground of my Invercargill school. We hid down the side of the house, obscured from view by trees and a concrete fence, and went to work on the tunnels my brothers and I had been digging. I told my classmate to hide or run if Mum appeared, and when she eventually became suspicious about why I was avoiding her – 'What are you doing down there?' – my classmate and I scattered into the bushes. I was later forced to confess that I'd invited a worldly to our home. My new friend never came back after that, although we kept playing together at school.

Grandma Edith was just as rigid with the rules. She'd take me and my siblings to the playground down the road from her house, but we knew we weren't supposed to interact with any non-Brethren children. Grandma would swoop in to take us home if she thought we were being too friendly.

I soon discovered other ways I was different from my worldly classmates. They and almost all other outsiders had boxes called televisions that showed moving pictures. Our neighbour had one in his garage, and if we positioned ourselves just right in the backyard we could catch glimpses of people and places flashing across the screen. We had to be discreet, because Mum and Dad would shout at us if we were caught. Televisions also appeared at school sometimes, when my classmates had to watch what they called videos; my teachers were under strict instructions to remove me from the classroom before pressing play. I burned with shame as I sat in corridors, on benches or even – if there was nowhere else for me to go – with my back turned to the rest of the class, blocking my ears so I wouldn't be polluted. Later, a different kind of boxed technology arrived in the classroom: teachers called them computers, and I was hazily aware of something called the internet that could tell you anything you wanted to know – this, the Brethren proclaimed, was even worse than TV.

The rules shifted and changed over the years, depending on leaders' whims and technological developments, which meant that keeping up with them had become an intricate dance. At one point, a ban had been placed on attending university, which meant Brethren could no longer become doctors, but they generally respected the medical establishment and were allowed to undergo modern treatments. Heart transplants were forbidden, though, and for some strange reason members were allowed to receive blood transfusions but banned from donating blood themselves. A list compiled when I was a kid – 'Rules for the Brethren' – went on page after page detailing all the things that were mandated and forbidden. Not only were Brethren not allowed to listen to the radio or prerecorded music, but even recordings of Brethren – like those I'd heard of Grandma Lottie and her male accompanist – were marginal. Men weren't allowed to have facial hair, and women were supposed to wear silk headscarves whenever they left the family home. Other rules included:

No shared driveways.
No parachute jumping.
No owning dairy farms.
No getting married without priests' consent.
No social contact with anyone outside the church.
No piloting aeroplanes.
No reading novels.
No voting.

No hobbies.

No having lunch at school.

On the rare occasions my parents relented and decided it was OK to go to the beach – usually when it was cold and deserted – we kids weren't allowed out of the car until Dad had checked to make sure there were no scantily clad swimmers nearby. If he spotted someone in a bikini or Speedos, we were bundled straight back home.

Many Brethren obsessions revolved around sex and the notion of purity. Premarital sex was forbidden, as was any kind of kissing, petting and even hand-holding; young people of opposite genders weren't allowed to be alone together, even if they were engaged to be married. According to the church, nobody could be trusted to resist sexual temptation.

The Brethren also paid careful attention to racial purity. Most New Zealand assemblies were exclusively white, and we looked down our noses at Māori people. Racist slurs were commonplace in the church; it was a shock when I later realised there was a smattering of Māori members. I knew there were Brethren assemblies in other countries but I was surprised to learn there were Black Brethren of African descent living in places like the Caribbean, along with a handful of Indian Brethren living in Mumbai. The number of Brethren of East Asian descent – out of a worldwide flock of tens of thousands – could be counted on one hand.

The Brethren justified their ban on what they considered to be interracial marriage by saying it wasn't suitable for people from different cultures to marry and procreate, but this racist doctrine was full of holes. It was fine for a white Brethren member from New Zealand to marry a white member from New York, while that same white New Yorker was banned from marrying a Black person in their local assembly – even if their families had known each other for generations and had much more in common. For the purposes of culture, the Brethren were divided into 'white' and 'everything else', meaning that Indian Brethren could seek out wives among Brethren of African descent. If a white member could prove they had non-white ancestry, they were permitted to marry a non-white member, because, according to the church, the purity of the bloodline had already been tainted; this led white prospective partners of non-white members to scour ancestral records.

It took a few years for me to piece together where all these rules were coming from. As a child, I had a dawning realisation that we all lived in awe of someone called Mr Hales from Sydney. John Hales was the 'Elect Vessel', considered to be God's direct representative on Earth; he was the latest in a long line of Elect Vessels going back to the origins of the church in the 1820s. Disobeying Mr Hales was tantamount to disobeying God himself, our parents told us, when we asked curious questions after church services. 'Mr Hales can do no wrong,' they said. 'There's more chance of the sun not rising than the Elect Vessel failing.'

My dad knew this Mr Hales. When Dad was twenty he'd been to Sydney for cancer treatment, and Mr Hales had driven him around for the afternoon – an 'immense privilege', Dad told us, full of awe, on one of many occasions when he described the encounter. Some of the Elect Vessel's austere religiosity seemed to have rubbed off on Dad.

Directives from Mr Hales were interpreted and enforced by local Brethren leaders, several in each assembly, who were usually referred to as elders or priests despite having had no formal pastoral training. He often went on global tours, where he would lay down instructions for the Brethren he visited. I quickly learned there were harsh consequences for anyone caught breaking rules or ignoring instructions, and my siblings and I became accustomed to people abruptly disappearing from church. One time, Mum had to explain that we weren't allowed to talk to the Brethren family who lived around the corner, because their youngest son was being punished. If we went past their house we had to look straight ahead and avoid eye contact or conversation – a lot to wrap my head around when just a week earlier I'd been building a Lego castle on their kitchen table.

Brethren being punished like this were 'shut up', a form of religious quarantine. The offender would be banned from attending church services, and other Brethren forbidden from having contact with them. It was as though a barrier had been placed over a bridge, preventing anyone from crossing. The offender would be left in limbo while the priests assessed the gravity of their sins and determined whether they were suitably repentant to be allowed back. This could drag on for months or even years.

Being 'withdrawn from' was even worse. If a person was shut up and refused to repent, the priests would move to this second stage. It wasn't just quarantine: it was excommunication, a complete eradication from the Brethren community. The bridge was now burnt down. Afterwards the excommunicated member would be mentioned only in hushed whispers as a warning to others. I got used to seeing pictures that had people cut out of them; a relative's wedding photos had been chopped in half, with the remaining pieces showing a solitary bride. Sometimes, if a sin was considered bad enough – such as adultery or treachery – the priests would skip the shutting-up stage and go straight to withdrawal. Through the 1970s and 1980s, when the Exclusive Brethren were much quicker to withdraw from people, members who had experienced excommunication almost outnumbered those who hadn't. Some of those punished members were readmitted when priests determined they had served their sentence and showed repentance; it was technically possible to come back from being withdrawn from, although much harder than coming back from being shut up. As a child, I wondered what happened when someone came back and their family had already cut them out of pictures. The brutality of those earlier decades had eased somewhat by the time I was a kid in the 1990s, but it was still a very real threat.

Someone who had been excommunicated was called an 'out', a lower class of person than the worldlies. An out who spoke publicly against the Brethren slid down even further and became an 'opposer', the lowest of the low: their destiny was hellfire and brimstone – and there was no return.

If a Brethren member's excommunication was announced during a meeting then the gathered Brethren wouldn't sing a hymn to close the service, as was their normal practice. Excommunication was no time for joyful songs.

When I was in primary school, a local Brethren father was shut up for reasons that were never quite clear to us children. His daughter was in my year level, and while he was confined I was banned from speaking to her, even in the classroom. It didn't matter that Carla hadn't done anything wrong: she was living under the same roof as her father, which meant she was tarnished by association. Her mum, also tarnished, stopped picking up her daughter at the main school entrance when the end-of-day bell rang; the shame of being ignored by other Brethren mothers was too much for her to bear, so she waited for Carla in a back alley on the other side of the school.

My childhood was punctuated by fear that I would be shut up or withdrawn from for some real or perceived transgression. It was generally accepted among the Brethren that no child would face assembly discipline until they reached twelve years old – 'the age of responsibility' – but even that wasn't a hard and fast rule; as a young kid I'd heard of priests in other cities shutting up children as young as nine for being involved in corruption.

The Brethren often told stories of the 'rapture': Jesus would return triumphantly through the clouds and sweep up the faithful to join him in heaven. Anyone found unworthy would be left to suffer the terrors of a godless world before being cast into hell – and I lived in fear that when the rapture came, I would be left behind. In my nightmares, everyone around me would start floating to heaven; I'd frantically jump as high as I could, desperate not to be abandoned, but I never succeeded.

We were all told over and over again that the Exclusive Brethren fellowship was the only place where we would find love and acceptance. The world outside, we heard, was cold and hard, and church leaders told us at meetings that it would 'chew you up and spit you out'. To be cast out into that world was to lose everything – and more than anything, I was terrified of losing the people I loved.

*

'Isn't he just like George?'

Those words were a mystery to me as a child. I had no idea who George might be and even less of a clue as to why people kept comparing me to him. But I quickly learned that being like George wasn't good: it was said when I misbehaved and the adults didn't think young ears were listening.

Headscarved Brethren women had pointed and laughed when I ran away from Mum during a service at Hamilton's Peachgrove hall. It's one of my earliest memories of rebellion – I was a headstrong preschooler trying to escape the tedium of church. Evading attempts at capture, I fled up the main aisle as fast as my short legs would take me, then padded around the outer ring of the hall, looking for a way out. Mum shrank with shame; Dad was furious. My naughtiness at church became a recurring theme, and he would sometimes drag me out kicking and screaming. In the foyer I'd get a dressing-down or a sharp smack – 'Behave yourself!' – before Dad allowed me to return red-eyed and subdued.

My parents weren't the only adults I disobeyed. During a visit to Anna and Rob in Auckland, I refused to get ready for a bath one night. I yelled in protest and wedged myself behind the upstairs toilet. In frustration, after repeated remonstrations, Rob – normally mild and gentle – dragged me out and dropped me fully clothed in the tub, saying, 'You're having a bath whether you like it or not!'

Dad ruled with an iron hand, never afraid to assert what he believed was his God-given dominance as the spiritual head of the household. One evening when I was aged three or four and refusing to settle for the night, Dad tied me to the bed. Being strapped down under the sheets wasn't enough of a deterrent – I dragged the mattress with me as I tried to escape.

It wasn't just us kids under Dad's thumb. I once stood at my bedroom door, watching in fear as Mum was shouted at in the bathroom. I was much too young to understand what was going on, but there were frightening flashes of Dad yelling and Mum crying.

Beyond our restrictive home, my awareness of worldly life had got off to a halting start. In an end-of-year school report when I was seven, my teacher described 'very good writing skills' but commented that my knowledge of current events needed development. It wasn't for lack of interest on my part – those kinds of things were just never discussed at home. I got a kickstart the following year when a team from *The Southland Times* visited the classroom at Surrey Park School in Invercargill. It was my first encounter with journalism, and I soaked up the stories, going on to proudly win the Newspapers in Education Study Award that September. Another few years passed by before I realised the Brethren taught that the press was evil.

At home and at school I pored over encyclopaedias and atlases, soaking up stories of faraway lands. This was fact-based learning, permissible for Brethren, and Mum helped me pinpoint Luxembourg on a map of Europe. I dreamed of visiting this strange small country wedged between Belgium, Germany and France. For a Brethren boy, though, that trip would never be possible. Brethren weren't allowed to travel overseas without permission from church leaders; international holidays were banned, and when travel was necessary for church meetings or business activities, it was only allowed to countries where the Brethren had a presence. There were no members in Luxembourg. Similarly, we could only travel to other places within New Zealand to visit relatives, conduct business or attend church meetings.

Avid reading got me into all sorts of trouble. There were books that were permitted and books that were forbidden, although I didn't care much about that distinction. Anything supernatural was strictly off limits; the Harry Potter series was considered satanic. Mum admonished me when she discovered me hidden away reading *The Lion, The Witch and The Wardrobe*, passing down a warning she'd learned from her own grandmother: 'Nana Ruth always said The Chronicles of Narnia were blasphemous.' Non-fiction books were better than fiction, although even that had caveats: a writer's religious or political views could quickly disqualify them. I soon learned that if pages of a particular book were stuck together, it was probably to shield my eyes from an unsuitable paragraph. Some Brethren families carefully painted over swear words with correcting fluid. Occasionally, Dad and Mum would raid our bedrooms to make sure we hadn't brought unsuitable books home from the library – so I got better at hiding them, usually somewhere in my bedroom.

I loved imagining other worlds, and thought playing make-believe was fun – although I quickly learned from conversations at church that none of the other little Brethren boys dressed up in their mother's clothes and shoes. Honey the Bear and Wally the Wombat were often joined by a large collection of dolls; Mum snapped a picture of me fast asleep as a young child, surrounded by dolls and soft toys, my red cowlick curling over my forehead. On rubbish collection days in summer, I stared in fascination as shirtless men ran along the street, throwing bags into a truck that went stop-start, stop-start past our front yard. I couldn't get my tongue around 'rubbish truck' – we called them 'rukker kucks', a family joke that stuck for years – but their visits were an exciting window into a life beyond the church. I wondered what would happen if a Brethren boy wanted to be a rubbish truck worker, and I felt strangely drawn to the athletic men. This was my secret. I knew I could never tell Mum that I daydreamed about inviting them to sit in our yard for a tea party with my teddy bears and dolls.

Growing self-awareness made me painfully shy. I desperately wanted to fit in: to watch videos in class, eat lunch with the other children, and play with worldly friends without having to look over my shoulder. As the knowledge dawned of how weird I must seem to my classmates, I became terrified of public speaking, even hiding in our garden to avoid Year 2 speech day. This extended to church: at communion and prayer services, I was too scared to get up and pray as was expected of all boys from the age of five; my younger brother beat me to the microphone, then an even younger brother stepped up. It wasn't that I didn't want to participate – I wanted to blend in at church, more than anything – but crippling fear kept me bolted to my seat. At the end of these services, the congregation would sit in silence and stare at me expectantly to see if today would be the day I finally made my move. When we got home, it was always clear Dad and Mum were disappointed: 'It's such a shame you're not contributing to the holy fellowship yet.'

I was eventually pushed into public prayer by an elder. He waited until my parents were away, then unexpectedly picked up the microphone at the end of a service: 'I think Craig would like to pray for us tonight.' I twisted my shoes into the green carpet with embarrassment, but there was no escaping the several dozen expectant faces that stared back at me; the only way out of this nightmare was to stand up, close my eyes and offer a short prayer: 'Our God and father, thank you for bringing us here tonight, and pray for Mr Hales that he be given the strength he needs. In Jesus's name, amen.' Humiliation overrode my fear, and after that I was away.

The following year at school, I got up in front of the class without hesitation. 'Very good effort in speech competition,' a teacher wrote, as I scooped first prize. It was an early lesson that appearances had more impact than feelings. I went on to claim writing and poetry prizes, and Aunty Anna, a trusted confidante, encouraged me as I began to find my voice through our letters. This newfound confidence came with its downsides: 'Craig has a strong, determined personality,' noted a Year 6 teacher. Another teacher observed that I became 'extremely stubborn when unhappy in the class'.

As I grew older, I started to connect the dots: the man we'd heard in Grandma Lottie's recordings was the mysterious George to whom I had been compared as a child whenever I was being rebellious. I learned that he had been Lottie's husband, which made him my grandpa. He was Anna's younger brother. George had been withdrawn from when my mum was thirteen, and she hadn't seen him since. This explained why Lottie lived without a husband and might cry if she heard the recordings.

Even worse, George was against the Brethren – one of the terrible opposers we kept hearing about. He had dared to challenge the Elect Vessel's authority. We were told he had hurt Lottie deeply and abandoned the family. George loomed in the distance as an evil person who shouldn't be talked about, a story that made threats of excommunication seem very real. I imagined what might happen if I met a similar fate: 'Be careful what you say,' I told myself, 'or you might end up like George.'

2.

WATCHING DAD AS I GREW UP TAUGHT ME THAT VIOLENCE was how some things got dealt with. He thrashed me, and I lashed out at my younger siblings, a horrible cycle where punching and kicking was the ultimate demonstration of anger.

One afternoon when I was only eight, a petty sibling dispute boiled over soon after Dad got home from work. Angered by his heavy-handed attempts at justice, I screamed at him: 'Fuck!'

I had never sworn in front of Dad before. Swearing was a terrible yet exotic thing done by worldly kids, and I thought this word was the worst of them all.

From the look on his face, it was as though the ground had parted for the arrival of the devil himself. I realised I'd made a grave error and high-tailed it for the backyard, with Dad – still in his work overalls – in close pursuit. I made it as far as the washing line before I tripped and fell. He closed in.

I was used to being severely smacked, but this was different. Dad left me lying on the ground and lined up his steel-capped boots: *thud, thud, thud.* I wrapped my arms around my head, sobbing and screaming as his kicks thumped into me.

Later, bruised and terrified, I curled up in Mum's arms, crying as she tried to tell me everything would be OK.

Not long after that, a couple of Brethren kids came round for a playdate. Childish rough-housing turned to name-calling, and I ran off and shut myself in my room. But Victor and Blake wouldn't let me get away so easily; they banged on the bedroom door, shouting taunts. Full of rage, and with nowhere further to run, I opened the door, punched Victor in the face and slammed it closed.

I'd broken Victor's nose. There was no hiding what I'd done when he turned up at church in a face cast: everyone saw me as a violent child, and I was marched around to his family home for a humiliating apology while our mothers made awkward small talk and pretended there was no bad blood. Nobody thought to ask what was going on in our home – it was just a black mark against my name, one that lingered for years.

One of the many problems with beating your kids is that eventually they get big enough to defend themselves. As the oldest child I was the first to put this to the test with Dad. He was slender and wiry, and at ten I was solidly built enough to try my luck.

Dad had chased me into my bedroom for a beating and was incensed when I dared strike back with a punch. Standing up to him was like dumping a jerry can of petrol onto a bonfire. Blows rained down indiscriminately, and in the scuffle we fell to the floor where we writhed around throwing punches. I wasn't quite big enough to match his strength, so I grabbed his pinky and bent it back as far as I could – in the heat of the moment,

I figured breaking his finger was the only way this nightmare would end.

'David! Stop!' Eventually, Mum's helpless screaming got through to Dad.

Ashen-faced and panting, he rolled off to one side and looked at me in disgust. 'We're going to have to call a priest.'

To me, this was the worst possible outcome: the intervention of a priest was the first step towards someone being shut up or withdrawn from. I was still under the nominal age of twelve for 'assembly responsibility' but feared that wouldn't be enough to save me from public punishment. My fear of Dad was eclipsed only by my fear of being excommunicated, and I sobbed in terror as he went to find the phone. I would be the one in trouble; he was the head of the household, so I was supposed to respect his authority no matter what.

'Please don't!' I said. 'I'll be good, I promise!'

When my tearful pleas fell on deaf ears, I ran sobbing into the night. Brethren discipline required a priest to first talk to the guilty party; using my childhood logic, I figured that if he couldn't talk to me, I couldn't be shut up. I huddled, terrified, in a neighbourhood alley in the dark, weeping as my mind churned through worst-case outcomes. How would I face the other Brethren kids at school if I was shut up?

Eventually I plucked up the courage to creep back through the streets and survey the family home. The coast appeared to be clear, so I snuck through the back door and put myself to bed.

The next day, Mum told me it didn't look like I was going to be shut up – but she added that I needed to be a better boy. For weeks I lived in fear that the priests might change their minds.

*

Dad swung through emotional extremes and was rarely affectionate. Tortured by his relationship with God, he thought the reason he felt terrible was that he wasn't close enough to his heavenly father.

As kids we'd often hear him awake well before dawn, down on his knees in the living room, loudly remonstrating with God as he tried to overcome his negative thoughts. By 6 am he'd be off to work, but then at 8 am he'd drive all the way back home to read us the Bible over breakfast to make sure our own relationships with God were off to a good start. Dad would continue this relentless cycle until he drove himself to the point of collapse; one morning, we woke to an ambulance in the driveway, and paramedics cutting away his clothing with a pair of scissors: they were checking his vitals after he crumpled in a heap on the floor. Mum tried to reassure us: 'They need to take him to the hospital for some tests, but everything is going to be OK.' The doctors told him that he needed to rest up and not be so hard on himself. But he hadn't been home long before he started doing the same thing. Again, doctors told him to rest and the cycle continued.

At the time, I didn't know it was strange; to me, this was just how my father behaved. Years later, though, I would piece together how deeply traumatised Dad had been by his childhood. Grandma Edith – his mother – was a farmer's daughter from Motueka, and Dad's early memories revolved around happy trips to visit her parents, known to the grandchildren as Papa and Mama. Then, suddenly, those visits stopped. Papa Archie had said something in church that the leaders didn't like, and he was withdrawn from by his own brother; Mama Barbara was also withdrawn from when she refused to leave his side. Edith was tormented by cutting off her parents, but Brethren rules were clear: talking to excommunicated relatives was out of the question.

When I was a kid, I knew that a woman called Mama Barbara lived in Motueka; she was my last surviving great-grandparent, but she'd been thrown out of the church long before I was born. Edith stoically refused contact with her mother for more than twenty-five years, hiding her sorrow behind a stiff upper lip. But I did see her crack, just once. I was around at her house after school when the phone rang; it was her sister, Aunty Jossy, calling with the news that their mother had died. My grandma's face crumpled, and she briefly wept – an extremely rare display of grief.

The loss of her parents wasn't the only trauma Edith had endured. A few years after they were withdrawn from, her husband had been shut up and then withdrawn from for a farcical sin. Brian, who owned a bike and mower shop in Hamilton, had printed an ad that showed a woman mowing her lawn in a bathing suit.

Brian and Edith assumed his punishment would be short, so she stayed living with him, which meant she also went under assembly discipline. But my grandparents agreed their five teenagers should be billeted with other Brethren families, as there was no sense in forcing them all under discipline while Brian sorted out what he saw as a minor misunderstanding. At least this way, the children would be free to continue going to church meetings and socialising with their friends and cousins. This was common Brethren practice when parents were shut up, driven partly by a belief that kids needed to be in 'pure' households where they wouldn't be contaminated. Uprooted from family, the children lived under the dark cloud of believing their parents had done something terribly wrong. This could drag on for years, depending on when elders decided to readmit the parents – and sometimes they never came back.

Edith and Brian's plans to return fell apart when she got pregnant. Even though they were both shut up, they were supposed to be sleeping in separate beds – the rule was that couples under assembly discipline must abstain from sex. The pregnancy was therefore damning evidence that my grandparents weren't ready to be received back into the holy fellowship. Their punishment stretched on for four long years as they raised a son in the absence of his five older siblings. Meanwhile, those three brothers and two sisters were being shunted around different Brethren households in Hamilton, made to feel like outcasts and treated as second-rate compared to the children of the families with whom they lived.

Edith, by then greying in her mid-forties, gave up on ever returning to the Brethren with Brian. Forced to choose between her husband and her children, she bent over backwards to be accepted back into the church before her eldest daughter's wedding in July 1983. The Hamilton elders strung Edith along before saying they didn't think she was ready to return quite yet, and my aunt had to get married at her uncle's home. Just a few weeks later, the elders readmitted Edith.

As she cobbled together the wreckage of her life, it continued to crumble. Brian, devastated that she had abandoned their marriage of more than twenty years, fought for custody of their sixth child, while the Brethren threw their backing behind Edith in the ensuing bitter legal dispute. While she was mostly successful – shared visitation tapered off after a few years – her other children were trickling away. Her eldest son had been excommunicated for rebelliousness, and her second daughter had made an escape, fleeing years of spiritual and emotional abuse.

To cap it all off, my dad – third in the family – was diagnosed with non-Hodgkin lymphoma at twenty, not long after Edith was finally readmitted. A chance visit to the doctor for an unrelated injury had revealed a lump in his groin. He briefly became a Brethren celebrity – the child of a broken home, facing yet another test from God – and was shipped off to special meetings with church leaders. He was told he only had a fifty per cent chance of survival and probably wouldn't be able to have kids. The aggressive treatment crushed him further; he was never quite the same after having to stand up as the man of the house while enduring rounds of chemotherapy and supporting his mother in court.

As a kid I didn't appreciate how terrible Dad's youth had been. Family implosions were normal in the Brethren, and those who experienced them were expected to chin up and carry on; Mum, too, lived with the trauma of having an excommunicated father. Poor Dad struggled along, believing the reason he felt so miserable was that he wasn't close enough to God. This was a typical Brethren mentality: the pain of losing loved ones was considered righteous suffering, a form of martyrdom, and nobody in the church addressed the cause.

Dad had many layers. When he wasn't depressed or enraged, he would go out of his way to help others. He was in his element as he toiled away at housework for Mum; it raised Brethren eyebrows that he was doing what they saw as women's work like folding laundry and doing dishes, but Dad didn't seem to mind. Mum, however, was mortified when a senior leader questioned why her husband was doing housework.

I don't remember him being affectionate with us kids, but he showed his love in other ways. The enormous play hut he built in our backyard was the talk of the neighbourhood: two storeys high, it had swings, a slide, and a flying fox that zoomed over the lawn and finished with a swinging bump against the corner of the house. Worldly kids stared wistfully – they knew we weren't allowed to invite them in.

When I got interested in gardening, Dad helped me dig my first vege patch. The two of us got stuck in with a shovel, then built a timber hothouse and painted it white. As we worked side by side, Dad told me stories and explained how all kinds of practical things worked.

He was always busy, but when he was helping you with something he had a knack for making you feel like you were the only person who mattered. Small memories stand out: his look of deep concentration as he tried to solve a curly challenge, his patience when we kids didn't quite understand, and his broad grin when it all worked out in the end. I found it hard to reconcile this version of him with the one who lashed out at us.

*

School was my one respite from Brethren circles. As I approached adolescence and started finding my voice, I figured out how to be friends with the worldly kids in my own weird way, treading a fine line socialising with them in the classroom while knowing we could never eat together or hang out after the final bell rang. From Year 7 to Year 8, as I turned eleven, I felt as though I'd sailed from the bottom of the class pecking order to somewhere near the top. Mostly this change in social status was the result of talking back to teachers and cracking jokes. 'He has many talents but often lets himself down by making uncharitable comments,' wrote my Music teacher in a 2001 report, noting that my 'attitude could be improved upon at times'. My homeroom teacher summed it up: 'He has a quick and ready wit but has yet to learn when sarcasm is appropriate.'

At school I could test boundaries and challenge authority without fear of excommunication. I didn't care what teachers thought of me – unlike the priests, they had no power to cut me off from my family and friends; they were just worldlies who didn't deserve my full respect, and I took delight in needling them. I chuckled inwardly with glee when one teacher, furious at my impudence, called in the principal and said, 'Please remove Craig from this classroom before I do him physical harm.' My fellow rabble-rousers cheered me on.

But I knew it was never going to last. At twelve, I was pulled out of the public education system. My worldly friends wrote sad farewell notes in my yearbook; I'd always known this day would come, and it felt as though my world was shrinking. The church took a dim view of worldly high schools, so like most other Brethren kids my age, I transitioned from the beginning of Year 9 to learning at home via correspondence. Gone was the classroom banter, my new friends, and the exasperated yet patient teachers. I was stuck at a blue-panelled desk tucked in a corner of the bedroom I shared with my brother Caleb, alone with my thoughts and the tedious home education packs sent from the Correspondence School – a method of government learning usually offered to students in remote locations but utilised by the Brethren.

The use of homeschooling was a relatively recent development for the Brethren. My parents and their peers had gone to regular high schools, rubbing shoulders with worldly students for an extra four years. That was ended in the 1990s by Australian John Hales, the Elect Vessel, who said it was unsuitable for Brethren teens to continue with mainstream secondary education when moral standards in society were declining.

By the time I started high school, the Brethren were starting to realise they needed a better arrangement than pushing teens into homeschooling. Many of us struggled with the lack of face-to-face learning, and a couple of families in Invercargill dared to send their kids to a regular high school – a black mark against them. While I was sad to have lost my worldly school peers, it was unthinkable to me that people would ignore church teachings like this. Once, in a fit of self-righteousness, I got up at a meeting and prayed that God would care for Brethren students at worldly high schools. Incensed, one of the said students promptly got up and prayed that God would support kids struggling with homeschooling. It felt personal, but we were just parroting what our parents were saying at home.

As I finished my first year of homeschooling, the Brethren were on the cusp of a new education era. Taking their lead from Sydney, where John Hales had spearheaded the opening of a church school, the Brethren in Invercargill started an education trust as they set out to do the same. None of the trustees had any experience in education; they made things up as they went along. When the trust bought a boxy weatherboard house on St Andrew Street, opposite the sports fields of Waverley Park, we all pitched in for weekend working bees to turn it into a makeshift school. Three small, cold bedrooms became classrooms painted in dull beige. The gardens were ripped out and turned into lawn, and lesson packs were stacked up in former wardrobes.

In order to comply with government regulations – and thus receive government funding – the Brethren had to hire worldly teachers for their new school. University education had been banned by the church decades earlier, which meant there were no qualified Brethren teachers. I often wondered what these worldlies thought, being brought into a peculiar little church community and asked to educate children without stepping on religious toes. Male teachers were banned from wearing shorts, and female teachers had to wear skirts or dresses of 'a modest length'. The Brethren used a religious exemption to prohibit teachers from joining trade unions. These rules and many more, for both staff and students, were spelled out in the school's 2003 handbook.

Each week in my second year of high school, we spent two days working on similarly designed correspondence courses as the year before, and on the other three days we gathered for classroom lessons in which teachers would review the course content and answer any questions. They couldn't deviate from the rules in the handbook, which decreed that the theory of evolution was 'regarded as a falsehood'. Dancing was forbidden, as were 'any other body contact activities' – that meant absolutely no tackle rugby or bullrush. Computers were out of the question: 'The Trustees regard occupation with and the study of computers damaging to the proper development of children's minds and only serve to reduce and limit their thinking capacity to be conformed to programs and the manipulation of keyboard and screen. It is regarded that computers in many fields represent a misuse of physical and natural phenomena created by God.'

By the time I started Year 11, my third year of high school, the Brethren were streamlining their education efforts in New Zealand. The local trust in Invercargill was rolled into a nationwide programme; our school was rebranded as the Southland campus of Westmount School, a network of fifteen sites where Brethren students were taught a curriculum approved by our leadership. Finally we ditched the correspondence courses: Westmount offered five days of classroom learning a week. The Brethren families who had sent their children to worldly high schools relented and enrolled them at our school. But even then, there were just seven students in my class.

Brethren education was as crushing to me as the public system had been liberating. My academic achievements kept pace, but coming first out of seven felt meaningless. 'Craig is an extremely capable student, but must not rest on his laurels,' a teacher noted in a report when I was fifteen. What was the point of trying when I knew I'd never go to university? I wouldn't even need to find a job, because I had guaranteed employment at Dad's tyre shop. The Brethren took care of their own. One small silver lining to this bleak time was that our family had moved into a much larger sprawling brick home on a two-acre block of land, so I did at least finally have a bedroom all to myself.

Brethren students had no choice in what subjects we studied during those final two years of school. There were the basics – English, Maths, Science – and beyond that we were forced into an array of classes that the trustees thought would be useful but which I despised. Already well ahead with the required credits to pass Year 11, I pleaded with the principal and trustees that I be allowed to drop out of Architecture, which I hated with a passion. I would have much rather taken up Sewing or Cooking, but those classes were reserved for the girls. When was I ever going to use Architecture? But my pleas fell on deaf ears. 'It's character-building,' they told me, 'to do things you don't like.'

I figured the only way I could get out of Architecture was to behave so badly that the teacher refused to have me in the classroom. That poor man. I made those lessons intolerable: talking back, slamming doors, asking deliberately stupid questions. Whenever he told us to use a pencil with a fine tip, I'd dig out the thickest, darkest pencil I could find to smudge up the page; if that didn't upset him enough, I'd outright refuse to do the work and be as disruptive as possible, sitting back with my feet up on my desk and cracking rude jokes. 'I'm not gonna do any of this today,' I'd say. 'You can't make me.' This battle of wills dragged on for several weeks, until he caved and went to the principal. 'I can no longer have him in my classroom,' he said. I could barely hide my glee: it wasn't personal, and a part of me felt sorry for the teacher, but I felt like I'd been left with no choice. I was allowed to pick up a Correspondence School paper studying Latin, under the supervision of a Latin-speaking teacher, while my male peers toiled on with their maps and drawings.

Soon afterwards I was once again in trouble for talking back, this time in Accounting class where I'd been rude enough to the teacher that she also refused to have me back. I was suspended from school for more than a week, and I couldn't return, the principal said, until I'd apologised to the teacher. Being stuck at home was supposed to subdue me, but I enjoyed the sleep-ins. When my teachers sent me schoolwork, I sent it back unopened. Poor Mum didn't know what to do.

This led to my first official visit from the priests. Known as 'priestlies', these experiences were feared by young Brethren: two or more church elders would shut themselves in a room with you and grill you about your sins. I've never worked out who called in the priests – it could have been my parents, distraught at my rebellion, or the teachers escalating the problem to the Brethren trustees.

I found myself trapped in the spare bedroom. Three chairs had been pulled in and set up awkwardly beside the bed; I was beside the window, with two priests sitting opposite, interview-style. They were between me and the door, so I had no chance of making a run for it. These were familiar faces: I took communion with them every week, and they were both distant relatives.

I squirmed awkwardly as the men reprimanded me: 'Why are you acting like this? This isn't how Brethren should behave. You'd better submit to authority and accept what you're being told to do.' They asked if I had any sins I wanted to confess; I stonewalled. Eventually the exchange came to an awkward finish. It didn't feel like they'd achieved anything, and I was confident they weren't going to shut me up. I went back to school after writing an insincere letter acknowledging I had been rude to the teacher without actually apologising.

I wasn't the only one in the church bumping up against rules. The trustees themselves were struggling to fit their version of education into New Zealand's national curriculum, but in order to qualify for government funding, some Brethren restrictions had to be eased. For instance, the English curriculum included a module on film studies, meaning we had to watch a movie or fail that module. I'd never seen a movie, so it was hugely exciting when our teacher rolled out a video player and TV. We watched *Rabbit-Proof Fence*, an acclaimed Australian film about Aboriginal girls torn from their families by racist government policy. My classmates and I were much too naive to comprehend the themes and had no clue how movies worked. During a closing scene, when the sisters are shown as old women, a student asked our teacher if the filmmakers had waited for the actors to grow old.

*

My high school years had been marked by upheaval in the church. Elect Vessel John Hales died of cancer in January 2002, and there was a brief uncertain period where we weren't sure who the new Elect Vessel would be – nominally the Brethren believed that they were revealed by the Holy Spirit, but the dying leader usually signalled who he supported as his successor. It soon became clear that John Hales's son Bruce Hales Jnr would assume power over the Brethren worldwide. Not everyone was happy about this, and we heard stories from overseas of people being withdrawn from for challenging the authority of the Hales leadership, but in New Zealand most of us were excited to be following a fresh and more youthful face. Bruce Hales Jnr immediately set about putting his own stamp on the church, introducing new rules and scrapping some that had been enforced by his father. There was even a new name for our leader: now we talked about our 'Man of God', and the Elect Vessel designation was retired.

During this time, the Brethren were agitated by their hatred for the Labour government led by Helen Clark. An unapologetic feminist, Clark had won office in 1999 as New Zealand's first elected female prime minister. She presided over a programme of progressive social change that included the legalisation of sex work and the introduction of civil unions for same-sex couples. I heard Brethren privately expressing death wishes against Clark and other socially liberal politicians; when the prime minister was left bruised and shaken after an aeroplane door blew open on a chartered flight, the Brethren said that if we'd been praying harder, Clark would have fallen out. Later that year, a group of a dozen or so Brethren teenagers burned an effigy of the prime minister atop a bonfire at a Saturday evening gathering of Brethren families in Invercargill.

Civil unions were a particular sore point for the Brethren. Ironically, church protests and prayers against the legislation were what allowed me to learn that the gay community existed.

Until then I hadn't known there was a label for men who were attracted to men, although it was unthinkable that such a label might apply to me. Who were these men living in such sin? How were they able to ignore God's rules about finding a wife and starting a family? Didn't they know they were all going to burn in hell? We prayed their souls would be saved – we also begged God to stop the bill from passing through Parliament. When civil unions became law in 2004, when I was fifteen, local priests told us it was because we hadn't been showing enough faith.

By 2005, when New Zealand went to the polls, Brethren fury was channelled into organised political action around the country. Members donated time and money to centre-right candidates for the National Party in a bid to boot Labour from power – a bizarre move, considering that Brethren had banned themselves from voting for more than a century. Even though we still weren't allowed to cast a vote, it was suddenly OK for us to actively campaign for a change of government. Brethren ran leaflet drops to support National candidates, organised telephone push-polling, and drove a concerted attack campaign against the Labour and Greens parties.

It all went badly wrong when the Brethren's secretive association with the National Party came to light just a few weeks before election day. National plummeted in the polls and lost the election; newspapers filled with speculation about why a fringe religious group had been trying to sway New Zealand politics.

The Man of God told us repeatedly that the press was wicked and that we shouldn't be reading the news, but these events were too fascinating for me to ignore. The Sunday newspapers in particular were reviled, but I snuck home copies of the *Sunday Star-Times* and combed through them for reports that analysed the Brethren's political endeavours, painstakingly saving them in folders. What on earth had the new Man of God been thinking?

*

When I was sixteen and in Year 12, Mum spent weeks in hospital after surgery to remove her gallbladder. She'd been having issues with gallstones and it all finally came to a head. I was struggling at school, acting out and talking back to the teachers, then driving to the hospital after class to pour my heart out to Mum. She lay pallid and grey in a surgical ward yet still gave everything she could to make sure we were supported.

Was she afraid of dying? 'No.' If she was going to die, did she want us to call her dad, George? 'No.' I loved Mum dearly and couldn't wrap my head around how she expressed little affection for her dad, who at one point she'd loved just as much as us kids loved her.

My six siblings and I needed our own dad to step up and make sure we were OK, but as Mum lay in hospital he spiralled even deeper into his depression. One awful morning he drove himself to exhaustion and collapsed again; this time he crumpled in the kitchen, cracking his head open on the bench as he fell. My brother Caleb found him lying on the floor in a pool of blood, and once again we had to call an ambulance for him. But this felt worse than his previous episodes – he'd never needed to be stitched up before, and now Mum wasn't there to pick up the pieces.

Later that day, as Dad was treated at hospital, we heard that Mum was being rushed into emergency surgery again. There had been problems post-op, and her abdomen needed to be reopened immediately. The doctors said they couldn't guarantee she'd survive.

I went through the day feeling numb, waiting for a phone call to let me know whether I still had a mum – and, for that matter, a dad. What's a teenager supposed to do in a situation like that? How do you prepare for the possibility of becoming the eldest of seven orphans? My teachers were as kind as they could be, but I couldn't properly open up to them about my trauma and grief because as worldlies I felt they wouldn't understand.

When Mum came home from hospital she was bedridden, too weak to do anything more than watch as Dad's mental health continued to deteriorate. He shut himself in his wardrobe for days at a time, obsessing over books of Brethren teachings as he cried in the dark for God to show him the way forward; occasionally he'd emerge and shout at us for not being well behaved.

One evening he became very upset about us not eating dinner together as a family – it was difficult to get nine people showered, dressed and fed simultaneously before the seven-thirty church service. He demanded we all arrive at the table at the same time.

We made it happen – no mean feat – and sat there expectantly, waiting for him to read the usual pre-dinner Bible verses. Instead he stared at us blankly, then slammed the Bible down and shouted, 'I can't do this!' As he stormed back to the wardrobe, the rest of us ate in stunned silence.

I was in an impossible situation. According to Brethren doctrine, Dad was still the head of the house, and we had to respect his authority even if he was no longer capable of exercising it. I couldn't understand where he was coming from or what he was trying to achieve. I was a headstrong teenager with issues of my own, years away from any empathy for the huge pain he lived with. I resented him for traumatising us and for his double standards: if I lashed out, the priests got called, but if Dad lashed out, we had to submit to his authority.

Dad became suicidal, and talked about wanting to end his life. I remember at least one occasion when he disappeared into the night and Mum was distraught. We had no idea where he was: had he hung himself in the cemetery, drowned in the river or jumped in front of a train? As the eldest son I was supposed to shoulder responsibility, so I took it upon myself to comb the streets of Invercargill, pushing aside a rising lump in my throat as I scanned parks and beaches for my father's body. I felt very alone on that late-night mission. The severity of Dad's depression was brushed over by the Brethren, and nobody offered to help me with the search.

Finally one Friday night at a local priest's house, it all got too much for me to shoulder on my own. He was a fatherly figure – more of a mentor than a priest – and I felt safe confiding in him. Our conversation moved to the privacy of his study, and

I poured out my woes about how I was struggling to cope and that it was too much to handle as a sixteen-year-old. But instead of offering support he told me to man up: 'You have a duty of care to your six younger siblings, and it's probably also time you took on a bit more responsibility in the family business.'

I couldn't believe what I was hearing. I was barely holding my own life together, struggling with school and a nagging realisation that I wasn't attracted to girls. The civil union debate had brought home to me with awful clarity that anyone who might be gay would never be accepted by the Brethren. It took everything I had to push my fears aside, and this priestly order seemed like too much to ask. How was I supposed to help care for six siblings when Mum was still very weak physically and Dad was incapacitated mentally? And what did I know about stepping into a tyre shop? But it was clear that I didn't have much choice. A few months later, I left school and pulled on a pair of overalls.

The local priests weren't the only Brethren authorities telling me what to do. Around that time, I formed a connection with a genial elder, Athol Greene, on one of his visits to host special meetings in Invercargill. He offered support to many young Brethren – he was also the father-in-law of our Man of God, Bruce Hales Jnr. During his visit, Athol ditched the usual custom of inviting prominent leaders to join him for dinner on the Saturday; instead, a group of trouble-making teens was assembled to dine with him and Roger Kirkpatrick, a Brethren doctor and senior leader who was also a relative of the Man of

God. This generous gesture stuck with me, and I kept in touch with Athol. He was always happy to take my calls, a reassuring grandfatherly figure.

When I told Athol about what was happening with my parents, he backed the local priests. In an afternoon phone call from his home in Penrith, New South Wales, he said that because my grandfathers had been withdrawn from, neither of my parents had fathers. 'You have to be the grandfather for your parents,' he told me.

My head was reeling as I sat on the edge of my bed, picking at the light green pattern on the covers. How was I supposed to parent my parents? I was only sixteen!

Athol said he empathised with me – 'I had no dad, buddy' – and promised he would stand behind me as I shouldered this immense responsibility: 'Give it all you've got,' he told me. 'The Lord will honour you.'

There was no time for dwelling on my sexuality or for reflecting on the contradictions and foibles of Brethren doctrine. I was too busy fretting about our family and trying to hold things together at the tyre shop, where I was thrown headlong into a retail sales environment.

At least my job reopened the door to more contact with worldlies. While Brethren weren't allowed to eat, drink or socialise with non-Brethren, we were still allowed to hire them at our businesses. I had long conversations in the shop with a worldly colleague called Ben who had been raised seventh-day adventist and was still religious, and I opened up to him one afternoon as we cleaned the tyre-fitting machines. 'I'm not sure whether I fully believe in Brethren teachings,' I told him – a huge admission – 'but I think I'll stay in the church because it's where all my friends and family are.' Ben was quizzical: 'Surely you should belong to a church because you think it's the right place to be, not just because it's the easiest option?' I didn't know how to respond to being called out like this.

That year almost crushed me. I knew I didn't belong, but there was too much going on for me to fully explore what that meant. As curiosity and rebellion drew me to the world outside the Brethren – and as I was pulled in different directions by frightening suspicions about my sexuality – grief and chaos kept reeling me back home.

3.

NEARLY TWENTY YEARS HAVE PASSED SINCE THAT TIME IN MY life. I'm sitting at my kitchen table, surrounded by boxes of letters, diaries and photo albums: two centuries of records that document my family's Brethren journey. I've built a reputation as someone who's interested in family history, and have inherited several large collections that add to what I was able to copy before leaving the church. Carefully inked missives on yellowed writing paper reveal stories of heartbreak and division. Over the past few years, I've been on a mission to examine those stories and bring the truth to light, interviewing dozens of relatives and former Brethren to try to understand my family.

Grandpa George – the wicked opposer to whom I'd been compared as a child – was far from the first person in our family to find himself on the wrong side of the Exclusive Brethren. In 1920, just over sixty years before he was withdrawn from, his own grandfather faced excommunication after speaking out against Brethren leadership. In fact, though my parents were devoted members of the church, both sides of our family come from a long line of protesters.

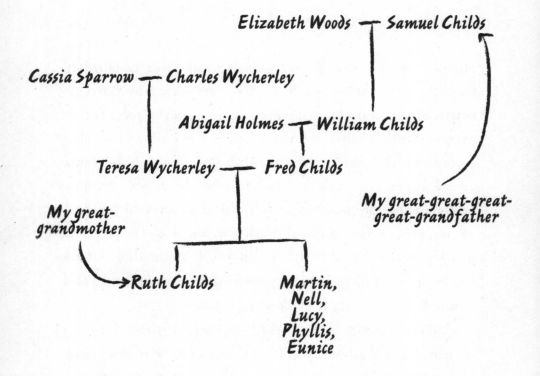

Elizabeth Woods ── Samuel Childs

Cassia Sparrow ── Charles Wycherley

Abigail Holmes ── William Childs

Teresa Wycherley ── Fred Childs

My great-
grandmother

My great-great-great-
great-grandfather

Ruth Childs

Martin,
Nell,
Lucy,
Phyllis,
Eunice

As a child I was deeply curious about our family history, but the stories I heard were never enough for me – and always told with a Brethren slant. Was this person a devoted church member? Did they ever show doubt in the leaders? Did any of their children go astray? Grandma Lottie told me there was no need for us to learn about relatives who weren't Exclusive Brethren. Unsatisfied, I started doing my own research, talking to older relatives and poring through boxes retrieved from their basements and cupboards across New Zealand. My parents were vaguely aware of my growing interest in genealogy but too distracted to fully comprehend its scope. Some photos were cut to pieces because zealous church adherents had chopped out kin who had betrayed the faith. Some letters had annotations from younger generations about whether they included good Brethren beliefs, while some relatives referred mysteriously to records that seemed to have been destroyed.

The Brethren were a tight-knit community, and my great-great-great-grandparents were still within living memory. Some forebears had been gospel preachers, venerated by later descendants; a few, like my grandpa George, were personae non gratae. Others trod a fuzzy middle ground, remembered as lukewarm followers.

There was no middle ground for Alfred Theodore Childs, my great-great-grandfather on Mum's side, who was excommunicated in 1920. Fred, with his piercing gaze and bushy white beard, cut a commanding figure. As the son of a missionary and the son-in-law of another prominent Brethren leader, he was well connected in Brethren circles. But he walked away from it all in protest, concerned that the conservative church in which he had been born and raised was becoming 'inflated with false doctrine'. This crisis of faith was a milestone in a journey that had begun on the other side of the world more than a century earlier. In a thread that runs through my family history, Fred was affected by the decisions of his grandfather Sam.

*

Samuel Childs – my great-great-great-great-grandfather – was a well-to-do businessman from London's merchant class. Born out of wedlock in 1787, Sam was an impressive figure with wavy black hair and thick dark eyebrows, exuding confidence in a gilt-framed oil painting he sat for in his late forties. But for all his material success, he was a troubled man, preoccupied with whether God would judge him for the circumstances of his birth.

His unease with his place in Christendom dovetailed with growing religious dissatisfaction in Britain and Ireland. Some Anglicans felt the Church of England had become stale, heading down the same liturgical path as Roman Catholicism. These protesters rejected the concept of organised religion in favour of a simpler ascetic faith, and they gathered for informal meetings inspired by, as they saw it, the Bible alone.

Tormented as he was by church teachings on parenthood and legitimacy, Sam must have been relieved to find a community of Christians who had thrown out the old rule book. Through the 1820s and into the 1830s these freethinkers loosely coalesced, among them John Nelson Darby, the youngest son of the Darbys of Leap Castle. With his privilege, charisma and piercing dark eyes, he stood out as a prominent voice. Fellow Brethren founder George Vicesimus Wigram was a family friend of Sam Childs.

Darby and Wigram's group soon came to be known as the Plymouth Brethren, in recognition of the rebels' early connections to Plymouth, a port city on the south coast of Devon. The Brethren movement spread rapidly, and sometime after 1841 Sam moved with his wife and the youngest of their thirteen children to the Berkshire town of Reading in the Thames Valley. A Brethren meeting room had been established there in 1840 – the Blue Room on Queens Road – and Darby was a frequent visitor.

Even in those early days, trouble was brewing within the group. Brethren followers argued over how to interpret and apply scripture, and a loose set of rules began to take shape. In 1836 – the year Sam's last of four sons was born – a prominent Brethren member was concerned enough to pen a letter to Darby warning that if the group continued on its path it would be consumed by 'doctrine and opinion'. Darby – whose mysticism had taken a moody turn after he fell from his horse and suffered a head injury – paid the warning no heed.

Tensions erupted in 1848 as the Brethren movement underwent its first bitter split. A comparatively liberal side believed it was acceptable to continue fellowship with other Christians who held slightly different beliefs, and this side became known as Open Brethren. The Darby and Wigram camp, meanwhile, believed in rigid enforcement of doctrinal boundaries and became known as Exclusive Brethren. Brethren gatherings up and down England were forced to choose sides, with friends and relatives cleaving over who was correct.

This divide put the retired Sam Childs in a difficult spot. The 61-year-old had relocated to Reading, only for much of the congregation there to turn against his long-time friends Darby and Wigram by establishing an Open Brethren meeting. For Sam, a gruff grandfather with bushy white whiskers, there was no question about where his allegiance lay. By 1853, he'd given up on Reading and moved his household back closer to London. There, he set about constructing a home in Sunbury on land adjacent to Darby House, an estate owned by the family of the emerging Brethren leader. This was much more comfortable territory.

Sam and Elizabeth's youngest son William – my great-great-great-grandfather – came of age at this new home in Sunbury, surrounded by a clutch of servants and older sisters. Sketches and tintype photographs of young William show a dandily dressed boy with deep brown eyes and brown hair slicked neatly away from a left-side parting. As he soaked up adult conversations about business and religion, he must have listened in wonder as Darby held forth during visits to his relatives and Brethren followers.

Ambition drove William from an early age. At eighteen he was in the family candle-making business, keeping scrupulous records of wages and supply costs. The following year he was off on world adventures, writing of his distress at discovering the exchange rate when he crossed the US–Canada border at Niagara Falls. But for young William, much like for his father, religion was never far from mind. Impressed by Darby and

Wigram, he was inspired by these charismatic leaders to leave the family business behind and become a Brethren missionary.

Having already visited North America and Europe, William set his sights on the West Indies. Britain's Caribbean colonies were prime targets for religious proselytising, and he was determined to help start a Brethren movement there. His fiancée Abigail, also a devout Brethren member, took a bit more persuading; it came as a shock when William suggested they begin their married life in Jamaica. Her fellow Brethren pushed her along, with an elder writing in 1863 to encourage the move. When they married in Jamaica the following year, William described himself as a Minister of the Gospel. The service was at an Anglican parish church – it would be years before the Brethren were permitted their own marriage celebrants – on the grounds of Mount Holstein, a colonial estate that just decades earlier had been a forced home for hundreds of slaves. Now the slaves were free – and prime targets for preaching. William and Abigail set to work.

As a child, I heard proud stories of how our forebears had been blessed to host Darby himself when he visited Jamaica in 1869. William and Abigail believed they were doing God's work in converting former slaves – ancestors of the Black Caribbean Brethren I would learn about more than a century later – and such visits from senior Brethren leaders bolstered their efforts. I found it wonderful to imagine these founding fathers under the same roof as my ancestors, and I boasted about this connection as a child when we hosted other Brethren families for weekend dinners.

William and Abigail's family grew alongside the fledgling congregation. By the time George Vicesimus Wigram made a visit to Jamaica in 1871, their third child had been named in his honour. But the toddler George Wigram Childs was sickly, and William and Abigail struggled with his health even as two younger brothers arrived in quick succession. The youngest, Alfred Theodore, became known as Fred. When he was just a baby, the family abandoned their missionary life in Jamaica and returned to England for the health of young George – but to no avail. He died a few months later.

In a family photograph taken not long after George's death, Abigail looks exhausted. Her once rounded cheeks have hollowed out, and her thin frame disappears into a black floor-length dress. William, no longer a dapper young gentleman, stares pensively to the left with those same deep brown eyes, clutching a surviving son who shrugs in discomfort. Those ten years had been rough.

As he mourned his lost son, my great-great-great-grandfather threw himself into Brethren affairs back in the thick of things with Darby and Wigram in England. Disturbing reports were emerging of the wayward direction taken by the fledgling Brethren movement in New Zealand, a far-flung colony in the South Pacific where only a few decades earlier the Crown had signed a treaty with Māori tribes. Darby's friend and Brethren associate James Deck had shipped out there some twenty years prior – ostensibly for his health, although letters show he was deeply pained about the split between Brethren followers in 1848 and perhaps saw the new colony as an escape.

Free from the watchful oversight of Darby and Wigram, Deck had set about establishing his own version of Brethrenism. A charismatic preacher with a long flowing beard, he drew large numbers from mainstream Christian churches whose leaders saw him as a threat to their congregations. Deck welcomed all, never bothering to draw a distinction between Open and Exclusive Brethren. This worked fine for twenty years, but as shipping routes and communication improved, word filtered back to England of the freewheeling nature of his movement.

Darby and Wigram grew increasingly concerned with setting New Zealand straight. In 1871, Wigram journeyed to the colony and undertook an extensive tour, trying to determine which Brethren meetings should be classified as Exclusive and which Open. He reported approvingly that the assembly in Christchurch appeared to have the greatest loyalty to the Exclusive side, but he remained concerned overall by the lax approach taken by the New Zealand Brethren. On a subsequent visit in 1874, he fretted that the assemblies were being tainted by 'the heartiness and rough and ready nature of the society'.

It's little wonder then that Wigram and Darby sought to install loyalists among the New Zealand Exclusive Brethren. They needed devotees who would preach the correct strict doctrine and pressure other members to toe the line. This was the perfect opening for William Childs, a proven loyalist with connections from childhood who had shown he was willing to depart for distant shores in support of the Brethren cause.

Not long after Wigram's second visit, the Childs family once more set sail from London, this time to make a new home in Christchurch. Darby paid a visit the next year, following insistent requests from James Deck, who remained an old and familiar friend despite their divergent beliefs. My great-great-grandfather Fred Childs, aged three and a half, likely watched in wonder as the elderly Darby and Deck shared a pulpit at the meeting room in Christchurch.

*

Fred, bright-eyed and blond, had a happy upbringing. The New Zealand Brethren were a warm and welcoming community, and by the time the Childs family posed for portraits when Fred was seventeen, his mother's cheeks had filled out again. That day, Fred wore a crisp white shirt with a buttoned vest and swept his hair back from his forehead, eyes and mouth turned in a subtle cheeky grin. A promising life lay ahead.

The week before his twenty-sixth birthday, Fred's wedding to Teresa Wycherley, who was known as Tess, took him even deeper into the Exclusive Brethren fold. Darby and Wigram had died by then, and control of what was known as the London Meeting shifted to Frederick Raven, a father of nine, bearded and with brooding dark eyes, who had famously refused to accept honours from Queen Victoria and the British Admiralty. Fred's father-in-law Charles Wycherley, a prominent Brethren figure in Wellington, was 'a Raven man through and through'.

As I sift through our family records, I discover a letter to Fred from his sister-in-law Sophia four months after his wedding in 1898. Writing from England with loopy blue penmanship, she references the family's sadness that Fred's eldest brother has drifted from the fold: 'Poor Will. We must go on praying for him ... He is missing so much.' Sophia praises Frederick Raven's 'simple' teaching and 'consistent' preaching, although there's a hint that not all is rosy among his followers: 'How sad it is that he [Raven] has been so misunderstood.' To me, this is familiar language – more than a century later, I was taught as a child that most people who oppose the Brethren just don't understand them. The supposed misunderstandings of Raven's doctrines prompted further divides through the last two decades of the nineteenth century, as members left in protest. In 1890, Fred's missionary father was among a group at the Worcester St hall who rejected Raven's teachings, leading to a split in the Christchurch assembly. But Fred, now married into a family of Raven loyalists, stayed true to the Exclusive Brethren cause.

He and Tess spent the first few years of their married life in the sparsely populated Akatarawa Valley, surrounded by parks and forests. After their family quickly grew to six children, they moved south to Upper Hutt – closer to Wellington city – and life became a whirlwind of Brethren meetings and families.

Then tragedy struck: Tess died suddenly from meningitis in 1916, leaving Fred a solo father of six. Unable to cope, he turned to his extended Brethren family, and the children were scattered across the country to stay with relatives.

My great-grandma Ruth and her siblings were eventually reunited when their father remarried in 1919 and gathered his children back together in Wellington. Their stepmother also had two daughters living at home, so the family swelled to ten under one roof. This was a shock for Ruth, who had become accustomed to a quiet life with her elderly grandparents and spinster aunt.

As domestic squabbles consumed Fred's children, storm clouds of a different kind were brewing among the Exclusive Brethren. Frederick Raven had died in 1903, and in the years following his death the leadership mantle had passed to an Irish linen merchant in New York. James Taylor was only in his thirties; like Fred, he had been left a widower, in his case with five young children after his wife died in childbirth. The Brethren told admiring stories of how he cared for his family, pushing a pram with one hand in public while he handed out gospel tracts with the other. Taylor's new teachings were controversial – and Fred, like his missionary father, was beginning to have doubts. Not long after Fred's second wedding, a London elder called Mr Giles attempted to raise the alarm in a widely distributed pamphlet: Mr Giles warned that the Exclusive Brethren were at risk of becoming a 'vast hierarchical system' dominated by Taylor 'to the exclusion of any who cannot agree with him'. Fred agreed with Mr Giles.

Years later, I heard stories of how Fred had gone along with 'the Giles division'; although still a conservative Christian, he agreed that Taylor's dogmatic new direction was a step too far.

Even so, Fred faced an agonising decision. His family had been closely aligned with the Exclusive Brethren for almost a hundred years, spanning four generations from his grandparents to his children.

The consequences were swift when Fred told his local Brethren community that he didn't agree with the leadership of James Taylor. Fred was withdrawn from, along with others who supported Giles. His second wife and the eight children they had between them were also excommunicated. But the price was worth it for my great-great-grandpa: his immediate family was free, or so it seemed.

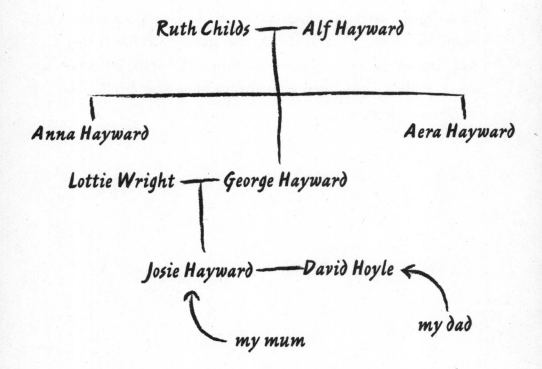

4 ·

GOING THROUGH THE FRAYED LETTERS AND NOTEBOOKS, I come across a stack of small bound diaries starting from 1918. The words bump up against each other in lettering so tiny I take pictures of some pages so I can zoom in. Slowly, a love story emerges.

The diaries were written by my great-grandparents, one of whom was Ruth Childs, Fred's second-eldest daughter. By 1928, she was a shy 22-year-old with curly brown hair and sparkling brown eyes. She attended the midday wedding of her friend Grace Bauckham, a sticky affair in the breathless heat of Wellington's summer. After the happy couple set off on their honeymoon, a group of wellwishers – unwilling to let the celebrations end quite yet – decamped to the home of Grace's aunt. It had been a long day, and Ruth was tired. Moving away from the crowd, she sat on a box outside and made small talk with another guest.

Alf Hayward was a dark-haired daredevil, an outgoing 23-year-old who loved to be the centre of attention. His slight ten-stone frame belied the energy he commanded in a room, and his escapades contrasted with Ruth's relatively sheltered life. Infamously he had almost died on the icy slopes of Mount Ngauruhoe after setting off against a guide's advice. His daring stories were a breath of fresh air to Ruth as they chatted on those backyard boxes.

Like Ruth, Alf had grown up in the Exclusive Brethren. As work took him away from the family home in Ashhurst, he explored other denominations – in those days it was still possible for Exclusive Brethren to try other churches without being penalised, although it was forbidden to participate in the communion part of their services. At various points he worshipped with the Presbyterians, the Methodists, the Salvation Army, and even the rival Open Brethren, the less restrictive group that had broken away back in the late 1840s.

To the consternation of his parents, Alf decided to break bread with the Opens in Whanganui. 'Breaking bread' was the terminology used to describe becoming an official member. Prior to the 1960s, being born to a Brethren family didn't guarantee membership: a young person still had to ask to break bread around the age of eleven or twelve and have their application considered by the assembly. Alf noted in his diary how he was baffled by the reaction of his father and stepmother to his joining the Open Brethren: 'Dad <u>grieving</u> about my decision. <u>Grieving</u>, mind you!'

Ruth, too, had experienced the animosity between Exclusive and Open Brethren. Her father, Fred, and their family had found fellowship with the Opens after leaving the Exclusives, and this had cast a long cloud over relationships with their Exclusive relatives. At that time the Exclusives didn't expressly forbid contact between members and non-members, but an attitude of 'them' versus 'us' was spreading through the flock like cancer, and cousins and uncles berated Fred's children for leaving the Exclusive fold.

Ultimately, Alf and Ruth had the Open Brethren to thank for their chance meeting at Grace Bauckham's wedding. Ruth's family had settled into services with the Open assembly at their small weatherboard meeting room on Vivian Street in central Wellington, and Alf arrived a few years later when the postal service transferred him to the capital. But although he became an occasional visitor to Ruth's family home, he was too busy planning his future to pay much attention to the quiet young woman he'd met at his cousin's wedding. He pulled long shifts at the radio station atop Te Ahūmairangi Hill, dreaming of going overseas as he rambled through the hills on his lunchbreaks.

It came as a 'tremendous surprise' when Alf was assigned to the navy in the summer of 1930 as a telegraph operator aboard HMS *Nucula*. He stayed loyal to the Open Brethren as he travelled the Pacific, seeking out the Open meeting in San Francisco just before Christmas. Over the next two years, as HMS *Nucula* crisscrossed the Pacific, he documented his adventures in careful spidery handwriting. On one trip, as the weather cooled past the equator, he described how he 'lay in a lifeboat for an hour watching the stars & dreaming dreams of NZ, home, & Roma!'

Roma, a Presbyterian reverend's daughter, was Alf's love interest back in New Zealand. They'd known each other for a decade, and as their romance blossomed she received gifts from family in anticipation of impending nuptials. Then, two years after Alf first set sail, he abruptly ended the courtship. Roma was shocked when he told her their romance was 'crippling me spiritually' and he no longer thought she would be a suitable wife. His aunt laid into him for being so disrespectful.

A short time later, his tail between his legs, he threw in his seafaring adventures and accepted a post to the Chatham Islands. There, on a remote windswept archipelago almost nine hundred kilometres east of Christchurch, Alf licked his self-inflicted wounds and reflected on what might have been.

His relationship with Roma was news to me. I grew up hearing of his devotion to my great-grandmother, and there was never even a whiff of romances that came before her.

As the letters and diaries carry on into the early 1930s, I read about how Alf's deep spiritual searching eventually brought him back to Ruth. Not much had changed in her life since that brief conversation in 1928. Now twenty-seven, she was still very sheltered, even though twelve years had passed since her family walked away from the Exclusive Brethren. She had seemed an oasis of calm when Alf crossed paths with her again as he passed through Wellington en route to his self-imposed exile in the Chathams, and the pair soon struck up a correspondence as spiritual friends.

Alf poured out his woes to Ruth as he built a life on the island outpost. 'It is just as hard to keep "unspotted from the world" down here as it would be in Wellington, if not harder,' he wrote, describing how he was still tempted by unspiritual affairs. Alf, a wireless operator, resolved to give up his personal wireless set and stop listening to radio entertainment, because all he needed was 'two-way communication with a risen Lord'. Ruth pushed him along in his spiritual endeavours and rebuked him for wasting too much time on worldly pleasures; a chastened Alf acknowledged he had been 'spending whole days on the beach, going shooting & fishing': 'Things not exactly sinful, but, as you had feared, taking up precious time which should be given to the Lord.'

Alf 'utterly failed' to keep up with his Bible readings, and his letters ebbed and flowed as the months stretched into years. A months-long silence would be broken by a twenty-page missive describing his trials and tribulations in granular detail. Ruth redoubled her efforts in prayer, and Alf came to see his spiritual penpal as a 'very near, dear friend'.

What had started as a spiritual friendship turned to romance. Alf wrote wistfully about his dream of settling down in 'a little quiet home where the Lord will be honoured & his people are welcome'. A gold-framed picture of Ruth soon sat on his dressing table, alongside one of his mother, Annie: 'photos of the two dearest friends I've ever had on earth'. He wrote to Ruth: 'When the mail came I sneaked away from the office & went along the cliffs with your letters, just to be right away from everybody and have you all to myself. It was such a glorious day & the sea was so beautiful … it was just as if you were by my side all the time.'

Alf and Ruth's shared Exclusive heritage was a mixed blessing. His parents were still in the more restrictive church, as were many of Ruth's uncles and aunts, and the couple faced ongoing pressure to return to the fold. When Ruth travelled to Ashhurst in the summer of 1933 to visit relatives, she was interrogated by three elders about why she had deserted the church of her childhood. Alf was indignant – 'my dear Ruth, what a battery you ran' – and adamant he too would never return to a church that he saw as a 'pretty dead bunch'. Besides, he added, even if he and Ruth were to be recognised as Exclusives again, they would be promptly excommunicated for sharing communion with outsider Christians: 'If your dear Dad came over & broke bread, we would be "cut off", I suppose.'

But for all his criticism of Exclusive Brethren beliefs, Alf had his own judgemental religious streak. He told Ruth he despised the local Catholic priest 'and almost hate him for his damnable doctrines'. When the local Church of England minister died of a heart attack and Alf was asked by the magistrate to conduct the funeral, he refused as it would have meant reading the Anglican burial service: 'a dead, rotten lifeless thing'. He also took a dim view of the 'degraded' locals on the Chatham Islands, 'from the drunken reprobate of a doctor to the cheap little prostitutes at the hotel'. I find it unsettling to read such hatred interspersed with Alf's loving messages to Ruth.

*

When the couple eventually married at the Wellington registry office in 1936, they had drifted away from organised religion and settled into a quiet, home-based faith. Alf wrote: 'I'm a silly, sentimental, lovesick young husband, am I not? Fancy writing you a letter (and incidentally wasting a penny stamp) when you're only a few feet away from me in the next room! But you see this is the very first letter I've written at our new writing desk, so I want you to have it. Mr & Mrs Scott can have the next one if I can bring myself to the point of writing to them. I'd far rather come out into the kitchen and make love to you, my dear old curly-headed black-eyed darling ...'

When World War II broke out, Alf was posted to the air force but declared unfit for overseas duty and deployed instead to ground control at the Milson Aerodrome in Palmerston North. Alf and Ruth's two eldest children, Anna and George, grew up to the sounds of aero engines and flight experiences. A second daughter, Aera, was born shortly before the war's end. Alf was often away in the evenings but made the most of his time with the kids. Those were happy days during which they dabbled in the creek for crayfish, hung Christmas stockings, flew kites and learned chess. Alf and Ruth voted in national and local elections, listened to a radio broadcast of Princess Elizabeth's wedding, and enjoyed picnics and holidays with a menagerie of friends and family.

But Exclusive Brethren shadows were never far away. Alf's wartime stint in Palmerston North put the family within reach of their Exclusive relatives, including Alf's father, Ernie, and stepmother, Kate, in nearby Ashhurst. Alf and Ruth had mostly cordial relationships with these relatives, as contact between members and non-members was still permitted by the Exclusives.

It bugged Ruth that she and Alf still faced occasional pressure to return. In the summer of 1945 she described how her father-in-law had paid them a visit accompanied by an Exclusive elder who 'recommended us to try them for a month'. A few weeks later, Ruth visited an Exclusive friend and was surprised when another Exclusive woman arrived and pinned her in conversation: 'Ida talked "meeting" & justified their right position, & didn't I want to go back!' It was a relief when the host emerged from the kitchen with afternoon tea.

Palmerston North rang with celebration when the war ended. Alf was transferred back to the Post & Telegraph Department, and the family returned to Wellington with their three young children. Their new home in the suburb of Northland was just down the hill from the radio station where Alf used to work, and he delighted in taking his family for rambles through the bush there, finding happiness in the secret spots he'd enjoyed as a young man. Once again, there were dreams of what the future might bring.

*

Alf didn't think much of it when he noticed a lump in his neck. When it became uncomfortable, he saw a doctor and was told it should be removed. But Alf delayed the surgery twice because the dates didn't suit, and months passed before his doctor insisted he accept the next summons to Wellington Hospital. It was the middle of winter, the day before he turned forty-two, when he was finally scheduled for surgery. Nurses wheeled him, Bible in hand, to the operating theatre. As the anaesthetic was injected he read Psalm 25: 'In you, Lord my God, I put my trust.'

Alf never wrote 'cancer' in his diary, but after the growth was removed he stayed longer in hospital than expected. Ruth and the children arrived to celebrate his birthday in the ward, bringing 'cake, fruit, flowers, books, slippers, hankies & good cheer'. Then doctors broke the bad news: the surgery had not been enough, and Alf would need to undergo multiple rounds of further treatment.

Radiation wreaked havoc on his body, and he curled up in bed for weeks at a time, documenting each painful hour in shaky handwriting. Ruth struggled to sleep, lying awake listening to her husband's hacking cough. Each morning she got up early to do seemingly endless chores and play hostess to wellwishers who dropped in unannounced. She was under unimaginable pressure. In rare quiet moments, she wept in despair.

Alf and Ruth's tenth wedding anniversary in 1946 was a perfect storm: it poured with rain, Anna had mumps, Aera was cutting two teeth, and Alf was curled up in bed after another round of radiotherapy that morning. He'd picked up a lovely iced wedding cake on his way home from the hospital, but any thoughts of celebration quickly disappeared. By 3 pm all the couple could manage was to wistfully read through old telegrams and letters saved from their big day.

A pattern emerges as I read through Alf's diaries from the following few years. He'd bounce back from treatment, celebrate his recovery and return to work at the postal service – then, months later at a check-up, doctors would deliver the bad news: his cancer had returned. There were more surgeries and radiation treatments, and months-long periods of sick leave. Alf and Ruth retreated ever further into their religious beliefs, finding solace in their red leather Bible. They gathered around the family organ to sing hymns with the children – and they agonised over what God was trying to tell them.

Their vulnerability reopened a door that had been closed for many years. As they struggled to survive, the Exclusive Brethren in Wellington took fresh interest in their circumstances. They had rebuffed the church for decades, but now Alf was willing to accept any help that was offered. The local Exclusive congregation was full of relatives and childhood friends who rallied around the family, chipping in with food, childcare and financial assistance. Alf appreciated the support and would occasionally attend Exclusive services at College Street; in those days non-members were permitted to attend, although they had to sit at the back and weren't allowed to speak.

Ruth was much harder to persuade, resolutely staying home even when Alf started taking the children along to the services. But the pressure ratcheted up as her husband started attending meetings every Sunday and then on weeknights as well. Even so, Ruth was bewildered when he told her in the summer of 1949 that he'd decided to return as a member. They'd just been on a romantic getaway to the Marlborough Sounds without the children, a blissful two weeks of swimming, picnicking and napping, during which Alf had said nothing about his intentions.

His wife spent the next six weeks in torment, describing her daily grief and despair over Alf's return to the dogmatic church of their youth: 'Grieved that Alf has taken a step I feel I cannot – Why!' The couple spent long nights by the fire, debating Exclusive Brethren beliefs well past midnight as their children slept. Ruth penned a long letter to her father Fred, now in his seventies, knowing he would understand her concerns. But she showed the letter to Alf, then had a change of heart and ripped it up.

Twelve days later, she sat down to write a very different letter to her dad. She had finally capitulated: after twenty-nine years of distaste for the Exclusive Brethren and six weeks of relentless pressure from her sickly husband, Ruth would also be returning to the church. She told Fred that after 'hours of darkness' she believed God wanted her to follow her husband: 'I feel now, father, you are dearer to me than ever, but He is first. I believe the Lord has enabled me to write this letter.'

She had made her stand, but her emotional torment continued. 'Feeling yearning over Father,' she wrote plaintively four days after declaring her position to Fred – and then, eleven days later: 'Spent some time just tossed with doubts. A few tears.'

*

As Alf's cancer progressed and medical options fell away, my great-grandparents became even more convinced that true healing lay in faith. Increasingly, they relied on Exclusive Brethren support. Alf kept a 'kindness journal' as his condition worsened, detailing every gift the family received: a leg of hogget from Colin Whitten; a bag of oranges from Mrs Clow; an electric bed-warmer from Henry Senior. As the months passed and he grew sicker, he was forced to summarise: 'kindness & love untold from many, many of the dear Brethren'.

In the spring of 1951, Alf visited Wellington Hospital. The assessment following his weekend stay was bleak: his treatment could go no further, and it was time for him to return home, 'take peace' and prepare to die. 'Five doctors all agreed,' Alf wrote. He was furious, resolving that faith alone was the key to winning his years-long battle with cancer: 'I believe <u>God</u> I will do so in the face of 500 doctors if need be!'

Ruth, too, spurred on by her renewed all-or-nothing faith, was convinced the answer lay with God and decided after prayer to put Alf 'on a complete liquid diet of fruit & vegetable juices'. This fast was to last for forty days: 'a scriptural period'. For more than two weeks, Alf had nothing but juice. Local Exclusive Brethren brought around boxes of produce, which Ruth juiced, juiced and juiced. Alf was allowed one cup of tea each day at 3 pm as a special concession, but after ten days even the tea disappeared. He noted that he was going 'weak at the knees' and rapidly losing weight.

Alf's religious fervour neared delirium, and he refused to accept that death was approaching. On the fourteenth day of the fast, he went a step further and decided the palliative medicines he'd been prescribed at the hospital were hindering his faith – giving up all medications would show faith in God's ability to command a healing miracle. 'The doctors, having given me up, I've given up their remedies too! ... The sleeping tabs & painkillers are down the drain.'

Racked with cancer, starved for a fortnight and now feeling every shooting pain, Alf's ruined body fought on for a few more days: 'Pain is purifying.' Three days after giving up his medication, he dragged himself from bed to shuffle up and down the back lawn with five-year-old Aera: inhaling, walking twenty steps, then exhaling, every breath a painful exertion. 'I could feel the pulsing, tingling life in almost every nerve,' he wrote, 'and virtue seemed to flow from her warm hand into my gaunt, emaciated frame.' Later that evening, Alf noted triumphantly that he was beating his cancer: 'The tide has turned.'

His diary ends there. The following day has a short message in Ruth's handwriting: 'Alf very ill indeed.' He died five days later.

Ruth was in shock. She and Alf had been living in denial, but when it became clear he was very sick they had sent the children away. Ten-year-old George was staying with another Brethren family when he was woken early one morning and informed his father was gone. As tears fell, he was brusquely told, 'Don't cry.'

Meanwhile, thirteen-year-old Anna bore the brunt of Ruth's grief. Anna knew her mother had prayed for Alf and believed he would recover, and now it was clear that Ruth was utterly shattered in her faith.

Another month went by before Aera learned of her father's death. Alf and Ruth had sent her to stay with an uncle and aunt in Napier, half a day's journey from Wellington by train. Her dad, gaunt and sickly, had clung to her as he said goodbye from his bed, but Aera had wriggled free in frustration, keen to get on with what she thought was a holiday.

When Ruth arrived with Anna and George to collect Aera at Christmas, she flew around excitedly. 'But,' she said, 'where is Daddy?'

Her older siblings looked uncomfortable and told her, 'You'd better ask Mum.'

Ruth took her youngest daughter on her knee, hugged her, then broke the news with a tremble in her voice. 'Darling, Daddy has died.'

Aera was devastated. She had no idea he'd been so sick and felt she'd been cheated out of saying a proper goodbye.

My heart aches for the grief suffered by those three children who lost a parent, just as I had feared I might lose mine.

*

Ruth had always struggled with being a mother. Before marrying Alf, she'd had a very cloistered life with little experience relating to children. Whenever her offspring misbehaved, she worried she wasn't doing enough to teach them to be God-fearing Christians. In her diary, during the wartime years with Alf at the aerodrome, she wrote, 'Children were good except for bed jigging which is strictly forbidden. Then they romped on my bed & tore the curtain. I gave them both a hiding & went into miseries myself.' Such beatings happened frequently throughout George's upbringing.

I know all too well what it's like to cower on the ground as a parent's blows rain down; I've felt the terror of not knowing when it will stop and being powerless to fight back. George was particularly affected by one night-time beating after his older sister tattled on him for saying, 'Mummy's mad.' Ruth, incensed that her children would comment on her anger, gave her son yet another thrashing as punishment. For George, it was the ultimate betrayal: he and Anna were supposed to stick up for each other.

Around the time of Alf's death, Ruth's diaries make for sad reading. 'Feel very depressed,' she wrote. 'No good reason for it.' These words could have been lifted from my own experience of living with a mentally ill parent. Ruth had little support as she suffered from depression and faced the loss of her husband. Without Alf to help balance her moods and with the struggles of a newly single mother, she became increasingly stern towards her kids, even as she yearned in her diary for 'more grace and patience'.

For the children, life in the Exclusive Brethren became the new normal. They were baptised into the faith – an awkward encounter for Anna, a gangly eleven-year-old, who sat in the bath fully clothed while an elder scooped water over her at the family's weatherboard bungalow in Miramar. George was rapidly indoctrinated. When he was taught an Indigenous war dance at school, he was petrified it may have caused him to be possessed by demons; he threw himself at the end of his bed to pray and renounce the 'spirit of the Maori haka in the name of the Lord Jesus'.

Anna and George spent much of their adolescence in conflict with each other. My aunty told me that when she had her first spiritual experience – 'I think I was about sixteen' – one of the first things she felt she needed to address was that she didn't get on with her little brother. Anna spent a night in prayer, and in the morning she realised that she loved him. After that, she made a concerted effort to get on better with him. But George missed the memo and still tried to aggravate her.

Anna, full of spark, with round-rimmed glasses and coiffed brown hair, was banned from going to university because she was a woman, even though she had excelled at school. Her non-Exclusive relatives were disappointed: Anna was clearly a star student, and her aunt made her feelings known in conversations with the wider family: 'what a waste of a very bright girl'. It was a different story for George, who was allowed to enrol in an Engineering degree at the University of Canterbury. In 1960 the Exclusive Brethren still permitted university education for men, although it was beginning to be frowned upon. George, however, ignored the gathering storm and was determined to set his own path.

*

George was a hit when he started visiting Christchurch in preparation for his university studies. Tall and athletic, with an impish grin, he became known as a ladies' man who wasn't above playing footsies under the table with girls he fancied. His musical abilities put him in high demand for Exclusive Brethren gatherings, and he was often asked to bring his piano accordion from Wellington. The Wright family in particular welcomed his musical talents. Johnny Wright was a famed pianist within the church, known across the country, while his eighteen-year-old daughter Lottie played the Hawaiian guitar and had a very clear, quavering voice like an opera singer.

George and Lottie weren't an obvious match. A demure brown-haired girl of Irish heritage, Lottie lived and breathed her faith, and was known as a stickler for the rules. She kept George at arm's length when they first met, refusing an invitation to join him for a walk; her parents held private concerns about this sweet-talking charmer from Wellington. Lottie's early rejections must have come as a surprise to George, who was used to getting the attention of girls who caught his eye. But his reputation preceded him – Lottie wasn't going to get mixed up with a boy like that.

Her opinion of him didn't shift until she heard that he had publicly renounced his wayward behaviour. In fact, the matter had been somewhat out of George's control. An elder had unexpectedly confronted him during a public church meeting, and eighteen-year-old George, put on the spot, had hurriedly pledged his loyalty to the system.

Once past her initial reservations, Lottie fell madly in love with George. Letters and postcards flew back and forth between the teens while he was still living in Wellington. George became a frequent weekend visitor to Christchurch, catching the overnight ferry from Wellington to Lyttelton Harbour. They'd spend as much time together as possible, and when he departed he'd book a window berth so he could shine his flashlight towards Lottie until the last possible moment. She would watch his waving torch until the boat rounded the end of the pier, then take the train journey back to town on the verge of tears.

The Exclusive Brethren were shifting and changing as George and Lottie's romance blossomed. The New York linen merchant James Taylor had died in 1953, after fifty years atop the Brethren hierarchy, and had been succeeded by his son James Taylor Jnr who became known as Big Jim. When Big Jim's daughter Consie married a Sydney accountant, Bruce Hales, in 1958, an aspiring leader was thrust onto the global Brethren stage. Those were heady days in the Exclusive Brethren. New York was a long way from Australia and New Zealand, and Bruce rapidly assumed de facto leadership of the Australasian Brethren on behalf of his distant father-in-law. After his brother John also rose to prominence, the siblings crisscrossed the antipodes, enforcing Brethren doctrine.

George and Lottie's engagement brought them squarely under the gaze of the Hales brothers. Lottie's father, Johnny, a much-loved man of Irish heritage, was well regarded enough to be a keynote speaker at 'fellowship meetings', special church events where members would gather from across the country. He became close to Bruce and John as they rose to power – and he wasn't afraid to hold his own with them, famously rebuking John for driving too fast down the motorway.

There were early warning signs that the Hales brothers would cause problems for George and Lottie. When Bruce visited Christchurch in the late spring of 1960, Lottie was perturbed to hear him say it wasn't right for young Brethren to leave home for education in another city. This led to her having a back-and-forth with George over whether he should cancel his planned studies; she told him there was no reason why he shouldn't stop.

He stuck to his guns, but a much larger problem loomed: Bruce also strongly disapproved of young Brethren having long engagements, directing couples to marry as quickly as possible. He was renowned for singling out young people at meetings and asking why they weren't married yet. On one occasion he asked a couple who barely knew each other if they would wed, and they married just a few days later. Refusal may have led to excommunication. Young Brethren lived in fear of being pointed at next.

George's hand was forced after Johnny visited Sydney in the summer of 1961. There, Bruce told him that his daughter should marry George immediately – and if they didn't want to, then she should break off the engagement.

Lottie was mortified. She confronted George on his next visit to Christchurch and told him this was surely a test of their loyalty to the Brethren. He again pushed back – he was a teenage student, he argued, and it made no sense for them to rush into marriage.

She pulled off the engagement ring and handed it to him with an ultimatum: 'We're not allowed to have a long engagement.'

It was a fateful moment for George. Unwilling to let Lottie go, he held the ring briefly and gave it back to her. 'Well, let's get married then.'

George wrote to another Brethren leader in Sydney for guidance on how the occasion should proceed, and the response was clear: 'we follow what is done in New York'. The rules flowed thick and fast: sensible shoes, no need to invite family from out of town, no fancy white dress but just a new best dress worn for the first time. 'Everything is to be on a spiritual level,' the leader added. George's spartan aesthetic occasionally went too far, even for Lottie, and two weeks before the marriage she wistfully wondered if she might look too plain on her wedding day. He wasn't having a bar of it, writing to her: 'You're adorned for me so it's what I want that matters. And as far as I'm concerned the plainer the better.'

This level of control was fairly typical among Exclusive Brethren in 1961. Members were encouraged to confess their misdeeds at meetings that sometimes stretched until almost midnight. Lottie, a self-righteous teenager, dutifully tattled on the Christchurch Brethren in conversations with George, describing how her peers were 'absolutely broken' after being punished for sins including fornication and 'dressing like the world'.

But Lottie herself, now nineteen, wasn't immune to temptation. As her wedding day approached, her interactions with George became increasingly amorous. During one of his visits, the young couple went too far one evening after Lottie's family had gone to bed. Nothing serious happened – just a bit of fumbling, really – but in the cold light of day it felt like the end of the world to my nineteen-year-old grandparents.

Overcome with guilt, George confessed to his mother, Ruth. She shared the news with a Brethren elder in Wellington, who promptly wrote to one of his counterparts in Christchurch. Lottie also confessed to her parents; they told the local elders, who arrived on a Wednesday evening to grill her. She told the elders how the young couple had laid down together and she'd let her young fiancé put his hands down her neck, but promised them that through God's mercy it hadn't gone any further. George was sick with worry about how matters would play out, losing his appetite as he waited for news from Christchurch: 'No breakfast again this morning.'

The elders unexpectedly decided the young couple's misdeeds weren't bad enough to warrant public attention. They told Lottie the matter could be closed in private so long as her and George's stories tallied and they'd told the full truth.

Sixty years later, I wonder how Grandpa George would feel about me reading these personal letters. His horror and shame seem a world away – yet strangely it feels as though his letters, carefully saved for many years, have brought us closer together.

Being spared public shame was a huge relief for George and Lottie, inspiring the nineteen-year-olds to recommit to their faith. It was, Lottie told George, a reminder that their marriage would be sacred before God. 'The main thing is that I'll have you always with me, and me with you.'

5.

MY CHILDHOOD FEELINGS OF BEING A ROUND PEG IN A SQUARE hole intensified as I grew older. Still, it seemed safest to try and fit in, so as I went through puberty I played along as best I could when my Brethren peers spoke about girls. I never got 'the talk' from my parents – by the time Mum finally tried to talk to me about sex, I'd already been told by the worldly kids at primary school and looked it up in the dictionary. I believed sex was shameful, but taboo topics were like catnip to Brethren kids. We whispered crude jokes to each other and laughed. Secretly I wondered what my male peers saw in the opposite sex that I didn't. Why were they so obsessed with breasts?

When I realised there was a word for men attracted to men, at first I refused to consider whether it might apply to me. We all knew that gay people were perverts, and it was eye-opening and frightening to wonder if I might be one of those deviants – it was awful to contemplate! Try as I might, though, I couldn't push the thought away. The puzzle pieces of my life began to fall together into a damning picture of who I was: my fascination with the shirtless rubbish collectors, my sense of being more at home with the girls at school, and now my complete lack of attraction to what the boys referred to as 'tits and fannies'.

Boys were the first thing I thought about when I discovered masturbation – such an ugly word, filled with shame. I feared I'd be shut up or withdrawn from if my parents found out how much I enjoyed touching myself. It was too risky to indulge in the house, where I still shared a bedroom with Caleb; instead, I'd sneak around the back and into the garage. Fear and pleasure coursed through my veins. I knew I had to stop at a certain point – we'd all read the Bible verse about the sin of ejaculating onto the ground – but one sunny afternoon, tucked amid dusty boxes and tools, I misjudged and watched in horror as an unfamiliar white watery substance splashed onto the floor. Racked with guilt, I confessed to Mum immediately; she gave me a stern lecture but thankfully decided not to tell Dad.

In 2006, when I was seventeen, my heart pounded through my chest the first time I saw an ad from a gay man in the personal listings of *The Southland Times*, the newspaper I'd been introduced to at my worldly primary school. I'd never before been presented with an opportunity to connect with a gay person; although I was still a long way from acknowledging I might be one myself, it was enticing to think that at the end of that phone number was a man who liked men.

For days, whenever I got the chance, I stared at that number. Then I plucked up the courage to call it from our family landline. I had no intention of talking to him; if he answered I planned to hang up immediately. As it happened, the call went to voicemail, and I listened wistfully to the short recording. For the next hour I called the number over and over, tucked away in the study, listening to the message from someone who didn't seem ashamed of who he was. What was his life like, I wondered? Did his parents still talk to him?

Later that afternoon, he called back. Mum answered the phone and was bemused when a stranger wanted to know why he'd missed so many calls from us. I told her I'd been calling a wrong number.

The gay sex hotline I called several months later was much harder to explain away. It had also appeared in the personal listings, and I was emboldened after getting away with my previous calls. There wasn't much to it, really – just a prerecorded story about two guys hooking up in a youth hostel – but it was the closest I'd come to a gay experience.

As soon as I'd hung up, I realised my mistake: there would be no disguising the 0900 number on our telephone bill. I spent weeks waiting for the envelope to arrive in the mail, then snuck the bill to school and ran it through the office shredder. My victory was short-lived, though, as Mum became suspicious when the bill never arrived and requested a fresh copy from the telco provider. Dad confronted me, and I wept as I admitted I'd made the call, promising him I wasn't interested in 'those things'. He threw his arms around me in relief – the only time I remember him hugging me – which only made it worse. How would he react if he knew I might actually be gay?

The first time I met another gay person face to face, I was in my overalls and aged almost eighteen. I had regular contact with worldlies in the tyre shop – an escape from relentless Brethren observation – and I'd fitted a set of tyres to a nurse's four-wheel drive. When she returned to pick it up, I told her she'd also need to book in for a wheel alignment. She nodded and said, 'I'll tell my partner, and she can bring it back next week.'

My ears pricked up. Why was she referencing her female partner as though it was the most normal thing in the world? I longed to ask her what that was like. How had they met? Did people ever react badly when she talked about her partner? What gave her the courage to talk about the relationship so openly? But I was still deep in the closet, and she drove away without any idea of the impact she'd had.

*

I met Paul through the personal listings in *The Southland Times*. More than a year after calling the gay sex hotline, I'd plucked up the courage to go a step further.

My crushing fear of being excommunicated was eclipsed by exploding hormones, and I was desperate for connection: physical connection, yes, but also emotional connection with someone who understood how I felt. I made an excuse for why I needed to go out that evening – it was the autumn of 2007, a few days short of my eighteenth birthday – and dialled the number from a pay phone on Tay Street. I'd learnt my lesson.

To my surprise, Paul agreed to meet and invited me over to his home. Fortunately it wasn't near where any Brethren lived; members operated like a spy network, and I knew it would be reported back to my parents or the priests if my car was seen parked on an unexpected street.

The first thing I noticed about Paul was his shoulder-length blond hair – Brethren men weren't allowed to grow their hair long, so this marked him out as a worldly. Welcoming and friendly, he ushered me through to a dimly lit room where a purple mosquito net hung bunched up over a neatly made bed.

I could barely speak. Part of me was terrified, knowing I was about to cross a point of no return. I also thrilled with anticipation at being so close to another man as we undressed. What did he think of my body? Would he take the lead and show me what to do? How was I supposed to know where to put my hands and whether he was OK with it?

Our encounter was awkward, over almost before it began. I was too embarrassed to tell Paul it was my first time.

Guilt swept through me. I slunk furtively back to my Toyota Corona, hidden up a side street across the road from Donovan Park, and my stomach churned as I scanned for any Brethren observers. Had I been followed? Would my sin be discovered? I didn't know what I'd been thinking. All my life I'd heard terrible warnings about people being cast from the flock; now I was sure my turn had come.

After I snuck home through the back door, I couldn't sleep. Convinced my life was over, I shut myself in the study and with shaking hands called Daniel Hales in Sydney.

The Hales family was still the pinnacle of Brethren fellowship. Daniel's father, John Hales, had died a few years earlier, and Daniel's younger brother was Bruce, the new Man of God. Daniel knew I was the great-grandson of Johnny Wright, who had rebuked John Hales for speeding all those years ago. I knew that if I could plead my case to anyone, it would be directly to the Hales family.

Daniel, a grey-haired, cardigan-wearing businessman, listened as I told him in a trembling voice that I had something terrible to confess.

I could still feel Paul's body pressed against mine, my hands running through his long blond hair, and I tried desperately to push his face out of my mind. In a state of shock, I couldn't bring myself to tell Daniel what I'd actually done. But to my surprise he was kind, fatherly almost, and calmed me down. 'Whatever you've done,' he said, 'there is a way through, and it surely won't be as bad as you fear.' He told me to take my confession to Peter Hickmott, one of the Invercargill elders, and be honest with him about what had happened – 'tell him not to do anything without talking to me first'.

The next morning I was shaking as Peter closed the door to his study. I barely noticed the autumn clouds or the well-pruned rose bushes lining the path outside. Peter was an awkward man; he and his wife didn't have children, and his owlish spectacles and halting nature belied the power he was accumulating within the Brethren system. The Man of God himself had stayed in this house, and I knew that anything I told Peter would be repeated directly to the Hales brothers in Sydney.

Peter questioned me closely as I revealed my misdeeds, just as Grandpa George had revealed his fifty years earlier. Who touched what? What went where? How many times? I felt unclean; I wished the floor would open and swallow me. Soldiering on, I gave every last detail I could think of, with one crucial exception: I denied I was gay. I pretended that I'd been 'experimenting' in a foolish youthful misstep that had no deeper meaning. Peter must have had his doubts, but he kept them to himself.

After our meeting, I waited on tenterhooks – pacing my room, unable to engage in conversation – as Peter conferred with Daniel. I was bracing for the axe to fall, knowing I could face public humiliation and excommunication. When the edict finally came back, I was astonished: like George and Lottie all those years ago, I was told my confession showed God's spirit was working in me and the matter of my misdeeds could be 'closed' in private.

*

Overcome with relief and encouraged by Peter Hickmott, I set out to confess every last sin I could think of to bring myself closer to God.

It wasn't long before I found myself back in Peter's home, there of my own free choice but knowing his expectation was that I would 'get right' with God. Although nothing would ever be as terrifying as that first confession, it was still a huge step for me to talk to Peter like this. I wondered what he would think of the things I had to tell him. Was there a chance I could be shut up or withdrawn from? And what if he talked to Daniel again, and they changed their minds about whether I was a good person?

Peter served me whisky during those late-night confession sessions, pouring top-label Scotch from the drinks cabinet. I'd head over to his large two-storey house after church on a Friday evening, telling Dad and Mum I needed to spend time with a priest, and we'd drink at his large wooden dining table as I mustered the Dutch courage to confess a slate of newly remembered sins. This alcohol consumption was considered normal: the Brethren were heavy drinkers, with booze woven into our daily lives. It helped move things along – my wickedness was too much to bear while sober. How else could I face what a terrible person I was, full of dark thoughts and desires?

Peter, like all Brethren priests, had no formal training in pastoral care. His primary Brethren assets were his wealth and his proximity to the Man of God; the respect he received had nothing to do with whether he was equipped to care for vulnerable teenagers. There was also an enormous power imbalance: I knew that he held all the cards when it came to making decisions about my future with the Brethren and therefore my loved ones. So much was at stake as he poked and prodded me with questions about my sins. Was I sorry? How many times had I committed this particular transgression? Had I told anyone else about it? Were there any witnesses?

I looked back over my teenage years and into my childhood, thinking of all those I had wronged and the evil thoughts I'd had. There were so many sins that I wondered if I'd ever be able to remember and confess them all. But did I even deserve to be forgiven? My confessions were accompanied by apologies to those who had been on the receiving end of my sinful behaviour. I tracked down former teachers and apologised for misbehaving in their classes. I ran into a former neighbour in the supermarket and apologised for shouting insults across the fence as a child. I said I was sorry for being rude and disrespectful to Brethren I didn't like – and there were plenty of them.

Whenever I walked down the street, I stared straight ahead in order to avoid the surrounding temptations. I was determined to scour my record clean so God had nothing to hold against me.

As I cleared my slate, I hoped that the burden of my sin would lift. But I still felt guilty when I woke up each morning; I couldn't shake the feeling that I wasn't worthy and didn't belong in the Brethren. God was supposed to be loving but felt just as distant as ever; now I understood how Dad must have felt on those lonely mornings as he cried out for God in the dark. Like Dad, I reasoned that God must feel distant because I still wasn't trying hard enough.

As the months passed, I went to great lengths to uncover former misdeeds, endeavouring to leave no stone unturned – if this confession wasn't the final breakthrough, I'd tell myself, then maybe the next one would be. But it was all to no avail. As confessions stacked up with no breakthrough moment, I realised with a crushing reluctance that I couldn't keep ignoring the biggest sin of all.

Even after that first sexual encounter, I tried to tell myself I wasn't gay. I was just curious, I reasoned, and fooling around with a guy was less risky than with a girl. It was common for young Brethren to be forced into marriage after being caught 'defiling their purity' – and divorce was forbidden. I knew of couples my grandparents' age who had endured fifty years of loveless marriage after being caught in drunken encounters as teenagers. Ultimately, though, this fear was a red herring for me. The real reason I'd fooled around with a guy instead of a girl was simple: I wasn't into girls.

Being gay was a different type of sin. Everything I'd confessed had been relatively straightforward: transgressions that could be forgiven and not repeated. But being gay? That couldn't be forgiven. It spoke to who I was as a person. It was what the Brethren called 'original sin' – pegged not to an event but to the innate wickedness humans inherit as descendants of Adam and Eve. Tackling original sin was a big deal. Surely, though, this was what was holding me back. I would never get close to God while I was keeping such a dark secret.

It was another Friday night when I felt I'd built up the courage to tell Peter. I was at his house after the evening service, and he once again offered me whisky. We were at his dining table, as had become our custom in the three months since I'd made my first confession. It was midwinter, and a sharp westerly swept through that seemed never to stop blowing in Invercargill. Trees near the coast sloped to one side, twisted by a breeze as relentless as my Friday confessions.

Peter's wife made herself scarce that night; it must have been clear I was building up to something important. He poured me a stiff Scotch, then another, then yet another, as we made awkward small talk: 'How are things with your parents? Are you feeling more settled at work? Have you read the latest ministry from Sydney?'

I shifted nervously in my seat, struggling to keep my thoughts straight as the alcohol buzz hit. My guilt, normally a hard rock, was untethered and floating in a fuzzy cloud – I dreamed of permanently softening the edges of my guilt like this. There was no denying the rock, though. I knew I had to come clean, although even under the influence I was unable to say the words. The rock was too big, the enormity of my sin too shameful to be spoken aloud.

Eventually, in drunken shame, I asked Peter for a pen and paper. My confession was too dreadful to come out of my mouth, but perhaps I could muster the courage to write it down – and this way, I wouldn't stumble over my words.

Peter quietly retrieved a notepad and ballpoint from the nearby dresser. We both knew this was a big moment. Much less affected by the alcohol than I was, he seemed to know exactly what was going on.

Teetering on the edge of an emotional precipice, my fingers clammy with fear, I scribbled on the piece of paper. Then I pushed it across the table towards Peter, knowing my life was in his hands.

His face was expressionless as he read the two words: 'I'm gay.'

*

Athol Greene, the Man of God's father-in-law who I saw as a grandfatherly figure, consoled me after hearing the news of my confession. Athol was one of a small number of people who were told; Peter also shared the news with two other priests in Invercargill, along with the Man of God, Bruce Hales. His brother Daniel was told too, as an update to my earlier conversation with him, and Athol because Peter knew I was close to him and trusted his advice.

I almost couldn't bring myself to call Athol again. What would he think now he knew I was a degenerate? Would he still be supportive and grandfatherly, or was I no longer deserving of such kindness? To my surprise, he jumped in with commiserations, telling me it was still 'very likely' that I'd get married, have children and be a successful Brethren father: 'You'll solve this problem, mister,' he said.

I trusted these elders but was terrified of the news spreading. Even if I wasn't going to be shut up or withdrawn from, the Brethren rumour mill could bring about social ruin. Determined to keep a tight lid on the secret, I made a detailed list of everyone who knew I was gay: their name, the date they'd found out, and who had told them.

Besides the senior leaders, my parents were the only others on the list – although they never addressed it with me directly. I knew that they knew, and they knew that I knew they knew, but we avoided talking about it. I often wondered what they thought, but I didn't dare ask. Were they devastated to learn their son was a deviant? Did they feel betrayed? Were they relieved I'd confided in the elders, and did they trust that the Man of God had things under control?

In some ways, I was lucky: it wasn't that long since the Exclusive Brethren had treated gay people as demon-possessed. If I'd confessed twenty years earlier, I would have been withdrawn from immediately. The church's thinking had shifted partly because societal views had changed; the Brethren were acutely aware that their perspective on gay people was out of step with that held by the rest of New Zealand.

Peter Hickmott was as kind as he knew how to be: 'You're not evil, you're unwell.' With the Man of God's encouragement, he told me I'd been struck with a deep sickness that needed to be treated. Our Friday night confessions became prayers. At that dining table, still drinking Scotch, we pleaded with God to work in my heart and save me from the curse of homosexuality: 'Please, God, show me the way forward,' I would beg. 'I'll do anything!'

In his own way, Peter only ever acted out of love and concern as we swept through my whisky-soaked confessions and prayers.

He was doing the best he could with what he believed to be true, and I never doubted he had my best interests at heart. I trusted him when he told me I needed to go to the doctor for blood tests: 'We need to make sure you don't have AIDS.' There was no talk about whether I'd done anything that had put me at risk; for all I knew, it was possible to contract HIV just by touching another gay person.

My skin crawled with shame when I visited our family GP – it was almost as bad as my fateful confession, except this time I was sober. The doctor asked a few questions and told me there was almost zero chance I had HIV, but I was under priestly orders to insist on the test. I almost cried with relief when the result came back negative.

Peter genuinely believed I was broken – as did I – and thought he was doing the right thing by working with me to change my sexuality. There was clearly no future in being an openly gay man, and we knew the consequences if I kept acting on my lustful desires: I'd be struck down by God and burn forever in hell.

*

God was mysteriously absent as the weeks dragged into months. I'd been convinced that confessing my sexuality would finally allow me to be at peace, so it was a shock when I remained lost, confused and very much gay. I didn't want to be gay – nothing would have made me happier than miraculously being 'cured' of my gayness. But no matter how hard I prayed or how many sins I confessed, it didn't happen. The Friday nights at Peter's home were having no effect. This was dispiriting, and I wondered if I'd be condemned to a lifelong struggle of suppressing my sexuality and also my doubts.

Doubts were considered a sin by the Brethren. Popular refrains from the church leaders included 'We'll do the thinking, you do the doing' and 'If you don't understand it, don't question it'. Allowing ourselves even the smallest of doubts, we were told, could lead to the unravelling of our faith; we were told not to pick at the thread, but to stitch it right back in and pretend it never came loose in the first place.

I felt guilty for having doubts and tried to double down on my beliefs, but I found it difficult to understand many of the rules I'd been raised with. 'Satan is prince of the airwaves,' we were told; a teaching that began in the Taylor years. This was used to discourage aeroplane travel by Brethren, but eventually they became avid flyers. Then it was used to ban access to radio broadcasts, including – for a while – the frequencies used in garage-door openers. Digital cameras were also forbidden and then suddenly permitted. We were told that all television programmes were products of the devil; there was no allowance for people exercising their discretion in deciding what was suitable. When my parents built a house to fit our large family, they were forced to construct around the shell of an existing home because completely new constructions were forbidden. The Brethren also fussed over hypotheticals – for example, if you were in a car crash and needed to call for help, was it OK to make a call on someone else's mobile phone when use of them was forbidden? We tied ourselves up in knots trying to keep abreast of what was allowed.

The daily church meetings weren't getting through to me. They were supposed to bring us closer to God, but I found them depressing and confusing. Instead of admitting this, I started preaching at Sunday services, taking the microphone and trying to persuade the gathered Brethren of something I did not believe. My sermons were carefully rehearsed in the bedroom mirror as old nerves flared up, and expectant faces stared as I said that our community was the only place where we could truly be close to God. It felt like the ultimate hypocrisy: what did I know about getting close to God?

On a visit to Auckland to see my aunty Anna and cousin Lindy a few months later, I was asked to preach at the main Brethren hall on Coronation Road. This was far beyond anything I'd tackled before: delivering a sermon in the largest meeting room in New Zealand, with capacity for more than two thousand people. I had no idea why I'd been asked – I was just a teenager visiting from the other end of the country, and there were hundreds of men more qualified than me. But I wasn't given the option of saying no; clearly they thought I'd have something worthwhile to say. Perhaps news had filtered through that the Man of God himself had been involved in efforts to get me back on the straight and narrow. The Brethren loved nothing more than a redeemed sinner story arc.

That Sunday evening, I couldn't escape the attention of the crowd gathered in the windowless brick hall. In Auckland I'd normally have been sitting somewhere around the eighth row, well back from the leaders, tapping my foot on the green carpet and shuffling restlessly on the black vinyl seats as I waited for the interminable services to finish. But preachers were elevated to prominent seats, so that night I was called out publicly and told to sit in the front circle with the elders. I grasped my black Bible and hymnbook as I made my way over to sit among the Auckland leaders.

A sea of Brethren surrounded me when my turn arrived. I walked the few short steps to the microphone, trying to breathe, and pushed my nerves down as far as possible. I told my audience which Bible verse we were going to read – so far, so good. I preached a familiar message about getting close to God and being grateful we were in the only true church. Then, after a sentence about how worldlies thought sinning was fun, without thinking I added an aside: 'Of course, sinning *is* fun.'

There was a gasp. A ripple of laughter ran through the room. Was I really telling the biggest assembly in the country that sinning was fun? There was no move to seize the microphone. While the young people laughed, elders in the front row watched with raised eyebrows, waiting to see where I would go with this.

'The thing is,' I said, 'while sinning is fun, all those worldlies out there will have to pay the price when they burn in hell for their sins. So we're much better to do without the fun now, and then we'll be rewarded by spending eternity in heaven with God.'

The elders visibly relaxed. My delivery had been unorthodox, and we weren't supposed to admit that sinning was fun, but I'd got there in the end. It was a narrow escape.

*

Away from the preaching and backslapping, doubts crept through my mind like shadows at dusk, swirling together with curiosity in an intoxicating dance. But when I started asking questions, I was quickly shut down. That was perplexing to me – the Bible recounted how Jesus, aged twelve, had sat questioning his elders in the temple; if that was good enough for Jesus, I reasoned, surely questions were OK. During group conversations after church meetings, I openly challenged some of our teachings while my fellow Brethren awkwardly shuffled their feet. 'Why can't we be left to make our own judgements about what TV shows are OK?' 'Why is it OK for Brethren to campaign for political parties but not OK for us to vote?' Questions like these were a direct challenge to the divinely appointed Man of God.

It was deeply isolating to have doubts when everyone in my community was supposed to be moving in lockstep. There was no diversity of thought, and disagreement was tantamount to treason. I didn't know how to find others who shared my doubts – most were too afraid to speak out, and if I had revealed my true feelings to someone, there was a chance they would have reported me to the priests. A careless word could have got me excommunicated. For most Brethren, the only path was just to keep quiet, but as the church tried to control my understanding of the world, I was already grasping the scope of what lay beyond.

Athol did his best to head off my doubts when I tentatively shared them during our phone calls. He said I should stay loyal to Peter – 'the Lord has given him to you' – and that if I couldn't muster my own faith, I should fall into line behind Brethren whose faith was stronger than mine. As we continued our conversations, I from my bedroom, he from his home in Penrith, Athol warned that if I allowed any doubts, the devil would try to get me to 'discount the Brethren'.

These chats with Athol weren't all doom and gloom. He was still optimistic that I would find a way through and settle down as a loyal Brethren member: 'Keep at it, son, just keep at it. We're going to win.' The key to this, Athol said, was to unfailingly follow the teachings of his son-in-law: Bruce Hales, the Man of God, a 'lovely man'. And then Athol added, 'He's Christ.' This sort of talk, while blasphemous to most Christians, was fairly common among the Brethren. They were increasingly putting the Man of God on the same level as Jesus himself, and Athol had no qualms about doing so.

'All you need in your soul,' Athol told me, 'comes from these great men.'

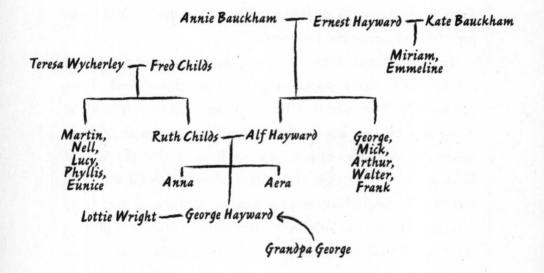

6.

AUNTY ANNA, GRANDPA GEORGE'S OLDER SISTER, ALSO HAD doubts about the Exclusive Brethren when she was a teen. Years of beatings and scoldings from her mother, Ruth, hadn't dampened her curiosity, and she wondered whether the Brethren were all they pretended to be. She felt she had never fully fitted into the system, and the first eleven years of her life – those spent outside the church – seemed like happier times.

After seven years as an Exclusive, Anna was outspoken during her teen years in the 1950s. But when she dared to ask questions, elders told her she was like the religious leaders of Christ's day who were so bound up in their doctrine that they didn't recognise who he was and contributed to his death. Being compared to murderers wasn't enough to crush Anna's spirit: she realised that fear was holding her in the Brethren, not love, and became determined to escape. She didn't believe in the diktats that Big Jim issued from New York, and she could see that a split was forming between senior leaders; she resolved to make her bid for freedom when the schism arrived.

Fatefully, though, she fell in love with a Brethren boy, and they wed in 1958. The wedding was a large family affair, with Brethren and non-Brethren gathered together, as was still permitted. Relatives from around the country were invited to celebrate at The Rowans beside Katherine Mansfield Park, a central Wellington reserve with neat paths and spacious gardens. The cherry trees were leafy green; summer was just ending, but the weather hadn't yet started to turn. Anna's uncles and aunts were all outside the Exclusive Brethren: none of Ruth's siblings had followed her back into the church, and Alf's five brothers and two sisters were also outside the fold. Some of the Hayward siblings had escaped to Africa, beyond reach of the Brethren; others had been excommunicated when it became clear they couldn't or wouldn't conform, much to the despair of their elderly parents, who stayed true to the faith.

Anna's grandpa Ernie Hayward, the patriarch of a now largely non-Brethren family, gave her away. He beamed with pride as he helped the nineteen-year-old bride off the running board of the wedding car, his walking stick also in hand. Anna looks radiant in her wedding photos: she's wearing a modest short-sleeved white wedding dress to just above the ankle, with matching hat, kitten heels and gloves.

It was a proud moment for Ruth. Anna's husband, Rob, was the son of Allan Simmons, an Auckland Brethren leader. Here, in Anna's marriage to a member of a prestigious Brethren family, was proof that Ruth's discipline and teaching had paid off.

Her sisters were happy for her – they knew how tough life had been since Alf died. While Ruth had leant on the Brethren, her sisters had been there for her too: babysitting, consoling and offering financial support. Although Ruth had gone back to the church their father had shunned in 1920, there was no question she was still part of their family. As they celebrated with her that day, they had no idea it was the last time they would be gathered together.

Cold winds of change were beginning to blow through the Exclusive Brethren. During the first half of the twentieth century, they had become increasingly connected, and the rise of inventions like the telephone meant global edicts circulated with increasing speed. Their Christian doctrine became more conservative as teachings of the early Brethren leader John Nelson Darby were reinterpreted and applied in a modern context. Yet for all their conservatism, it was still possible for members to socialise and interact with outsiders. It was also still permissible for members to directly challenge church teachings. Transcripts of meetings from that period show robust discussion, marked, as the years passed, by increasing deference to the teachings of the Elect Vessel James Taylor Snr the linen merchant.

By the time Taylor Snr died in 1953 – on a Sunday, aged eighty-three – he had become known among the Exclusives as 'The Beloved': a special man among men. Through the mid-1950s, there was no clear successor as Elect Vessel. His son Big Jim – the youngest of the family, also in the linen business – was seen as the standard-bearer of his father's legacy, but a number of other senior leaders were also widely respected and stood as counterweights. Meanwhile, Exclusive assemblies in far-flung places like Auckland retained a high degree of autonomy, and Big Jim's efforts to assert his newfound authority often fell on deaf ears.

Auckland became an early test case for the limits of his power. By the 1950s the city's Exclusive assembly had become one of the largest worldwide, and around a thousand members were regularly gathering in central Auckland for services at the East Street hall, a cavernous meeting room with a platform at one end. The Auckland assembly was a considerable base of Brethren power, and its leaders were prominent in hosting fellowship meetings across New Zealand and Australia – although many New Zealanders felt they weren't afforded the same level of respect as their Australian counterparts.

In 1951, this caused friction after an Auckland leader Jack Bishop gave teachings in the Victorian city of Geelong that ran afoul of established Exclusive orthodoxy on Galatians 6:1. This biblical verse addresses how to deal with a person caught in sin; Bishop said elders could hear confessions in private without bringing them to the attention of the wider assembly, which contradicted the teachings of public confession in vogue at the time. Bishop promptly apologised, but there was ongoing debate over whether his repentance was enough. For four years, the Auckland Brethren bickered over how to address the 'Jack Bishop Issue'. At East Street on Saturday evenings, they held special 'care meetings' where opposing camps thrashed out their arguments; these meetings became such a spectacle that Exclusives from nearby regions, including Northland and Waikato, would make special bus trips to observe the chaos as Auckland Brethren shouted angrily at each other.

From New York, Big Jim took a dim view of how the Jack Bishop Issue was handled, accusing the Auckland assembly of a 'reign of terror'. Matters finally came to a head in 1956, following an emotional Saturday night care meeting that had lasted four and a half hours, ending with an astonishing walkout that saw one hundred and fifty Brethren get up and leave in protest; these protesters refused to attend communion services the next morning, and many never returned. Ultimately, the Auckland challengers were remembered not for the substance of their concerns – Big Jim agreed the actions against Bishop had been 'harsh, legal, unscriptural' – but for the fact they had dared defy international Brethren leadership in the first place. When the protesters tried to plead their case to Big Jim during his visit to Auckland in 1957, their overtures were rejected: 'The Lord did not leave the saints at East Street when you did.'

As Big Jim placed greater emphasis through the 1950s on the need for loyalty to the Exclusive Brethren, he turned to the Bible to justify his position, focusing on an excerpt from the Second Epistle to Timothy. The author, whom the Brethren believed to be the Apostle Paul, had written a heartfelt letter to Timothy, an early evangelist in the coastal Greek city of Ephesus. The author, facing impending death, laid out instructions for keeping alive their fledgling Christian faith. In verses 19 to 21 of the second chapter, later translated from the original Koine Greek by John

Nelson Darby, Timothy's adviser describes how some vessels are better than others:

> Yet the firm foundation of God stands, having this seal,
> [The] Lord knows those that are his; and, Let every one who
> names the name of [the] Lord withdraw from iniquity.
>   But in a great house there are not only gold and silver
> vessels, but also wooden and earthen; and some to honour,
> and some to dishonour.
>   If therefore one shall have purified himself from these,
> [in separating himself from them], he shall be a vessel to
> honour, sanctified, serviceable to the Master, prepared for
> every good work.

Big Jim fixated on this section. It was, he believed, a directive from God that the Exclusive Brethren should be fully separating themselves from the 'wooden and earthen' vessels of worldly society – and, perhaps more importantly, even from other Christians who didn't share their exact doctrine. In fact, 'separating himself from them' isn't part of the original letter; that line was added by Darby, who believed it provided greater context. Most biblical scholars disagree with Darby's translation, while other translations – including the King James version – carry no such instruction to separate the vessels. But that didn't matter to Big Jim. To the Brethren, Darby was a direct representative of God, and therefore his translation must be correct.

This verse became the Brethren's mantra. When I was a teen, they quietly removed the brackets around the separation text, erasing any evidence of Darby's hand and making it appear as though the words were part of the original text.

In 1958, as Anna celebrated her wedding in Wellington, this hardline concept of separation was gathering steam. There was great debate over what separation from 'the world' might look like. Exclusive Brethren, Big Jim said, should cut themselves off entirely from those who weren't part of the holy fellowship. Relatives who didn't follow the separation doctrine should be disowned, membership of business associations should be renounced, and Brethren who were in joint ownership of property or business with non-members should cut those ties.

'Separation' was all about maintaining purity in the assembly and managing or eliminating perceived threats to that purity. The Brethren had an intense fear of the outside world, which led to a rejection of anyone who was 'other' – including fellow Christians – and a banning of most connections to outsiders. This extreme doctrine was about much more than social separation: it also cleaved the Brethren from outside society in structural, educational, financial and political matters.

In practice, separation meant it was no longer possible for Exclusives to buy shares, drink a cup of tea with a worldly friend, or live in a house that shared a wall with a non-Brethren neighbour. Members were forced to move out of terraced developments and live in standalone bungalows. Shares had to be sold immediately, and Brethren accountants and lawyers had to renounce their membership of professional societies. Anyone who worked with worldlies had to 'make a stand' and refuse to eat lunch with them in the smoko room. In time, this rule was applied so strictly that even excrement wasn't allowed to mix if it meant sharing a sewerage line with an outsider; when a Brethren family moved into a house that shared a sewer connection with the next-door property, they would dig themselves a new poo pipe in the name of separation.

Brethren leaders broadly agreed to implement separation but disagreed over how rapidly it should be introduced. In July 1959, at international three-day meetings in London's grand Methodist Central Hall, Gerald Cowell – a prominent and much-loved UK leader – proposed a more moderate line on separation. A photograph from the meetings shows Cowell, a bespectacled 61-year-old from the East London town of Hornchurch, holding forth from the lectern; dozens of senior Brethren men in suits and ties sit in tiers on the stage behind him. In front of him, out of the photograph's frame, more than two thousand men and women from around the world are packed into Central Hall. Most men on the stage appear to be listening attentively to Cowell – but Big Jim, seated immediately to Cowell's left, has his head cocked sharply to one side.

On the Wednesday afternoon, Big Jim snapped at Cowell during a discussion. This caused consternation among some of the gathered Brethren as they broke for afternoon tea at Caxton Hall, a ten-minute walk from the main conference venue. Over biscuits and cups of tea, members quietly discussed how taken aback they were by Big Jim's rudeness to Cowell, saying he had displayed a 'bad spirit'. But Big Jim strongly disagreed with Cowell's moderate approach to separation: God had spoken, he said, and the Brethren needed to move immediately. Families should be cut off, friendships with non-Brethren ceased, jobs resigned and households cleansed. The assembly must be pure.

Over the following months, Brethren had to choose between Cowell and Big Jim. The majority fell into line, and Cowell was excommunicated in 1960. Anna, who had planned to follow Cowell, was dismayed when her new husband stood firmly in the Big Jim camp. She faced an agonising decision: her freedom or her marriage. To stay with her husband, she would need to swallow her doubts and pretend she believed in Big Jim's teachings. Leaving the Exclusive Brethren would mean walking away from Rob, whom she adored. She decided it was too steep a price to pay.

*

Any lingering doubts my great-grandmother Ruth Hayward may have had about the Brethren had long since been dispelled. The church represented her most cherished connection to Alf's memory; one of his last wishes had been to live among the Exclusives. Each new ruling was a further test of faith, just as the fasting and pain medication had been in Alf's final days. Ruth embraced them all.

But the separation edict presented her most significant Brethren challenge yet. She loved her five siblings even though they were outside the fold. Her sister Phyllis had saved her invitation to Anna's wedding; in March 1959, just months before the separation ruling, she happily scrawled on it that Ruth had become a grandmother. But for Ruth, the sisterhood of blood had become less important than her spiritual brothers and sisters among the Brethren. As with her great-grandfather Sam Childs in the 1840s and her grandfather William Childs in the 1870s, there was no doubting where Ruth stood: she would hold true to the Brethren no matter the cost.

As details of the 1959 London meetings spread to New Zealand, Ruth agonised over how to break the news of separation to her sisters, drafting a letter to explain her position. 'I have been wanting for a good while now to speak freely to you all concerning our faith,' she wrote. As the letter took shape Ruth crossed out words, scribbled in the margins and rephrased paragraphs. She explained that her new understanding of Brethren faith meant she could no longer enjoy familial relationships with those who remained outside the church: 'There is only one fellowship, that of our Lord Jesus Christ, and if we are baptised to Him, then to partake in any other fellowship is sin … So I must judge such sin, and withdraw from it … This is a cutting off indeed, and grief to nature. But Christ, the Anointed of God, must have supreme place.' Ruth never again shared a cup of tea with her sisters.

Big Jim's separation edict cemented his power over the Brethren, and their separatist beliefs became more pronounced. In the 1960s, the church went in the opposite direction from

Western society, with new rules flowing thick and fast. Higher education was banned, radio and television were forbidden, and eating or drinking with non-members became grounds for excommunication. It was now unacceptable for women to wear hats, as had been the tradition; Big Jim ordered them to wear silk headscarves, and hair now had to be worn hanging down, to the shame of older women whose tresses were no longer as thick and full as they had once been. Women were also forbidden from styling or trimming their hair. Men were forbidden from wearing shorts. Gone were the days of asking for fellowship on the basis of personal conviction, as had been the case for Alf and Ruth; now a baby was considered to be 'asking for fellowship' when they first reached out for the bread and wine at a communion service. Previously it had taken effort to remain in the Brethren; now it took effort to leave.

These harsh new rules were devastating for non-Brethren family members who found themselves out in the cold. As I sift through letters from the early 1960s that describe the impact of separation, I'm shaken by the anger and grief of Alf's younger brother Mick Hayward. The only Hayward son still living near their parents in Ashhurst, he had a front-row seat as Ernie – my great-great-grandfather – and his second wife, Kate, were pulled into the doctrine of separation. Mick's daughters were nonplussed by the strange situation with their grandpa and grandma: for a while, Ernie and Kate still permitted them to visit but refused to eat or drink with them and insisted on going into a different room while they enjoyed their cups of tea. What was the point of inviting a grandchild over for their birthday if you couldn't share their cake? Then the visits stopped altogether. Mick, who had grown up among the Exclusive Brethren in Ashhurst but never formally joined, was incensed as he described to his brothers how the church was now treating him, his wife and their children: 'We have been slighted and insulted by the Brethren every way possible. Aunty Florrie refused to ride in our car, they refuse to shake hands, some look straight through me as though I don't exist.'

Grandpa Ernie, now eighty-three, was 'desperately upset' by the ban on eating and socialising with outsiders even when they were flesh and blood. Loving and hospitable, he wept as he explained to his grandchildren he could no longer see them.

Ruth, the sole remaining Brethren Hayward of her generation – although not a Hayward by birth – moved in with her elderly in-laws. She zealously stood guard to prevent the non-Brethren Hayward children from breaching separation by seeing their dad and mum. This led to a heated confrontation between Ruth and Mick.

When he arrived with his daughter to visit Grandma Kate, who was sick, Ruth refused to let them in. 'You can't come in here,' she told them, 'because you're an outsider.'

Mick wasn't having a bar of it. He pushed his righteous sister-in-law aside – 'Excuse me, Ruth' – and swept in to see his ailing stepmother.

Alf and Mick's youngest sister, Emmeline Hayward – withdrawn from as a young woman for 'worldliness' and 'wilfulness' – also received a cold welcome when she visited Ashhurst with her husband, Uani. In an account of her life, written years later, Em described what happened:

> We knocked. Ruth opened the door. As soon as she saw me she started to close it, I wish we had pushed it then. We heard the key turn, and she called out loudly, 'You can't come in here!'
>
> I knocked again, and how awful to see her actually closing the fanlights. Was she mad?
>
> Uani called out, 'Ruth, we are coming in, even if I have to break a window.' She quickly disappeared, and as we soon found out, she phoned the Exclusive Brethren elders.
>
> In the meantime my mother had struggled from her bed, and very unsteadily opened the door. Even now I cry. Her hair was snowy white, straggly and thinned out. She was almost blind, wrinkled, and oh so thin. She seemed so little. It just knocked me sideways. She was peering to see, and squinting out with one eye screwed up, as she said, 'Em, is that you?' Her voice was so weak, so sad, and so old.
>
> Dad was lying on the sofa, trying to focus through his thick glasses, his weak hands holding a walking stick that he couldn't use.
>
> Such a lot of misunderstandings and loss between us.

When the elders arrived, poor Grandpa Ernie began to weep.

'You are not in fellowship, so we can't have you here!'

His sobbing was so deep and each sob tore my heart into shreds ... It was the hardest thing I have ever done to walk out of that room so cut off, and unable to express my love.

Ruth, for all her rigid insistence on separation, still felt the pull of family ties. She found her faith tested when her niece Helen married in Wellington just before Christmas 1966. Ruth agonised over the thought of missing this event. Eventually she decided on a compromise she felt was permissible: she would not attend Helen's wedding service but would wait on the street across from the church to catch a glimpse of the bride and her family as they exited the main doors. Ruth sent a Russell Hobbs electric kettle as a wedding gift; it lasted more than forty years, a reminder to Helen of how her aunt still cared even when she felt she couldn't join the celebration.

Ruth's attitudes had hardened when she encountered another niece – Mick's daughter Robin – in 1969. Robin had recently graduated from nursing college and was working at National Women's Hospital in Auckland, a grand facility opened a few years earlier beside Cornwall Park. Robin was really thrilled when my aunty Anna came in to have one of her babies. Anna, by now a busy Brethren mother with hair pulled back in a sensible parting, a dimple on her left cheek, had just given birth to her sixth child and was equally pleased to see Robin. It had been ten years since the separation edict had torn apart their families, and this was a welcome reunion; she was perfectly happy to talk. Ruth, on the other hand, visiting from Wellington to offer motherly support, gave Robin a frosty reception and refused to acknowledge her.

*

As Ruth grappled with the consequences of rejecting her family, her children Anna and George were too busy raising their own to spare much time thinking about doctrine. For George, it was easier just to go with the flow. Distracted by three children, he didn't pay much attention as rules were introduced, slowly and gradually.

However, by the 1970s the siblings were having nagging doubts about whether the Exclusive Brethren were everything they claimed to be. Members were routinely excommunicated for minor infractions like wearing shorts or listening to the radio, and Anna agonised over the love and compassion that seemed to be missing from the increasingly hardline church. Part of her regretted not following Gerald Cowell when he'd objected to Big Jim's separation doctrine, which she thought went far beyond what scripture could justify.

In a bizarre twist, when Anna fell under church discipline in 1977 it had nothing to do with her doubts. The elders in Auckland discovered she and Rob had taken their children to sex education evenings five years earlier – Anna hadn't had any sex talks from Ruth and didn't want her own children growing up ignorant.

On the evening their eldest daughter, Kathleen, got engaged, priests turned up at the family's doorstep. They questioned Rob about those innocent classes and claimed he was evasive in his answers; that was enough for them to justify shutting him and Anna up so the matter could be investigated further. What was supposed to be a night of celebration turned to horror as the six eldest children were ordered to pack suitcases and then bundled out the door to stay with other Brethren families in Auckland – their parents feeling they had no choice but to comply. It was the last Anna saw of her children for eight months.

Like my grandma Edith, Anna sat heartbroken at home under assembly discipline while her eldest daughter's marriage was approved by Brethren elders. Kathleen had only just turned eighteen, and her grandmother Ruth, now living in Wellington, travelled to Auckland to be there for the wedding day in the absence of Kathleen's mother. Kathleen was the first of Ruth's grandchildren to marry – but how could Ruth fully enjoy the occasion, knowing her daughter Anna, missed terribly by Kathleen, was under assembly discipline? Ruth noted in her diary that it had been a 'very very happy occasion, yet a shadow in the background that Robert and Anna were not available'.

Anna, a busy mother of seven, had gone from a frenetic home and church routine to ghostly silence overnight. She was kept sane only by her youngest daughter, who at two and a half was deemed too young to be removed to Brethren custody. Being separated from her children was a lesson for Anna in what the church's punishment could look like. After that, she tried to do a better job of conforming to the rules.

My grandpa George – Anna's brother – mostly supported the Brethren practice of shunning rule-breakers until it happened to him. As Brethren misdemeanours went, it was minor: his wife, Lottie, had taken their three kids to swim at a nearby beach after school on a hot summer afternoon. Where she went wrong was also taking children from another Brethren family, as this was a breach of a recent ban on mixed bathing, which dictated that males and females should not swim together if they weren't from the same family. The local priests confronted George about it – 'Why did you allow mixed bathing to go on in your household?' – and he covered for Lottie to avoid throwing her under the bus. He hadn't even known about the beach trip, so it wasn't a question of whether he'd allowed it to happen, but he accepted the principle that a man should be responsible for his house and took his punishment on the chin.

George and Lottie were shut up at home for several weeks while the priests grilled them about the mixed bathing incident. To George's surprise, there was no deep spiritual searching or sympathetic comfort from the priests during their confinement; instead, it was all procedural-based on how to keep to the rules. He'd always assumed that being shut up before coming back to the meetings would lead to renewed faith and was an opportunity for spiritual cleansing. The priests, he had previously believed, needed to wait for some kind of breakthrough to show that he and Lottie were sorry and could be forgiven – but to his surprise, no such moment arrived. After a few weeks the priests decided the couple had sufficiently faced their sins; the men duly reported that George and Lottie could be 'restored to happy fellowship'. But George didn't feel any different to how he'd been before the experience.

After that, he paid closer attention as his peers were shut up and withdrawn from. There was nothing spiritual or Godly or encouraging about it, he soon realised. He came to see it as a crushing process; in his eyes, these people had been hammered down until they agreed not to make any waves anymore. Picking at the thread didn't end there – the doubts kept coming. As the 1970s rolled into the 1980s, one question about the Brethren kept rolling around his head: he wondered if somewhere along the line they had stopped being the one true church.

7.

ELECT VESSEL JAMES TAYLOR JNR'S PATH TO ALCOHOLISM WAS slow at first and then swept the Exclusive Brethren with a vengeance. Big Jim was a shy man; as he jostled to protect his father's legacy in the late 1950s and early 1960s, he found that having a few drinks of Scotch helped him get through the meetings, where he was expected to take a leading role. Until then Brethren had been largely teetotal, drinking in moderation or not at all, and most members had no frame of reference for seeing the effects of alcohol on one another. Hard liquor was up there with cigarettes as one of the vices of the world – until the script suddenly flipped.

Big Jim's 'few drinks' spiralled as he rose to prominence. By the time he visited New Zealand to host meetings at the Whangārei town hall in early 1962, he was openly encouraging previously teetotal Brethren to join him in taking up the bottle. The whole meeting centred around the idea that 'we should be free to drink', an astonishing turn of events for the gathered conservative Brethren farmers and small business owners, who had congregated to hear the Elect Vessel on his special visit from New York. Big Jim reasoned that alcohol was part of God's creation and therefore meant to be enjoyed by the saints. Nobody dared point out the obvious, but it was on people's minds: *Well, so is tobacco.*

Whisky-drinking soon became a test of faith: if you weren't doing it, then you were out of line with the Elect Vessel. Big Jim, previously shy, increasingly led riotous church meetings, while few Brethren recognised that he was in the advanced stages of alcoholism. Dignified old men were made to stand up and get publicly humiliated for not drinking; even pregnant women were forced to drink. Alcohol loosened your tongue, the logic went, so if you avoided drinking, it must mean you had something to hide.

The Brethren coined a number of absurd phrases to justify their alcohol consumption, and these were still regularly repeated when I was a teenager, decades later: 'Drink, and be free!' and 'Drink makes a strong man stronger and a weak man weaker.'

Big Jim's descent into alcoholism coincided with the rise of increasingly extremist doctrine. Separation was enforced with a brutal lack of compassion, and members who stayed out of trouble were held in place by the Three Fs: Fear, Finance and Family. One of the earliest reported suicides attributed to the doctrine of separation was that of Martin Lawson, who gassed himself in a North London garage in September 1961. Martin, a handsome, sensitive 21-year-old racing-car driver, had never been a member of the Exclusive Brethren but his parents were, and he often travelled from London to visit them in Hampshire for the weekend. The church intervened, ordering his parents to cast him out of the family for rejecting their faith – they complied, and the unthinkable happened.

Less than a year after Martin's death, Elsie and Winifred Rhodes drove to an outdoor reservoir with their beloved collie Bruie. Leaving Bruie in the car, they joined hands and slowly walked into the water. The sisters, aged fifty-eight and fifty-three, had been tormented by Brethren leaders in Staffordshire over their small egg farm, where they kept about 1500 chickens. According to British Egg Marketing Board regulations at the time, all eggs produced had to be stamped with a lion mark to show that the facilities had been inspected and the eggs were up to standard; without the stamp, eggs could not be sold via main distribution channels. The Brethren, under Big Jim, decreed that this harmless stamp was an impure link representative of the dreaded Mark of the Beast from a biblical prophecy in which mankind is forced to bear Satanic symbols. Elders shouted at Elsie and Winifred, a local newspaper reported, leaving them 'crying and shaking with fear'. The sisters let their family farm fall into disrepair as they changed from happy people into dispirited recluses. When their car was found near the lake where they had drowned themselves, their much-loved collie was still alive inside. A short note read: 'Be kind to Bruie, our dog.'

There's no record of what happened next to poor Bruie, but if he ended up with another Brethren household, chances are high that he also met a grim end. In the mid-1960s, not long after Elsie and Winifred ended their lives, another edict came down from Big Jim in New York. Pet ownership represented an emotional link that could come between a person and God, the Elect Vessel said, plucking a verse from the Book of Revelation: 'Without are the dogs, and the sorcerers, and the fornicators, and the murderers, and the idolaters, and every one that loves and makes a lie.' Dogs – and somehow all pets by extension – were at the same level as murderers and fornicators, he proclaimed. Following this, thousands of Exclusive Brethren worldwide disposed of their pets. My grandmother's family drowned their cat in the river. Guinea pigs met a grisly end. Goldfish were flushed down the toilet. Some Brethren families secretly kept cats but would lock them out of the house when church guests came to visit. In the 1990s, my siblings and I watched enviously as other neighbourhood kids played with their dogs, knowing that would never be possible for us.

By 1965, Big Jim's drinking was so heavy that he had to be hospitalised due to the effect of alcohol on his liver. But by the end of the decade, he was drinking heavily again. When he visited his daughter Consie Hales in Sydney for Christmas 1969, they drank until they were bleary-eyed. On a trip to Canada that same year, Big Jim emerged from his bedroom the morning after his arrival and spotted the host's whisky collection, asking, 'Can I have some of that with breakfast?' The host, astonished but knowing it was unthinkable to turn down such a request from the Elect Vessel, told him to go ahead – and watched in further astonishment as Big Jim filled a water glass with Black Label Scotch, then drank it with his bacon and eggs. Big Jim's host kept track that weekend: the Elect Vessel was drinking a bottle and a half of whisky a day.

In 1970, Big Jim hosted special church meetings in the north-east Scottish city of Aberdeen. He took centre stage, joined on the platform by around a dozen senior Brethren leaders from across Scotland and England. Many of them had whisky glasses by their side and sipped Scotch throughout the meetings. About five hundred Brethren were packed into the local meeting room, a silver-grey former Presbyterian church built of Aberdeen granite. It had a theatre-type layout, with rows of pews facing an elevated platform. Stretched in a semicircle around the hall was an upstairs gallery, its five or six rows filled mainly with younger people who had a bird's-eye view of the proceedings below. These were all loyal followers of the Elect Vessel: they'd got rid of their pets, quit working on fishing boats, cut off their non-Brethren relatives and become avid whisky drinkers. They had stuck with the increasingly demanding edicts for ten years and still believed Big Jim was the Elect Vessel, directly representing the Lord's will.

Even so, they were nonplussed by his rambling incoherence. 'You bum, you. You big bum. Scott! Bum! Scott! Bum! Scott! Bum! Scott! Bum! Scott! Bum! Now you have it. You never have it. You never had it so good. You never had it like this, you nut, you. You stinking bum! You stink! Why didn't you bring some toilet paper with you.'

Young married men whistled and stamped their feet as the jowled and balding septuagenarian took the gathering down a rowdy path. He joked crudely about other men's wives and made fools of senior leaders by ordering them around as though they were toy soldiers: 'Get up, Eric. Get up! Eric, get up. Sit down.

You never had it like this before. You stupid people here, what do you think I am? I'm a professor. Here, you. I'm not finished with you yet. You nut! Get up. I'm not finished with you yet.'

Ian Arbon couldn't believe what he was hearing. A twenty-year-old from the eastern English city of Peterborough, he was in Aberdeen with his family, invited to attend the special meetings by an uncle who lived locally. There was an element of group hysteria that scared Ian. High in the balconies with the rest of the young people, he had a direct view of Big Jim and his deputies on the platform. At the time, Ian never questioned why these holy leaders were consuming alcohol during a church service, as whisky-drinking outside of the meeting had become pretty well obligatory, an important part of showing you were 'approved'. He knew it wasn't normally done in the meetings, but he told himself that if the Elect Vessel was doing it, then it was OK.

That Saturday night, once church meetings had concluded for the day, Ian heard astonished discussion in the homes of local Brethren – in fact, the local members didn't talk about much else. They felt numb and didn't know what was happening; this was such a sea change from anything they had known before that there was a sense of shock.

When the five hundred Brethren gathered once more at nine the next morning, Big Jim was nowhere to be seen. A short explanation was made that he was unwell and had been forced to return to New York. Someone else led the service, a staid affair. Everybody was in a state of puzzlement, asking, 'What is going on?'

Gradually, the story emerged: the Elect Vessel had been involved in a major bust-up the night before and had been sent packing.

*

Big Jim had taken a liking to 35-year-old Madeline Ker, a Brethren woman just half his age, with a demure smile and shoulder-length dark brown hair. Madeline and her husband, Alan, had been invited to attend the special meetings in Aberdeen. They were originally billeted to stay with Brethren in nearby Laurencekirk, but their plans were rearranged at Big Jim's insistence so they could stay with him at the home of an Aberdeen leader, James Alex Gardiner, a rising star among the British Brethren.

That Thursday night, Brethren gathered in the Gardiner home were baffled as they watched Alan Ker lead his barefooted wife, clad in a dressing-gown, through to the Elect Vessel's bedroom. Alan then returned to his own bedroom alone, and his wife wasn't seen leaving Big Jim's room until six the next morning. That Friday evening she was again led by her husband to the Elect Vessel's bedroom around 11 pm, and again Alan returned to his own room alone.

When Big Jim wasn't in his bedroom with Madeline, he was holding court with whisky and women in the living room of the trim blue-and-white bungalow. A steady supply of hard liquor was passed around. As he became increasingly intoxicated on the Friday evening, he demanded that the women in the room sit on his lap one by one. A queue of them – some quite young, some married, some single – formed beside his chair, and husbands were forced to watch as the Elect Vessel fondled their wives' breasts, legs and bottoms. Several of the women wept as they awaited their turn, but Big Jim just joked about how their underwear prevented easy access.

Their host, Gardiner, was shocked by what was happening. As music started up again from an expensive electric organ – trucked in a hundred miles for the occasion – children were told to leave the room in order to shield them from the Elect Vessel's behaviour. Shame hung in the air as he sucked at a young woman's mouth; she did not respond in kind, and her humiliation was palpable as others watched on in horror. Her husband, feeling unable to defend her against someone so powerful in the church, bowed his head so he wouldn't see what was happening – but he found it impossible to ignore the slobbering kisses to which she was being subjected.

This wasn't new behaviour for Big Jim. Through the late 1960s, he would often demand that young women line up after church services for a 'holy kiss'. If any of them refused his advances, she was seen as being out of step with God's will.

That Saturday afternoon, as Big Jim took a break from raving at the gathered Brethren, Madeline was once more led to his bedroom. The hosts had tried to barricade the hall with furniture to block her path, but she and her husband forced their way through, cracking a large glass door pane in the process. When she came out of the room, she told Gardiner that Big Jim had ordered her to say their host was 'a son of a bitch and a bastard'.

Gardiner felt that he was in an impossible position: the Elect Vessel could supposedly do no wrong.

Later that evening, when Big Jim and Madeline did not emerge for dinner, the distraught host decided he had no choice but to confront the Elect Vessel. In a letter Gardiner wrote a week later, setting out his perspective on what had happened, he explained: 'I felt I had to find out what was happening in my house. I went through to Mr Taylor's bedroom and found Mrs Ker undressed and in bed with Mr Taylor. He had on his pyjama top which was open down the front.'

Big Jim was unrepentant. When questioned by a witness as to whether his behaviour was morally suitable, he simply replied, 'Yes.'

A horrified Gardiner insisted that Madeline and her husband leave immediately; from his perspective, this was in order to protect his house. Big Jim, enraged, tried to follow Madeline into the night, saying, 'She is my woman.'

Several Brethren men physically restrained the Elect Vessel. For these Scottish followers, it was a step too far to allow God's voice on earth to chase after a married woman who a short while earlier had been found naked in his bed. In the letter, Gardiner described what happened next: 'JT Jnr became very difficult, calling me "bastard", "son of a bitch" and to "all go to hell". I had to send for Dr Bill Thomson who had been attending to him for the last three to four weeks. JT Jnr became very quiet when Dr Thomson arrived and he was given an injection and tablets. Dr Thomson said that medically he was a sick man, but the moral side is a matter for the priests.'

Big Jim's son James Taylor III arrived in Aberdeen on a 1.20 am flight, having been summoned by concerned Brethren to take his father home. A few hours later, the Taylors were on their way back to New York.

As the Scottish Brethren reeled in shock, the church's crisis response kicked in. Senior leaders across England announced there had been an 'attack' on beloved Mr Jim, and they said the stories emerging from Aberdeen were malicious and false.

Ian Arbon was recalled home from Aberdeen with his family. His dad had received a phone call from the leader in Peterborough, who demanded they come back immediately and give an account of themselves. When the Arbon family showed up to the Tuesday night meeting, having rushed the 450 miles home, local elders asked whether they supported the supposedly treasonous Aberdeen Brethren. The Arbons were the only ones in the room who had been at the Aberdeen meetings. Ian, his father and his brother confirmed they stood with the Scottish Brethren. They tried to give an account of why they'd reached that view but were shouted down from all sides; they were then escorted to the door.

Feeling rather shell-shocked, the Arbon family waited outside the meeting room to see if anything else would happen. Over the next few minutes, about seventy people walked out and came over to the Arbons, wanting to know more about what they hadn't been allowed to say in the meeting room – of course, the Arbons were more than happy to tell them. Most of those seventy Peterborough Brethren were excommunicated for daring to question the purity and holiness of the Elect Vessel, and only a few returned.

Big Jim, meanwhile, dug in with his defence. Amid a flurry of letters between senior Brethren leaders accusing and defending the Elect Vessel, he wrote from his New York home: 'The charge made by that bastard Waterfall [a Brethren elder] that I was in bed with another man's wife is a dastardly lie. If I wanted to sleep with another man's wife would I go to Aberdeen – costing about $1,000? Brooklyn would be cheaper. Some Brethren have shown themselves to be boobs.' He also claimed that the tape recording of his obscene language on the Saturday in Aberdeen was doctored – 'It's a fake' – but that claim was rejected by his own New York Brethren, who concluded it was his voice 'without any doubt'. Ian Arbon heard it all with his own ears and was aware that faked recordings wouldn't have been possible anyway, given the recording facilities available in 1970 and the short time available to make them.

Big Jim's story shifted a few more times before he landed on an explanation for his behaviour in Aberdeen. It had all been a ruse, he claimed: he had only been pretending to be drunk and disorderly in order to flush out followers lacking in faith. Anyone who truly believed, he proclaimed, would recognise he'd been acting in love to preserve the holy fellowship: as we were often later told, 'To the pure, all things are pure.'

The Brethren in New York were responsible for investigating and enforcing assembly judgement, but censuring the Elect Vessel proved beyond them. He thumbed his nose at them, turning up drunk to meetings in the weeks following the Aberdeen incident, as a New York elder recounted in a letter: 'At the ministry meeting, Mr Taylor appeared bare foot, sat alternately clowning and dozing during the hymn, prayer and words.'

The brewing storm caught the attention of the press. When Big Jim brazenly invited Madeline Ker and her husband to visit him in New York a few weeks after their Aberdeen encounter, a *Daily Express* reporter was dispatched to ask the Exclusive Brethren leader for his version of events. Madeline and the Elect Vessel were found together at his house in Brooklyn, their respective spouses nowhere to be seen. Big Jim was in an armchair, clad only in underwear; he didn't seem bothered to have been disturbed in a state of undress, joking to the reporter that he'd better put some trousers on: 'But, quite honestly, I find it more comfortable just sitting in my underpants.' As the Elect Vessel denied having done anything improper – 'absolutely nothing happened in that bedroom that Mrs Ker and I are ashamed about' – he sat on the couch and posed for an astonishing photograph. He looked dishevelled, with a glass of whisky in his right hand and a large leather-bound Bible resting on his lap. He draped his left arm around Madeline's shoulder, resting his hand on her breast, and kissed her lightly on the cheek. 'I don't care what people say,' he told the reporter. 'She is a very, very pure person.'

This picture and the accompanying article were the final straw for many Exclusive Brethren in Europe and North America, who were already hearing from friends and relatives who had witnessed Big Jim's behaviour in Aberdeen.

*

The Aberdeen Division was one of the largest splits in Brethren history. Thousands walked away, including almost the entire Scottish congregation, which split off to form a slightly different version of Brethren fellowship. A 1970s estimate made by the Exclusive Brethren themselves suggests that one in four members left worldwide in the aftermath of Aberdeen.

A few months later, it became clear Big Jim would be too unwell to travel to Bristol for the universal meetings, an annual conference at which elders gathered from around the world. The Elect Vessel nominated a North Dakota pig farmer, James Symington, to lead services in his place. But before the Bristol meetings happened, Big Jim died aged seventy-one. Symington, one of his most ardent supporters in North America, used the occasion to stamp his authority on the church. He moved with brutal efficiency to crack down on stories about Big Jim's misdeeds, excommunicating those who questioned what had happened at Aberdeen. A new Elect Vessel had arisen, and dissent would not be tolerated.

The chaos of Aberdeen was muted by the time it reached the other side of the world. Leaders suppressed discussion so completely that New Zealand members like my grandpa George were only vaguely aware something had happened in Scotland. Even asking about it was grounds for being withdrawn from. When the Scottish Brethren distributed booklets in an attempt to explain, members were ordered to destroy the envelopes unopened under threat of excommunication; some ceremoniously burned a booklet on their doorstep to show their condemnation for its wickedness.

Aberdeen became mythological for the Exclusive Brethren. Just saying the Scottish city's name conjured up the spectre of attacks on the holy fellowship. Questioning the purity of Big Jim was unforgivable.

*

In 2006, when I was sixteen, the Brethren were just starting to allow internet access – although only to websites vetted and approved by a central church-controlled trust. That wasn't good enough for me, a deeply curious teen, so I snuck into an internet cafe and typed 'Exclusive Brethren' into Google. One of the first search results was the infamous picture of Big Jim Taylor and Madeline Ker. I was shocked to read about what had happened at Aberdeen; it was miles apart from the official version of events. We'd been told there was no transcript from the Aberdeen meetings because the recordings had been 'lost', but here were the audio files online. I thought that Big Jim's slurring nonsensical speech was far beyond what would be expected from an Elect Vessel.

Dad was horrified when I broached the subject of Aberdeen. Going to an internet cafe would usually have been kept a secret, but I had a burning desire to know the truth. As we stood in the backyard near the clothesline on a warm summer afternoon, both in our overalls after work, I pressed Dad on whether he knew what had really happened in 1970. He was confused, then defensive. 'Mr Jim was a pure man!'

That wasn't good enough for me. 'But there are pictures!'

A few months later, I was at a special church meeting with my parents in Wollongong, a coastal Australian city south of Sydney. After the meeting, Dad and I pressed forward to meet Bruce Hales, the seventh and current world leader, known as the Man of God. It was the first time I'd encountered him up close, a portly, red-faced man with snowy white hair. Dad wanted to ask him whether it was OK to readvertise our business in the Yellow Pages phone directory – a form of advertising that had been banned for Brethren businesses the year before, to calamitous effect for the family tyre shop. Our conversation with the Man of God was uneventful, and Dad was pleased to get special permission to advertise in the Yellow Pages again.

Then, as the Man of God manoeuvred into the front passenger seat of a waiting vehicle, Dad threw him an unexpected question: 'Mr Bruce, could you say something to set Craig's mind at rest about Aberdeen?'

I was mortified. Having doubts about Aberdeen was bad enough, but to have them revealed out of the blue to the Man of God was so much worse.

His reply was succinct. 'What it comes down to is the absolute folly of ever doubting the Man of God in the first place.'

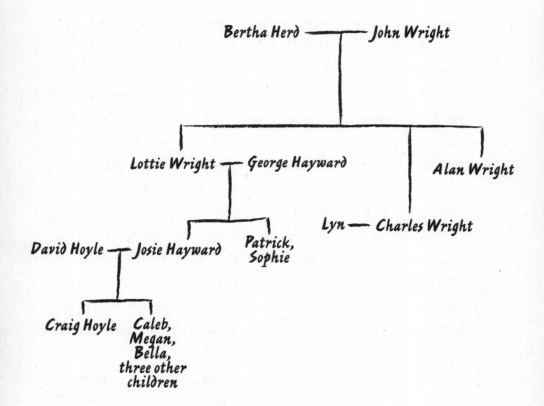

8.

'There's more chance of the sun not rising than the Man of God failing.' Those words echoed through my head as the Man of God slowly made his way up the aisle of the main Exclusive Brethren hall in Invercargill.

Hundreds of Brethren stood in hushed silence as the world leader, Bruce Hales, ambled in stately fashion across the green carpet. Loyal members guarded the end of each row of black seats to make sure nobody could approach him unannounced. What would those guards do, I wondered, if someone tried to push through? It had happened before – desperate Brethren throwing themselves at the Man of God to get his attention. He was God's voice on Earth, after all; if you were struggling to get close to God, then getting close to his direct representative was the next best thing.

It was a blustery Monday at the beginning of summer, several months after I had confessed I was gay. I was eighteen, and Bruce Hales had blessed us with a flying visit. Two years had passed since my awkward encounter with him in Wollongong, and I'd been doing my best to suppress any doubts about him and his predecessors. He was in fine form during those Invercargill meetings, joking around with the gathered Brethren and telling us how his father, the former Elect Vessel, had only tolerated black and white – no shades of grey allowed.

The local Brethren had gone to extreme lengths to protect Hales from the media when he'd flown in the previous evening. To evade any photographers lying in wait, his private jet was taxied into a waiting hangar; he was then escorted in a van with blacked-out windows – decoy vehicles travelled in separate convoys, so nobody could be quite sure of his whereabouts. Such measures were standard practice wherever Hales travelled around the world.

As the Man of God was brought to the meeting room on the Monday, Brethren were stationed on street corners to watch for members of the press, who were feared and loathed in the church. A large white marquee was erected beside the hall so God's representative could enter and exit the van without being seen. As if that wasn't enough, Hales was tailed by a bodyguard.

After the main service, I was among a small group of Brethren who gathered in anxious silence under that white marquee for private audiences with Hales. You could have cut the tension with a knife. One word from the Man of God could make or break someone, and it was a big deal to talk to him one on one. My recently confessed sexuality had been enough to put me on the list, and now here I was, hoping he would save me. In a white shirt unbuttoned at the top with its sleeves turned up, he seemed imposing but also very ordinary in his sweaty humanity. There was no doubt in my mind that he had the power to wave his hands and cure my sexuality.

As I stood there with my dad and Peter Hickmott, Hales held his black leather-bound Darby-translated Bible and told me in a broad Australian accent that while he sympathised with my predicament, there was no future in being gay. 'Never accept yourself for who you are,' he said.

It was another shock. Instead of curing me, he was suggesting I needed to fight my sexuality for the rest of my life.

He then instructed me to speak with a Brethren medical doctor, Roger Kirkpatrick, about treatment options. 'There's medication you can go on for these things.'

A cousin of the Man of God – his mother was a Hales – Dr Kirkpatrick was a Brisbane-based doctor widely used by the Exclusive Brethren. I'd met him a year or so earlier, when I had been part of the group of troubled young Brethren invited for dinner by Athol Greene. I'd watched in curiosity as Kirkpatrick knocked back whiskies and brushed off his wife when she reprimanded him for spilling food down the front of his white shirt.

I wasn't sure what to make of what I'd just been told. As the Man of God's convoy prepared to depart, he seemed distracted and pressed for time. He said he wanted to see me again.

Was this my lifeline? I'd been crushed by his suggestion that I was bound for a life of fighting against myself, but here was a glimmer of hope. I desperately wanted my homosexual curse to be lifted so I could fit in with the Brethren – people who had their flaws, yes, but whom I loved dearly and couldn't imagine a life without.

As soon as Hales left, I leaped at a local leader and told him that the Man of God wanted to see me again. He told me to follow Hales to his next stop: the special meeting in Oamaru, a town several hours north of Invercargill on State Highway 1. I would need to rush home and pack a bag so I could get on a bus with other Brethren.

Our family home was just a few hundred metres down the road from the Invercargill meeting room. I sprinted the short distance in my black trousers and white shirt, the standard uniform for special meetings with the Man of God. I ran inside and saw my cousin Lindy, who was staying with us for the occasion. She threw her arms around me with excitement when I told her Bruce Hales himself wanted to see me again – she knew what a big deal this was. My parents, only ever tangentially involved in my priestly oversight, and distracted by feeding and entertaining dozens of lunch guests, offered brief words of encouragement as I flew out the door. But I didn't care what Dad and Mum thought: all that mattered now was getting back to Bruce Hales.

In Oamaru that Monday evening, I waited for Hales at the front of the church but missed seeing him. There was a flurry of activity from local priests as I was decamped to the next special church meeting in Timaru, an hour further north. Because the Man of God wanted to see me, doors opened effortlessly in all directions.

The next afternoon I finally crossed paths with Bruce Hales again, this time at a local priest's modest two-storey brick home in Timaru. Once again, the Man of God was in fine form. He sat in the living room cracking jokes, whisky glass in hand, being served the finest food and liquor as he was passed letters from local members one by one; these letters contained the innermost thoughts and fears of Brethren members who felt that appealing to him was their final recourse. Hales, ensconced in an armchair below pictures of his father and other previous world leaders, read and commented on them in front of the dozens gathered, with scant regard for the privacy of the letter writers. He moved through them quickly, pronouncing judgement, giving advice and querying people's circumstances.

While Hales held forth, I was sent outside to talk to Dr Roger Kirkpatrick. He often travelled with the Man of God as a religious confidant, and was on standby to help any Brethren deemed to need medical help with a spiritual twist. Although many in the church felt more comfortable confiding in a Brethren medical doctor than a worldly one, doctors were a rarity in the fold and were therefore revered; the few remaining had qualified before the 1960s ban on university education. Being granted a consultation with Kirkpatrick came with the knowledge that you were speaking with the Man of God's cousin, which gave an air of divinity to what might otherwise have been a routine medical discussion.

That sunny afternoon in Timaru, Dr Kirkpatrick lowered his portly sixty-something-year-old frame onto a concrete ledge that ran alongside the driveway, partially obscured from the street by a green timber fence, and we talked in the shade of a large tree. His face was flushed pink, and I figured he'd been drinking; of course, the hosts had been offering alcohol to all their guests.

Kirkpatrick launched straight into grilling me about my sexuality. How long had I felt this way? Had I acted on my feelings? His questions soon became voyeuristic, and my skin crawled with shame. What had I done sexually with other people, how many times had we done it, and where? Did I prefer penetrating or being penetrated? Did I prefer a penis soft or hard? Kirkpatrick wanted to know whether I was sexually attracted to any Brethren – then he specifically asked whether I was sexually attracted to Peter Hickmott.

The doctor concluded by telling me my sexuality had to change. He said that because he was outside of his Australian jurisdiction, he couldn't prescribe any drugs; instead, he told me to pray hard to God for divine intervention.

The exchange left me feeling worthless and unclean. This had been no spiritual waving of hands but rather an invasive journey through my immature sexual experiences and desires. I endured it because this was what the Man of God wanted me to do – he had a direct line of communication to heaven, after all, so surely this must be the right path. My guilt and shame were my own fault. What else did I expect after committing such disgusting sins?

Back inside, my skin still crawling, I crossed paths with Bruce Hales again as he prepared to head to the main meeting hall in

Timaru, where followers were awaiting him. He asked me how the consultation had gone and told me he would be speaking to Dr Kirkpatrick about my case.

A short time later, at the official church meeting, I scribbled my notes as the Man of God held forth. Hundreds of Brethren sat around me in circular tiers in the windowless room, men and women separated under sterile fluorescent lights. Many of them, like me, were frenetically jotting down pronouncements that we thought applied to us. 'CHANGE,' I wrote on a scrap of paper I'd borrowed from the person beside me. 'We have to change.'

*

After returning to Invercargill, I only lasted a few days. I'd spent months waiting for the Man of God to cure me; when that didn't happen, the torment of facing a life fighting against myself was too much to bear. On the Friday afternoon four days after I'd packed a bag to follow the Man of God, I packed a bag to run away. To where, I had no idea, but the only thing that seemed worse than fleeing was staying put.

My brother Caleb grabbed my suitcase in the hallway and begged me not to leave. It was his last day of high school, and on Monday he was set to start work in the tyre shop. I'd lasted two years there with Dad – an agonising grind, believing I needed to pull my weight for the family. Now Caleb was on the scene, it felt easier to make an escape from that too. Mum cried as I rushed out the door, pleading with me to change my mind.

There was no plan. All I had to my name was a few thousand dollars I'd saved up from working in the tyre shop, in a personal bank account the Brethren couldn't touch. Trembling with fear, gripping the steering wheel, sporadically crying, I drove blankly up State Highway 1 from Invercargill, retracing the route I'd taken just a few days earlier. As the Southland fields gave way to the green hills of Otago and then to the flat dry plains of Canterbury, the shaking subsided. I made it to Timaru and pressed on.

I told myself there had to be something beyond the lifetime of misery that the Man of God was offering. But what? I had no clue how the world worked and was petrified that God would strike me down or run my car off the road. Who did I think I was, openly rejecting his plan? But then again, wasn't God supposed to love me? If so, why would he make me gay? I knew that I had always been gay. My earliest memories were of being different, and it seemed a sick joke for God to condemn homosexuality and then allow gay people to be born. Was he creating gay people just to make us suffer? A trickle of doubts became a rushing torrent as I raged at God for his cruelty.

After dark, and after more than seven hours of driving, I found myself in Christchurch. It was too late to get accommodation – and besides, I had no idea how hotels worked. I stayed in the car that night, my legs stretched out awkwardly under the steering wheel, and dozed restlessly. Adrenaline and anxiety got me through; I wasn't sleepy but knew I couldn't achieve anything until the world came back to life. It was a relief when the sun finally rose over the quiet cul-de-sac where I'd found refuge. This was a foreign experience: waking up in a city, completely alone, free to do as I liked, with nobody to insist on a breakfast Bible reading. I opened my Bible anyway through sheer force of habit.

I couldn't camp in the car forever, so my first mission was to find somewhere to stay. It had to be central, so I drove to Cathedral Square; I knew there was a church there, so I could attend the Sunday service the following morning. In the Brethren's eyes, going to a different church was almost as bad as being gay, but I wasn't ready to give up on God just yet.

As luck would have it, I found a youth hostel right across the road from the cathedral and paid for a bed in a dorm with five people. I wasn't bothered by sharing a room, well accustomed to being billeted in garages and rumpus rooms with groups of boys for special church meetings. I was taken aback, though, to realise that girls were also sleeping in the dorm room – the Brethren refused to let unmarried boys and girls be alone together, even if they were cousins.

The next step was buying a mobile phone. Personal mobiles were still banned; although the rules were beginning to change, it was still unthinkable to own a device that wasn't monitored by the church. But I had to have some way of connecting with the world. How was I supposed to apply for jobs if there was no number employers could ring me on? And what if I met new friends and wanted to stay in touch?

Besides, pushing my nagging guilt aside, I had another mission in mind. Once I'd bought a small brick Nokia, I headed back to the hostel and asked to borrow the local phone book. Curled up on my bunk bed, I combed through the listings, looking for relatives I'd heard whispered about but never met.

*

Charles and Alan Wright were the younger brothers of my grandma Lottie, who played the Hawaiian guitar and was pushed into a teenage wedding to Grandpa George.

Back in the 1940s, the three siblings grew up in a tiny house in what is now the coastal Christchurch suburb of Linwood. They were miles away from most other Brethren, surrounded by former soldiers and their families. The Wright children knew their parents were 'cracked' – Alan's word – but many of the returned servicemen around them were also damaged, so their 'wee bit dysfunctional' family fitted in just fine. Their father, Johnny, a short cheery man with thinning grey hair, was a gifted pianist. He'd been playing publicly from around the age of five, and people used to talk about him in reverential tones – he was one of those musicians who played music about a train, and you could hear it coming down the tracks. But their mother, Bertha, struggled with chronic mental health and cried every day, and the three children bore the brunt of her mood swings and paranoia when she thumped up the stairs on Saturday mornings and lashed them with poplar sticks. She was, they figured, 'just plain insane'.

Bertha wasn't alone in struggling with her mental health. As church rules rapidly shifted, Johnny was regularly shouted at by

Exclusive Brethren leaders, and eventually it became too much. Two elders were at the Wright family home in 1954 when Johnny finally snapped, lunging at a local priest and trying to strangle him, screaming that he was Satan. The kids watched in horror as their dad was wrestled to the ground; the priests held him down and called for backup. Then, with an absolutely terrified look in his eyes, Johnny was put in a straitjacket and dragged out to a taxi. He was forcibly held in hospital and subjected to electric shock therapy. Emerging weeks later a mere shadow of his former self, he tried desperately to piece together his mental wreckage.

With nothing left to lose, my great-grandpa Johnny found renewed solace in the teachings of the Exclusive Brethren. He had first joined the church in the 1930s, the only one of my great-grandparents not raised in it from childhood. Through the late 1950s and early 1960s, as the Hales brothers rose to prominence in Sydney and began enforcing the doctrine of separation, Johnny threw himself anew into being a 'servant for the truth'. The Hales brothers, seeing in Johnny a malleable vessel, welcomed his loyalty and rewarded him accordingly. He was personally invited to stay with them in Sydney and soon rose to host fellowship meetings. It was a remarkable turnaround for someone who had, just a few years earlier, been dragged out of his house in a straitjacket.

Johnny's sons, Charles and Alan, bore the brunt of his zealotry. Charles was forced to give up fencing because it meant belonging to a guild, then ordered to withdraw from his chemistry degree at university and reprimanded when he tried to start up a small electro-plating business: 'The Lord's not in that, so throw it all away,' his father told him. Alan, training as a carpenter, used to bring home small projects on the weekend to earn some extra cash, but that too was banned, leading to conflict. Alan was incensed that his ultra-religious father would sit reading a book and drinking whisky for hours at a time, but when Alan was out in the back room earning a bit of money, Johnny was suddenly concerned about him neglecting the Lord.

As I explore our family history, I'm curious about the parallels with my own upbringing. Uncle Alan and I both grew up with controlling, religious fathers who were mentally unwell. But why was Johnny so overbearing at home while being so kind to other Brethren? It might have been a fear of losing control. Whenever Charles and Alan did something that their father didn't understand, he'd stop them; he didn't like being out of his depth.

In 1968, Johnny's religious fervour came to an abrupt end when he died of a heart attack. He was just fifty-five.

Charles and Alan's sister, Lottie, had already married George and moved to Wellington, so it was just the boys at home with their mother. Free from Johnny's disapproving gaze, the three of them set about building a new life at a new home in St Albans, where they invited other young Brethren around for musical evenings. Charles hooked up a stereo system forbidden by the church, and it was quite marvellous for Brethren rebels who yearned for more from life. Bertha, free of an unhappy marriage and mellowing as she approached retirement age, turned a blind eye to her boys' escapades and happily cooked up beautiful meals for Brethren kids as they clustered around the stereo.

While the stereo somehow flew under the radar, Charles and Alan's great long sideburns drew more attention. Facial hair had been forbidden, but the Wright brothers – strong-willed young men with matching mops of curly brown hair – pointed out that the early Brethren leader John Nelson Darby had grown sideburns. His were difficult to ignore, given the pictures of him prominently displayed in every Brethren home – what had changed since then?

Charles and Alan put up a spirited fight when local elder Brian Suckling tried to take them to task at an assembly gathering in Christchurch. 'We are concerned about your sideburns!' Brian exclaimed.

Alan retorted that Brian should look first at his own son. 'His sideburns are longer than mine!'

There was a roar of laughter as Brian attempted a feeble rebuttal. 'His hair is fair, and it doesn't show up as much!'

As the microphone was passed around the hall, Charles pointedly told the elders to lighten up: 'God wanted his children to be happy.'

This sort of flippant talk was like waving a red rag in front of a bull. Local elder Allan Ivory quickly grabbed the microphone, pronouncing that the Wright brothers were evil and unfit for Christian fellowship. Somehow, astonishingly, a bit of facial hair grown as a lark had escalated to excommunication.

The Christchurch elders of the early 1970s perhaps underestimated the consequences of withdrawing from the popular Wright brothers. When Charles and Alan were given their marching orders, three other young men walked out with them in protest. As the five friends marched defiantly from the hall for the last time – knowing they were walking away from family and friends, likely to never return – one of them stopped at the back and shouted a final message at the priests: 'You're a pack of bastards, the lot of you!'

Charles and Alan's excommunication put Bertha in a difficult spot: the separation edict meant that if she remained living with them she too would be thrown out. That was a step too far for Bertha, who had lived her whole life in the Exclusive Brethren and was almost sixty. Her daughter, Lottie, was still in the church with three grandchildren, including my mother, alongside a wide network of siblings, uncles, aunts and cousins. But Bertha, a grandmotherly figure with smile lines and neatly waved grey hair, wasn't in a position to throw her sons out of the house – she'd recently sold the property to Alan, which gave the boys the upper hand. They stayed put; Bertha packed her bags and moved to stay in Wellington with Lottie and George.

My great-grandma only lasted two years there. She was disturbed by Lottie's zealous Brethrenism, and eventually it became too much. The final straw was finding out that Charles was married with a baby on the way – a grandchild that, under Brethren rules, Bertha would be forbidden from ever knowing. After waiting until Lottie and her family were out at the shops,

Bertha packed her bags once more. Sooner than expected, Lottie returned with the kids to find their grandma standing at the roadside with suitcases, waiting for a taxi. Lottie attempted a last-ditch intervention, but despite frantic calls to the priests, Bertha held firm: 'I'm going back to Christchurch to be with my boys.'

*

Decades later, when I packed my own bag and ran away to Christchurch, my sleuthing through the phone book turned up numbers for Charles and Alan.

My sudden appearance came as a shock: they hadn't heard from their sister for more than thirty years, and now here was her grandson out of the blue. I met them both later that day. Charles threw his arms around me in a bear hug and my apprehension quickly gave way to relief as he said, 'It's wonderful to meet you, Craig!' Here, I realised, was someone who understood.

Alan's children were particularly curious about who I was and where I'd come from. My cousin James, the same age as me, had grown up believing his aunty Lottie had died when she was young, which made my existence a conundrum. When James challenged his dad on why he had declared his sister to be dead, Alan flatly replied, 'She's dead to me!'

Uncle Alan, now a gruff white-haired cabinet-maker and ballroom dance teacher, had often made it clear to his children how he felt about the Brethren: 'If any members of the Brethren show up, just slam the door in their face.' But he was so pleased to see me that James was taken aback by the warm welcome I received. Alan's sympathy for my plight rapidly eclipsed any potential door-slamming. Remembering his own rapid departure from the Brethren, he offered me $3000 in cash to help me get on my feet, money he'd secretly stashed in the garage for emergencies.

Uncle Charles, a jovial chemist with shocks of white hair and a matching moustache, had taken a more moderate approach to his sister's memory. His children had grown up knowing their distant aunty Lottie was still alive, and once a year he'd raise a glass for a toast: 'Oh, it's Lottie's birthday today.' Like his younger brother, Charles was delighted to see me. My mum, just five when he was excommunicated, had been a favourite of his, even though he'd repeatedly told her off for bouncing on his wire-sprung bed. It was strange for Charles to imagine his five-year-old niece having a teenage son: *Gosh, fancy that*, he'd thought when I called, *one of Josie's children is coming to contact me.*

Also like Alan, Charles bore the scars from their time in the Exclusive Brethren, and he was occasionally overwhelmed by the sadness of his past. In his early married life he'd have such bad migraines that he'd need to go into a dark room and put a damp flannel cloth over his eyes. He didn't talk much about what was going on, other than to say that all his emotions were affecting him.

A small thing could provoke a seemingly disproportionate reaction. On one occasion, Charles had looked out the back

Above Left John Nelson Darby was a founding member who dedicated his life to the Brethren movement. His relatives lived at Darby House next to my ancestors Samuel and Elizabeth Childs.

Above Right Early Brethren leader George Wigram had known the Childs family for many years before my ancestors became missionaries, and a son was named in his honour.

Left Samuel Childs, my great-great-great-great-grandfather, worried that God would judge him for being born out of wedlock, and found solace in the early Brethren movement.

My great-great-great-grandparents William and Abigail Childs were missionaries for the Brethren movement. They are pictured here in Christchurch around the early 1880s with their four surviving children: Fred (my great-great-grandfather), Abigail Jnr, William Jnr and Joseph.

My great-great-grandfather Fred Childs with his six children in the 1920s, after they had left the Exclusive Brethren. *Rear*: Nell, Martin and Phyllis. *Seated*: Lucy, Ruth (my great-grandmother), Fred and Eunice.

My great-grandparents Alf and Ruth Hayward with their two eldest children, Anna and George (my grandpa). Alf was stationed at Milson Aerodrome in Palmerston North during World War II, and Anna and George grew up to the sound of aeroplane engines.

Alf and Ruth with Ruth's dad, Fred Childs. Fred supported the couple when Alf had cancer, but disapproved of their decision to rejoin the Exclusive Brethren.

Aunty Anna at her wedding to Rob Simmons in 1958. She had intended to leave the Exclusive Brethren as a teenager but stayed in the church to be with Rob.

Grandpa George, tall and athletic, was known as a ladies' man before he married Grandma Lottie.

My grandparents George and Lottie were just nineteen when they married in 1961. After George was excommunicated from the Exclusive Brethren in 1981, this wedding photo was cut in half to symbolise their separation.

My grandma Edith Smith, before she married and became a Hoyle. She stayed loyal to the Exclusive Brethren even when it meant losing her parents, her husband and two of her children.

My great-grandparents Willie and Rhoda Hoyle with their three eldest children in the 1930s: Arthur, Mary and Hubert (Snow). Willie and Rhoda would go on to have another seven children. Four of their ten children were excommunicated from the Exclusive Brethren.

Left Brethren world leader James Taylor Jnr, or 'Big Jim' as he was known, pictured with Madeline Ker, a married woman, in 1970. A scandal erupted after she was found naked in his bed. *(Daily Express)*

Big Jim denied any wrongdoing but the damage was done, and one in four Exclusive Brethren worldwide walked away from the church.

Jim Symington, a pig farmer from North Dakota, ruled the Brethren with an iron fist from 1970 to 1987. He faced significant health issues towards the end of his life due to the combined effects of diabetes and heavy drinking. He's pictured here with his wife, Beatrice, who was known as Trissie.

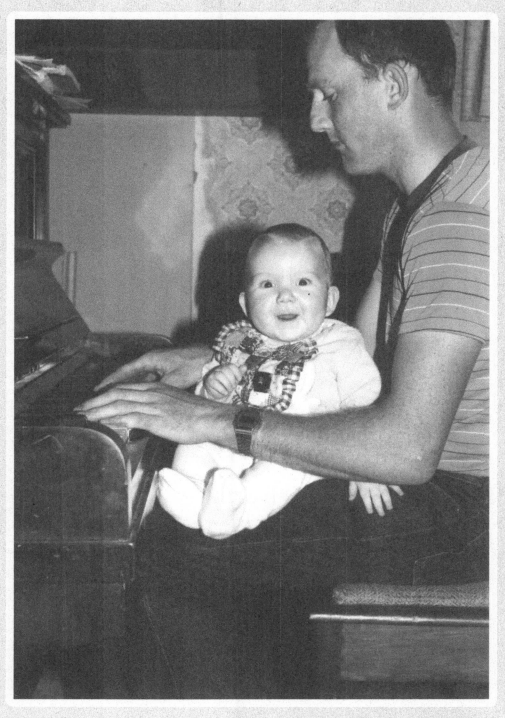

Me as a baby sitting on Dad's lap as he played the piano at our first family home in Hamilton in 1989. Music was a release for him.

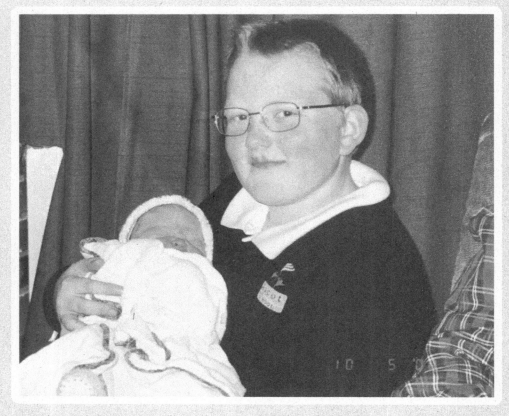

I was eleven when my sister Bella was born in 2000, the seventh and last child in our family.

Bruce Hales Jnr is the current world leader of the Exclusive Brethren, known as their Man of God.

Seven children born close together meant our family life was chaotic and fun. I'm at the back, second from left in this picture from 2002.

Meeting Grandpa George for the first time in 2009 was emotional for both of us – I was the first of his children or grandchildren he'd been able to hug for twenty-eight years. *(60 Minutes, TV3)*

Brethren doctor Mark Craddock was flustered and defensive when we confronted him in 2010 about why he'd prescribed Cyprostat to a healthy teenager. I'm standing to the left with *Today Tonight* reporter Jackie Quist. *(Today Tonight, Channel Seven)*

I marched in the 2010 Sydney Gay and Lesbian Mardi Gras parade with a group of others who had survived conversion therapy. It was a liberating experience.

I celebrated my twenty-first birthday with a rainbow cake in 2010. I'd been out of the Brethren for a year by then, and was ready to set off and see the world. The cars on top of the cake were a nod to the Brethren car chase I'd experienced in Sydney.

Uncle Charles and Aunty Lyn came up from Christchurch for my twenty-first. Charles had escaped the Brethren himself as a young man, and knew what it was like to start again.

Sarah Hall was the reporter who told my story for *60 Minutes*, and she and her husband, Grant, became parent figures outside the Brethren. This was taken at my graduation with a Bachelor of Communication Studies from Auckland University of Technology in 2013. *(Timeless Images Photography)*

Aunty Gwen Hoyle built a new life for herself after being excommunicated from the Brethren aged seventy. I'm pictured here with Gwen in 2009 at her hundredth birthday party.

Grandpa George and I bonded over our shared experiences leaving the Brethren, and we often discussed how it had impacted our lives. Here we are together in 2015.

George was also very supportive of my cousin Lindy, his sister Anna's granddaughter, when she was leaving the Brethren not long before me. The three of us caught up in Wellington in 2016.

It was a shock when my brother Caleb also came out of the Brethren, but we rebuilt our sibling relationship. Here we are hiking together in Hong Kong in 2019.

Uncle Hubert Hoyle, who was known as Snow, lost his wife and six children when he was thrown out of the Brethren. He looked on the bright side of life, though, and I enjoyed seeing him on visits to Melbourne. Here, he shows off his garden in 2015.

Above Grandpa George pictured a few months before his death in 2019. He's with his great-niece, my cousin Lindy, and her baby son, who was named in George's honour.

Left Uncle Alan Wright offered to support me financially when I left the Brethren. He said one of the things that made him happiest was giving his children opportunities he'd missed out on himself because of his Brethren upbringing. He's pictured with his grandson Oliver in 2021.

Aunty Dorothy, my grandfather's sister, escaped the Brethren as a teenager in the 1950s and never looked back. Here we are catching up for dinner in downtown Auckland in 2023. My partner, Ryan, is on the left.

window and seen a hedgehog trapped under the fence. He had burst into tears and said, 'Oh there's a hedgehog, the hedgehog can't get out!' His wife, Lyn, pointed out it would be easy to rescue the hedgehog with a shovel, and the critter was soon on its merry way. But, of course, Charles's grief went much deeper than a stuck hedgehog: seeing the poor creature struggling to escape had brought memories flooding back of how he'd been trapped in the Brethren.

I knew none of this about Charles and Alan when I turned up on their doorsteps aged eighteen. They were full of questions about what had happened in the church since their departure, and astonished to learn that Bruce Hales Jnr was now the Man of God – they remembered him as a tearaway teen from their father's trips to Sydney. In fact, Alan had enjoyed visiting Sydney pubs with the future Man of God, and my uncle had returned the favour when Bruce made his own trip across the Tasman, making a 'damn good fist' of pretending to be a good Brethren boy before they shot off to a nightclub and got 'thoroughly pissed'. The Bruce Hales in these stories was a far cry from the supposedly infallible Man of God I had been drilled to worship, who we were told had been sinless 'since the age of twelve'.

I turned down Alan's offer of financial support but accepted Charles's offer of a place to stay. I met him and Lyn for Sunday lunch at Riccarton House, and they immediately said I was welcome: 'We've got a spare room, and you're welcome to stay for as long as you like.' This seemed like a much better option than the cramped hostel dorm – even if he was an evil opposer.

As Lyn made up the spare room, I felt lucky to have landed on my feet.

Later that evening, as I sat in the lounge with Charles, there was a knock at the door. It was one of my cousins from the Exclusive Brethren, insisting I wasn't supposed to stay in a worldly home. 'Craig, we're concerned for your welfare, and your parents are worried sick.'

As strange as this was for me, it was even stranger for Charles, who found himself pulled back into Brethren-speak after decades of freedom. He was polite all the same, hiding his indignation that the Brethren had found out where I was, and at the presumption of knocking on his door and telling him he wasn't a suitable host.

I later discovered that the Brethren had deployed members to monitor airports, major centres and the inter-island ferry crossing in the hopes of spotting me. In other words, an informal network of spies had been activated at short notice to try and save me from eternal damnation. There had always been eyes and ears around when I was growing up, and this house call showed just how far their reach extended.

My cousin cajoled me into going for a late-night drive, then begged and pleaded as we argued back and forth about my place in the Brethren: 'Just come and stay at our house for one night, and we can talk about this again in the morning! At least you know who we are, and you'll be safe with us.' As we zigzagged through the dark suburban streets of Christchurch, I wavered. My decision to run away had been impulsive, and I had no idea what I was doing. Who did I think I was, trying to leave the holy fellowship? Even though I'd spat in their faces, they were showing me love and trying to bring me back. Besides, I reasoned, flattered by the attention, surely one night with my cousins wouldn't hurt.

After I hesitantly capitulated, we returned to break the news to Charles and Lyn. Whatever they were thinking, they masked it well, wishing me all the best as I packed my bags and departed as abruptly as I'd arrived. A fear clouded my thoughts when I walked out the door: would I ever be able to come back after rejecting their kindness like this?

'Just one night' with my cousins in nearby Rangiora became two and then three. They pleaded with me to give the Brethren another chance, and the pressure increased as the days passed – although I wasn't exactly coerced. As a confused teen, I had no reason to doubt they had my best interests at heart. My attempt to run away was doomed to fail, I told myself, and I was selfish and ungrateful for causing Mum and Dad such heartbreak. What had I been thinking, abandoning my family – and for what, being able to have sex? Was I really stacking up lifelong love against temporary lust?

Besides, I was discovering that the Brethren were more sympathetic to my plight than I'd expected. When in desperation I told my cousins I was gay, they threw their arms around me and said God would show us a way forward. Two more names were duly added to my secret list of people who knew I was gay, then two more. As the list inched past a dozen, it was a huge relief to get such a huge secret off my chest – that alone was enough to bring me to a happier place. Everyone – including my aunty Anna, one of the few Brethren I fully trusted, and her granddaughter Lindy – was sworn to secrecy.

I reluctantly agreed when my cousins suggested I get rid of my mobile phone to avoid the temptation of continued contact with my worldly relatives. We smashed it with a hammer in the backyard.

Even so, those worldly opposers remained too close for the Brethren's comfort. Christchurch wasn't considered safe for me; a week later, it was suggested that I go to stay with a Brethren aunt and uncle in Palmerston North, the city where my great-grandparents Alf and Ruth had faced sustained pressure to return to the fold. Exhausted and unsure of myself, I agreed to go along with the plan. It was easier just to ride the current – and selfishly it was nice to be the centre of attention for a change, after years of being told I needed to step up and take responsibility for others.

As I road-tripped to Palmerston North with my cousins, Brethren leaders in New Zealand were setting a plan in motion. Unbeknown to me, Bruce Hales had been alerted to my escapades, and a few weeks later I was 'invited' to travel to Sydney. It was the ultimate hook to reel me back in: beyond Christchurch, beyond even Palmerston North, and certainly well beyond the reach of any worldly opposers who might tempt me away again. Receiving an invitation to Sydney from the Man of God turned Brethren into minor celebrities. I was shocked and flattered, and Mum wrote to tell me how delighted she was that I was being granted such a privilege.

When a young person went to live in a different city for a few months, this excursion was known as an 'encouragement trip'. Scoring an encouragement trip to Sydney was a big deal – I'd caught the Man of God's attention, and he and other leaders were rolling out the red carpet to show me what a good life the Brethren could offer.

It never occurred to me that I didn't have to go – in theory I could have said no, but in reality it was unthinkable to refuse the huge honour. I was promised that the Man of God and I would finally finish the conversation we'd had cut short in New Zealand. Could it be that I just needed more time with him? Perhaps, after all, the Man of God would wave his hands and cure my sexuality.

9 .

Getting off the plane at Sydney Airport, I stared in wonder at the bustle of the international terminal. This was a long way from Invercargill. It felt like the capital of the world. At eighteen I found myself on an encouragement trip in the global epicentre of Exclusive Brethren activity, living under the watchful eye of Bruce Hales himself. Various Brethren families offered to have me stay and gave me temporary work – ostensibly motivated by kindness and friendship, although there was no doubt they were also acting as guardians and enforcers of our Brethren faith. Only a few of them were let in on my dark truth, their names added to my secret list of people who knew I was gay.

In the first few months of 2008, I kept detailed notes of church meetings with the Man of God. He relentlessly attacked the world outside the Brethren, including with dire warnings about 'Satan's printing presses': 'You pick up a newspaper and the evil is there. You don't have to read it.' These attacks were interspersed with reminders of 'the wretchedness of our own natural characters'. We needed to be broken, according to Hales, who warned it was time for young people to fall in line: 'If you're doing what's wrong, stop it! Cease to do evil immediately.' I jotted down page after page of warnings about the foolishness of leaving the Brethren: 'The world is hell, as far as I am concerned – these young people that go out into the world, they're going straight into the teeth of the devil.' And, chillingly: 'Better to die than to go on sinning.'

Hales also often talked about his father, John Hales, who had spent fifteen years as the Elect Vessel. His youngest son, having assumed the position of world leader, seemed determined to drive home to the Brethren that they had 'missed' the wisdom of his father, who was typically referred to by his initials, JSH. The references ranged from spiritual endorsements – 'JSH got delivered from Earth in his teens' – to domestic descriptions – Bruce Hales 'never saw JSH in a panic in the morning'.

One afternoon as I lamented the Sydney heat, I got into a spirited discussion with a group of young Brethren guys about wearing singlets under shirts. These locals told me it was 'part of the fellowship' for men to wear singlets, to which I retorted it was much too hot for an extra layer of clothing. One of them was a grandson of John Hales, and he rose up in indignation: 'Well, my grandfather said men should wear singlets – are you saying my grandfather was wrong?' Suddenly my view on singlets was a test of my faith. I had to start wearing singlets after that, lest I be seen as disagreeing with the legacy of John Hales.

As I found myself becoming disenchanted with the local Brethren, my encouragement trip was encouraging me in a different direction. It seemingly hadn't registered with the leaders who invited me to Sydney that the city was one of the world's rainbow capitals. For the first time in my life, I regularly saw gay and other queer people in public. A couple at Darling Harbour were a picture of languid happiness, sitting in the sun on a scorching day where the effort of moving seemed too much. One of them lifted his bare feet onto the lap of the other and leaned back in his chair. It was the first time I'd seen two men openly showing public affection with each other, and for a few seconds I stared in fascination. I couldn't imagine being self-assured enough to make such a bold statement to the world and to God. But I had to look away – I was with other young Brethren and couldn't risk being found out.

My temptations were still suppressed by the Three Fs: Fear, Finance and Family. Leaving the fold would mean starting again from scratch, and, material concerns aside, I loved my family dearly. I received pleading letters from my seven-year-old sister: 'I am missing you and I think you are missing me so why don't you come home … Me and you are a pair … You are my very favourite big brother.' I would be in Sydney for a while yet, though: the Man of God had plans for me.

On a warm Tuesday morning I was taken to visit Dr Mark Craddock, another senior Brethren member. It was my second guided consultation with a Brethren medical doctor. My meeting with Hales's cousin Dr Roger Kirkpatrick two months earlier had been a dismal failure, but this was another chance for the Man of God to oversee my treatment.

Dr Craddock, an older man with thinning white hair and a white business shirt, questioned me about my sexuality as we sat in the front living room of his spacious brick home in Oatlands. He told me he was sympathetic to my 'problem', adding that, 'Homosexuality is one of the hardest crosses a young person can be given to bear.' He explained that unfortunately he didn't know of any medication that could cure a gay person, but he was 'experimenting with a different drug on another young person' and 'waiting for the results of that'.

When Dr Craddock asked what percentage homosexual I thought I might be, I replied I was a hundred per cent gay. He scorned this idea, and I revised it, saying I was at least ninety-five per cent homosexual. He fixated on this, telling me I needed to work on increasing the five per cent of my makeup that was 'heterosexual'. In the meantime, he recommended I take a course of Cyprostat, a hormonal suppressant that cuts off the body's supply of testosterone, typically reserved for cancer patients and sex offenders. Dr Craddock told me that taking this chemical castration drug would reduce any urge I had to act out on my sexual preferences. He never explained potential side effects other than impotence.

It didn't occur to me to question his prescription. I was seeing him under orders from the Man of God, so I believed whatever Dr Craddock was doing must be God's will. He wrote enough repeats for me to continue taking Cyprostat for a year without needing to see another doctor.

When I went to fill the script, I felt intense shame and could feel the pharmacist's eyes boring into me as they surely wondered why I needed such treatment. I spent $348 out of my own pocket for the pills, which looked oddly unremarkable – small and white, in an opaque brown glass bottle – considering the huge impact they were about to have.

I swallowed the first pill as quickly as possible, desperate for a cure and willing to accept the impotence that followed. Over the next few weeks I found myself becoming tired, depressed, dizzy and nauseous, symptoms I initially put down to my moral struggle but eventually realised were being caused by the drug.

Not long after filling my script from Dr Craddock, I had a follow-up meeting with Bruce Hales. This would be a chance to finish the conversation we'd started in New Zealand two months earlier, and for the Man of God to check in on my progress. It was a huge honour to be invited to his office, but I felt mixed up and confused, and nervous about what he might say.

Walking through the gates of the Hales business premises felt like arriving to meet royalty. The father of the Brethren family I was staying with escorted me past neatly manicured hedges at Archway House, an office furniture business in the suburb of Ermington, 'Brethren central' in Sydney's north-west. In short order, I was walking into the Man of God's private office, a bland room with few personal touches: just a desk, a boardroom table and an assortment of cupboards around the walls. Tinted windows prevented anyone from peering in. He had his sleeves turned up, ready to do business, as a petrified gay teenager was ushered into a seat across from him.

We started with a prayer and a Bible reading from Romans – 'For thy sake we are put to death all the day long; we have been reckoned as sheep for slaughter' – then Hales launched into his questions. He wanted to know precisely when I had first realised I was gay: 'At what age were you conscious of being unsettled? When were you conscious of an inclination towards this other way?' 'All my life' apparently wasn't the answer he was looking for, so I said I guessed it must have been when I was around four, when I had watched in fascination as shirtless men cleared our garbage. Hales wanted details of when I had first started sinning and what had prompted me to confess my sexual misdeeds: 'Was there a crisis in Invercargill, or was it more of a crisis in yourself?'

Our conversation went on to range across all sorts of topics beyond my sexuality. I was told our family's tyre shop was an inappropriate business for Brethren to be engaged in – 'too much contact with the world' – and heard the Man of God's perspective on his experiences as a teen. 'I never really got involved in anything bad,' he told me. Perhaps those nights out on the town with Uncle Alan had slipped his mind.

My heart was pounding as I left the Man of God's office, my mind a mess of conflicting thoughts and feelings. Once again I'd been afforded the highest honour a young Brethren person could receive – a private audience with the Man of God – and he seemed so ... well, ordinary.

That afternoon, I wrote down detailed notes from our conversation while it was still fresh in my mind.

*

One Sunday evening I was invited to share dinner with Bruce Hales at a Brethren home in the suburb of Epping, where several dozen followers hung off his every word in the cosy living room. I was wedged between the larger-than-life Man of God to my left and even larger church spin doctor Tony McCorkell to my right; this was pole position for seeing and hearing everything that went on, as I drank with Hales just as Alan had forty years earlier.

The evening was jocular, with the Man of God in fine form. He was drinking Scotch and ice from crystal tumblers, just as Big Jim had enjoyed with his bacon and eggs. I watched in astonishment as Hales finished five glasses before dinner had begun – he could knock back whisky faster than anyone I'd ever seen. He switched to wine as we ate, then continued drinking after dinner. I was used to heavy drinking among the Brethren, but this was the largest quantity of alcohol I'd seen consumed in such a short space of time.

The Man of God didn't appear to be drunk, but his face was flushed and he had grown merry. Later that evening we gathered to sing around the piano, and 'Mr Bruce', as we called him, belted out his favourite tunes. There was awkward shuffling when someone got swept up in the merriment and suggested we sing 'Candle in the Wind' – we knew Hales had forbidden singing songs by Elton John because he was a gay degenerate. We looked to the Man of God for guidance, expecting him to admonish us and suggest a different song. To my surprise, he was right on board: 'Yes, let's sing that one!' I couldn't quite believe it as I watched Bruce Hales, the Man of God, break his own rule and croon along to 'Candle in the Wind'.

Alcohol consumption was rampant among the Brethren in Sydney, where I was told the spiritual worth of a man could be determined by the strength of his drinks. I knew we Brethren were heavy drinkers, but this was the first time I'd heard it so explicitly linked to our beliefs, with women also pressured to consume alcohol.

One weeknight, after a service at the main meeting room in Ermington, we spotted a police drink-driving checkpoint on a nearby busy road. The family I was with called back to relay the news to the gatekeeper and asked him to alert fellow Brethren as they left the yard. There was a chance people could still be over the blood-alcohol limit from the whisky they'd knocked back before the service, and drink-driving charges weren't a good look – best to take a different route home. This was just one of the tactics the Brethren had for avoiding drink-driving charges. At a dinner gathering in a private home, a relative of Bruce Hales advised that if we were ever in a crash and feared we might be over the limit, we should immediately go home and drink more whisky, then tell police we'd had a few drinks post-accident to calm our nerves – making it impossible to determine our blood-alcohol level at the time of the crash.

Some Brethren tried to push back against excessive alcohol consumption. During a later encouragement trip – this time to northern Tasmania, where I briefly worked in a Brethren welding factory – I attended an alcohol awareness seminar organised and run by local members in the small riverside city of Launceston. We'd heard whispered stories of people dying from alcohol poisoning, and it was felt the Brethren could benefit from some education on the topic.

After a church service, nearly a hundred members filed into a school hall and were walked through the impact that extended alcohol consumption could have on the body. As part of this, the Launceston Brethren provided lessons in how to pour a standard drink. A man was plucked from the audience and asked to demonstrate how he would pour a Scotch and Coke, and he dutifully filled half a tumbler with hard liquor. The educators then used a shot glass to demonstrate an official standard measure. We peered at the glass up on the stage – it seemed like there was almost no whisky in it at all. This was a long way from the drinking habits of the Man of God.

We later heard that alcohol awareness seminars had been banned from higher up.

*

I stopped taking the chemical castration drug after just a few weeks. The side effects were horrible; there had to be a better way. In a letter to Bruce Hales, I told him what I thought he wanted to hear: I had overcome my homosexual demons and was happy to return to New Zealand. 'The Brethren are the best place to be – I am now convinced of that – I know that nowhere else will I find the love & care I've experienced over the past few months.' Deep down, I wasn't sure what I believed anymore.

On a sticky summer afternoon in Brisbane, where I was attending one final set of special church meetings before returning to New Zealand, I saw the Man of God one last time. Once again, I was in the queue to speak with him. He was flanked by his cousin Dr Roger Kirkpatrick, the one who had asked me whether I was sexually attracted to Peter Hickmott.

Hales had a final warning for me before I left Australia: 'If you follow your own natural lusts you'll never get on with anyone – if you go into the world the only people you'll get on with are wicked people.'

I nodded along, but I doubted that was true. Although I'd been warned that being gay was an empty lifestyle, staying in the Brethren and living a lie also seemed like an empty life. And I'd seen enough of Bruce Hales to have doubts about whether he was all that was claimed by the church. The drinking, the contradictions, the threats – none of it lined up with someone who was supposed to be an infallible representative of God on Earth. I'd been told repeatedly that there was more chance of the sun not rising than the Man of God failing, but those words rang hollow to me now I'd spent more time with him. My stomach turned as I farewelled him one last time, waving along with hundreds of other Brethren as his motorcade departed.

*

I wasn't the only one in my family wrestling with doubts. Back in Auckland, my 21-year-old cousin Lindy was also struggling to reconcile the contradictions of Brethren faith. Her nana was my great-aunt Anna, the older sister of my grandpa George. Like me, Lindy had inherited the family curiosity. Why, she wanted to know, did the Brethren isolate themselves and refuse to break bread with other Christians? She was the kind of person who would find an injured bird at the park and bring it home to nurse back to health. There was so much love in the world, and she longed to share it with as many people as possible.

A few months after my final encounter with the Man of God in Brisbane, Lindy wrote a letter – five typed pages – detailing her concerns with Brethren teachings. Why couldn't we have pets? Why couldn't we donate blood? Why did the Brethren apply such 'complete cold severance' against family members who left the church? She also directly challenged the authority of Bruce Hales: 'I struggle to believe every word that comes out of his mouth is from heaven, I struggle to believe he is infallible and that he is God's only representative here on earth.' Lindy was aware of the immense cost of leaving the Brethren but said she could not in good conscience stay with a church whose beliefs she did not share: 'I want to be part of a fellowship that is more love-centred and demonstrates real practical Christianity, instead of one that claims great light but has not much fruit to show for it, and is more concerned about law-keeping than love.'

The elders in Auckland were unable or unwilling to respond to Lindy's detailed questions, so she forwarded her letter to the Man of God himself. He never replied.

When it became clear that Lindy would soon leave the church, Anna and her husband, Rob, called to see her one last time to say goodbye. On that dreadful day, Lindy curled up in grief, surrounded by family members begging her to stay. Lindy was absolutely traumatised, lying down and sobbing, feeling as though there was a knife between her shoulder blades.

After her nana arrived, Lindy looked at Anna in tears and told her, 'I can't do this – I can't cut you off.'

Anna, also distraught, kneeled and gazed deeply at Lindy with her soulful brown eyes, before leaning in to whisper in her granddaughter's ear, 'Lindy, I will never cut you off.' Rob, Lindy's parents and others around couldn't hear.

Lindy was taken aback, because Anna had never before articulated to her that she didn't agree with the principle of separation.

Those comforting words gave Lindy a tiny spark of hope. Leaving the Brethren, as she said, 'is like being pushed out of a plane in the middle of the night, and you can't see any lights down below, and you're in freefall falling into a black hole'. Anna's whisper was a thread of connection, and Lindy thought, 'I'm going to hold on.' She knew what she was hearing from her nana was powerful, but it also felt very fragile.

When Lindy left the Brethren, I was nineteen. Watching her make her terrible escape that summer profoundly affected me.

She had been widely loved within the church, and I watched in dismay as the disinformation machine quickly turned against her. Almost overnight she went – in the eyes of most Brethren – from being a gentle, loving friend to an evil, godless monster.

Her grandmother Anna was one of the few people with whom I could have an honest conversation. I confided in her that I was also thinking of leaving the Brethren, and she listened as I poured out my concerns and fears during lengthy phone calls. Anna never judged me nor condemned me as a sinner for doubting the Brethren. When I told her I was wondering about life outside the church, she thoughtfully worked through what that might look like, as well as the associated benefits and sacrifices.

Anna went to great lengths to protect her thread of connection with Lindy. She secretly bought a phone card from the local dairy so that calls couldn't be traced on the household bill, and she made excuses to avoid church services so she could call her excommunicated granddaughter while her husband was out. Anna would sit in her bedroom, talking to Lindy while watching up the driveway to see Rob's car lights as he returned home, at which point she would quickly hang up. She also re-established contact with her eldest daughter, Kathleen, now known as Kate, who had been withdrawn from in the 1980s.

I was still talking to Lindy too, in clandestine conversations my parents didn't know about, and we met secretly when I visited Auckland later that summer. Somehow the Brethren found out about this; the priests never addressed it with me directly, and there was no talk of my being shut up for contact with an outsider, but two weeks into the New Year I received a blistering call from Lindy's mother. She told me that her daughter was a 'liar and twister'. It seemed a particularly cruel thing for a mother to say about her own child. Lindy, too, was ripped into for daring to maintain contact with young Brethren still in the church, and when she tried to contact her family she was accused of 'breaking up Brethren families'. Shutting up had become less common under Bruce Hales, but Lindy had dared to challenge the Man of God's authority, which was still considered a grave sin.

Poor Anna had pledged her support to me and Lindy but lived in fear of what would happen if this was discovered by the church. Together, Anna and I agonised over how we longed to be freed from the Brethren. But she told me bleakly that any window of opportunity had long since passed for her. She could hardly bear going to church services, so she went as little as possible; when it was unavoidable, she sat near the back and tried not to cry.

In the end, we didn't spend long wondering what would happen if Anna's secret was discovered. I never knew how, but the Brethren found out about her support for Lindy and me, and Anna – a great-grandmother in her early seventies – received a visit from two Auckland priests who strongly reprimanded her for being a bad influence.

During a distraught phone call, she told me she had been reprimanded for keeping in touch with us; we were in tears at the sheer cruelty of it all. Anna was ordered to cut off all contact.

This tactic was supposed to help keep me in the Brethren, but instead it pushed me towards the exit. Of all the people who could have persuaded me to stay, Aunty Anna would have been the only one – and they tried to cut me off from her.

*

Over the next few months I began distancing myself from Brethren practices: attending fewer services, becoming more guarded, and bracing myself psychologically and emotionally for the break I knew would come. There was no way I could really prepare for the collapse of my entire life, but at least I could try to make it easier on myself. Surely losing friends wouldn't be so hard if I froze out some of them in advance.

As my church attendance tapered off, it became easier to avoid other Brethren, and I became more brazen about breaking the rules. One evening I snuck out to the movies, overcoming my fear that the spirit of God would depart from me as soon as I crossed the cinema threshold, as the Man of God had warned. I stepped backwards and forwards through the front door of Reading Cinemas on Dee Street, carefully gauging how I felt. No change – another piece of evidence that Bruce Hales was wrong! But I couldn't help wondering: what if I felt fine because the holy spirit had long since given me up as a lost cause?

Films were a wonderful, terrible thing. When I saw my first Harry Potter movie I was convinced Voldemort must be possessed by the devil – surely recognising that meant I still had a chance with God.

As I exited the cinema that Thursday evening, I carefully checked the surrounding streets. Even though I was becoming more relaxed about flouting the rules, it made no sense to be foolhardy. The Brethren spy network had eyes everywhere, and Dee Street was a main thoroughfare. My routine was well rehearsed: stand back and check out the windows to make sure nobody was on the footpath; pull a hoodie up over my head; slip out behind a group; slowly approach my car and avoid the final stretch until I was sure the coast was clear. I'd never been caught before – and this time, my caution paid off.

There, parked up near my car, was a silver Toyota Previa that I recognised as belonging to a local priest, Frank Moore. He was sitting behind the wheel, presumably to confront me.

Filled with indignation, I ducked into a nature strip and hid behind some bushes. Who did Frank think he was? Didn't he have anything better to do? I was determined not to let him win, although I was keen to avoid a confrontation. As I kept watch from the bushes, and sunset darkened the streets, I observed him periodically pulling out to drive around the block – not far, just a few hundred metres – surely to scan for signs that I was nearby. Perhaps I could make an escape if I timed it just right.

When Frank left for another loop, I took out my keys and dashed to the car. Hands shaking with adrenaline, I fumbled my way into the driver's seat and threw the transmission into gear. It was dark by then, and as I screeched off from the alley behind Wachner Place, I could see two beams of light as Frank's Previa pulled round the corner of an office block. I hurtled left around another corner and disappeared just before he came into view. Heart thumping, I broke into hysterical giggles. It all seemed so silly.

The saga didn't end there: the following evening, our family was invited to Frank's home for dinner. I knew my only way through was to brazen it out. He hadn't yet confronted me about my movie-going, and I was almost certain he had no idea I'd been watching him from the bushes. So what on earth was he playing at? If he wanted a round of Brethren chicken, seeing who would blink first, then game on!

I knew Frank wouldn't say anything in front of the others, so I made a point of sitting next to him and making small talk as part of a large group. 'How's work going? Lovely weather we've been having lately. Did you see the roadworks they're doing out on State Highway 1?'

Frank smiled politely and poured me a glass of whisky; I might as well have thumbed my nose in his face.

Defying authority like this was a radical move for a nineteen-year-old in the church. My entire life had been bound up with the Brethren, and as I picked apart their beliefs – mine too, until recently – I wrote plaintively in my diary that it was difficult to know where to turn: 'I feel like every tenet of the faith I have held is being torn to shreds, & there's almost nothing left to believe in.' Through those early months of 2009, my diary entries were guarded, as I was worried about people finding them and reading my private thoughts. But fear and emotion seeped through like a leaky dinghy cast adrift on an ocean of heartache: 'Over the last few months I have withdrawn into myself a lot, & one side-effect of this is that I have no-one to talk to anymore. Feelings are bottling up inside me, & I feel the need to get them out to someone or something, even if it is just a stupid piece of paper like this one.'

As the Brethren part of my life drew to a bitter and painful close, I decided to reach out to the local gay community. But would they be welcoming? What were gay people even like? Ultimately I believed I would find fresh fellowship and understanding among people who had undergone a similar journey to mine, but connecting with gay people in a small, remote city at the bottom of New Zealand was easier said than done – especially without proper internet access.

Invercargill's local newspaper, *The Southland Times*, was my only lead. Once again I turned to the personal listings, where every few months a brief message advertised a local rainbow support group. I'd watched those listings pop up for years, never daring to call the number. When I finally decided to reach out, I had to spend more than a month waiting anxiously for the next listing. I bought myself another unsanctioned mobile phone.

On the day the listing appeared, my hands shook as I dialled the number – and my heart flooded with relief as a friendly woman called Suzie answered the phone. It turned out she lived just around the corner, and she invited me over to have a proper catch-up. This was new territory for me, going into a worldly stranger's home – I'd seen inside Uncle Charles's house during my brief escape attempt, but he at least had a frame of reference for my Brethren experience and in my eyes wasn't a stranger.

Suzie opened her door and laughed. 'Oh, I know you – you fitted my tyres!'

To my surprise, the woman running the local rainbow support group was the proud lesbian who had casually mentioned her partner in that conversation at work a couple of years earlier. I'd longed to ask her then about what it was like being gay – now, she was inviting me into her home. 'Come in, I'll put the kettle on.'

I pinched myself as I wondered what would have occurred if I'd dared to say something back when we had first met. Maybe my whole coming-out process could have happened sooner if I'd known there was support just around the corner. I wondered aloud, 'Could you tell I was gay?'

Suzie laughed. 'There are plenty of gay people in Invercargill, you know.' Her partner, Lisa, was also warm and welcoming; they had kids my age, and it was such a relief to talk to parents who I knew weren't going to judge me.

Meeting other gay people, finally, was liberating. I went out on the weekends – secretly at first, then more openly, no longer caring about the Brethren spy network – and met gay couples living happy lives in Invercargill. These were people who had ordinary jobs, did ordinary things and had loving, caring partners – an existence Bruce Hales had warned me was empty and impossible. Invercargill's small gay community welcomed me with open arms and was full of sympathy for the turmoil I faced in choosing between the Brethren and being true to myself. Many of those I met had walked a similar road, even though they hadn't endured a Brethren upbringing.

Most, too, were happy to introduce me to their own friends, and I made new friends with the intensity of someone who knew that the countdown was on. Courtney and Mel were a couple I met through the rainbow group; Anastazia was a friend of a friend who lived near the tyre shop; Taniamaree was a former choir teacher from the Brethren school whom I'd run into again by chance. As the months passed, I saw that it would indeed be possible to live a happy and fulfilling life as an openly gay man, despite the Brethren's warnings. It was liberating to realise that my old doubts and fears weren't the only way of seeing the world.

As a world of possibilities opened up, I knew I had to leave the Exclusive Brethren as soon as possible. It was an agonising decision, and I needed to lay the groundwork carefully. I could try to manipulate the timing, but there were no guarantees, and I had to be prepared to cut and run at a moment's notice if I was backed into a corner or unexpectedly confronted. It was like juggling a live hand grenade.

Dad was furious as I scaled back my attendance at meetings. He was past the worst of his struggle with depression; he was just as religious as ever, though, and determined to assert his dominance as the head of the household. But I wasn't having a bar of it. What did he think he was going to do – physically drag me to church services? We were well past the days when he could make me comply through sheer force, and years of resentment boiled up as he ranted that I needed to submit to his authority. I rolled my eyes in disgust when I heard he'd asked at a public service for advice on how to compel his children to attend meetings; this prompted me to double down in my resolve to go to as few of them as possible. I wasn't quite ready to stop going entirely – most of my friends and family were there, and it was the only way I could regularly see some of them. Beneath my external rebellion, I felt frightened and vulnerable, and had to keep reminding myself I wasn't the bad sinner the Brethren believed.

Each previously mundane moment took on new meaning as I realised it might be the last. How suddenly would I need to depart? Who would take over the gardening I'd been doing around the house? What if I needed to know something about our family's medical history? I agonised over the logistics, suppressing occasional tears, wondering what would happen if and when I announced I was leaving. Would Dad and Mum change the keys immediately and call in the priests, or would I have time to gather my belongings? I made copies of anything meaningful, because once I was excommunicated there would be no chance of retrieving baby photos.

My parents, well aware of what was going on, watched helplessly as I laid the groundwork to leave. Dad swung between sullen anger and contempt, while Mum sat in her own quiet grief. By then the Brethren were less likely to shut people up at the drop of a hat, and it seemed like for a while, at least, the local priests were happy to sit back and let my parents try to resolve the situation.

At the beginning of 2009, one year after I'd been sent to Sydney, I planned a final farewell tour, driving two thousand kilometres from Invercargill to Cape Rēinga at the top of the North Island. From there I spent several weeks working my way down the country, visiting people I knew I wouldn't be able to see once I'd left the Brethren, although trying to see Anna without the priests finding out proved impossible. Dad objected to the trip; I said that if the church tried to stop me, I'd stay in motels instead. This was another open act of rebellion, as Brethren were only permitted to stay in other Brethren homes.

I wasn't quite ready to show my hand, and none of the uncles, aunts, cousins and friends I saw knew this goodbye was final. They were still dancing to the same Brethren tune; I was pretending to dance along but had long since given up listening to the music. In Wellington, I stayed the night with Grandma Lottie one last time. It was bittersweet to hear her voice raised in song as she plucked at her Hawaiian guitar – one last hug, one last laugh, one last grandmotherly tut-tut, and I held her tight before she waved me off with her usual 'Goodbye, laddie.'

When I arrived in the Wairarapa town of Masterton one weekend, I was asked to preach at the Sunday evening service. The Brethren assembly in Invercargill had stopped asking me to preach – it was clear I was 'troubled' – but the good folks of Masterton knew nothing about that. This was too good a chance to pass up. Taking to the microphone that evening, I read from the eighth chapter of the Gospel of John, in which Jesus pours scorn on the Pharisees for passing judgement on others. He urges them to abandon their preconceptions: 'Again therefore Jesus spoke to them, saying, I am the light of the world; he that follows me shall not walk in darkness, but shall have the light of life.' True light, I preached, was made up of all the colours of the rainbow working in unison. Diversity was critical, I told the gathered Brethren in Masterton; if we really wanted to find the 'light of life', then all must be accepted as equals.

Five days after my rainbow sermon, back in Invercargill, I called a meeting with the local elders. It was time for me to leave the Exclusive Brethren.

ALMOST THREE DECADES BEFORE I CALLED MY FATEFUL
meeting with the Invercargill elders, my grandpa George had his
own run-in with Brethren leadership.

In the spring of 1981, George was middle-aged, his hair
receding, as he approached a life-changing crisis. He'd become
increasingly concerned by the hardline teachings of Elect Vessel
Jim Symington through the late 1970s, and by 1981 he'd stopped
reading mandatory teachings from the North Dakota pig farmer
who had assumed power in 1970 – but George didn't dare
share his doubts with his wife, Lottie. He kept them to himself,
apart from very occasionally sounding out whether she had any
misgivings about the Brethren system. But any time he gave the
slightest hint that something was wrong, she reacted strongly in
defence of the church.

George agonised over how to address his concerns. Eventually
he decided the most effective path was to prepare a public speech
at which he would speak out and say his piece. He waited several
months for an opportunity to take the bull by the horns, feeling
trepidatious, but in the end there was no grand statement.

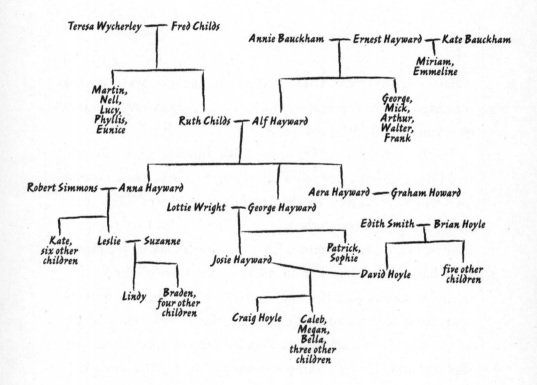

As George was leaving for work one morning, running a bit late as usual, Lottie confronted him with concerns of her own. She challenged him on why he hadn't been reading compulsory teachings from the Man of God. Would he do that soon?

George felt something snap. 'No,' he said, 'and I'm not going to be reading those white books anymore, because Mr Symington is the biggest rival minister of all.'

This was blasphemous talk. 'Rival minister' was the phrase used to describe leaders who weren't completely subservient to the Elect Vessel; it was treasonous for George to be levelling such an accusation against the Elect Vessel himself.

But George didn't stop there, saying, 'He's the biggest rival minister of all, because he's rival to Christ.'

Lottie was horrified. 'Well, I'm shocked to hear you say that, and I'll have to think about what to do now.'

Lottie, a bustling Brethren housewife with hair pulled into a sensible right-hand side part, didn't think about what to do for very long. Later that day she called the local priests and reported her husband as a traitor.

Two priests, Peter Hayman and Eric Boon, were on the doorstep that evening to interrogate George about his treachery. With the cat out of the bag, he felt he no longer had to keep himself in check and made his thoughts clear about the falseness of Symington's teaching.

The wheels of Brethren justice moved quickly when it became clear George would not back down from his blasphemy. A few days later, after a special assembly meeting, Peter Hayman knocked on the door once again, this time with grave news: George had been withdrawn from. The priest said, 'The Brethren have considered what you've said and the stand you've taken, and have judged that we can no longer walk with you in fellowship.'

The strangest thing happened as those words were pronounced: a great burden lifted off George's shoulders, and he suddenly felt free.

*

George and Lottie had been known among the Wellington Brethren through the 1970s for their fun, happy-go-lucky family. George, who didn't much care for putting on a show, was content to drive around in a battered old Austin. The car was so ancient that driving straight through water would soak the children's feet through the floorboards, so George weaved around puddles as the family went to communion services and prayer meetings at their local Brethren hall. My grandparents shared generously what little they had, and they often hosted Brethren gatherings at their weatherboard bungalow behind the white picket fence in Miramar. The house was chaotic, with books and musical instruments jammed in among a motley assortment of orange and beige armchairs.

Music was central to the family's life. George played the pedal organ and the piano accordion, Lottie had her Hawaiian guitar, their eldest children, Patrick and Sophie, were exceptional pianists, and my mother, Josie, the youngest – approaching her fourteenth birthday at the end of 1981 – grew up playing both the piano and the guitar. George's love of a good musical time hadn't abated since he started taking his piano accordion to Christchurch during his brief courtship with Lottie. Twenty years later he was still an enthusiastic leader at social gatherings; when the Brethren went on bus trips to church meetings in nearby Levin, he would sit in the middle of the back seat with his accordion, singing all sorts of humorous songs. Then, as night fell, he would give groups of mesmerised children astronomy lessons through the skylight of the bus.

But George and Lottie's happy home life sat against a backdrop of fear and control. Jim Symington was renowned for his harsh application of assembly discipline. Brethren worldwide endured a merry-go-round of excommunications and punishments; as a teen I heard people my parents' age refer to the Symington era as a 'holocaust'. Often there was no logic to who was discarded and who was spared – decisions were made on the basis of whoever managed to get on the phone fastest and put their version of events to Symington. George's mother, Ruth, my great-grandmother, recorded in granular detail how the Elect Vessel urged Brethren to purge their assemblies: 'Get rid of the troublers.'

Symington had a crude leadership style. In the 1970s, as he reinforced the ban on university education, he dismissively instructed members who had already undergone tertiary study to 'piss on your degree'. Some Brethren took the instruction literally.

Like his predecessor Big Jim Taylor, Symington became incapacitated by heavy drinking, and he was renowned for his love of raucous whisky-fuelled musical evenings. As in Big Jim's day, alcohol was liberally discussed during church services: 'Why should you drink a gallon of wine, when a cupful of whisky'll do you more good?!' At the height of Symington's power, he would hold forth at services in his North Dakota hometown of Neche, congregants clinging to his every word, then drive out into the countryside in his pickup truck and get plastered. On one occasion, a local non-Brethren farmer found the Elect Vessel 'totally blotto' up a back road near Neche after a big fellowship meeting. Symington, the neighbour later told other locals, 'didn't know where he was, or anything'.

It was commonplace for Brethren men to be thrown out of the church during Symington's reign of terror – many tried to return, with mixed success. The regular purges ripped families apart, leaving wives and children reliant on Brethren charity. The resulting divided households – mums and kids without their dads – were regarded as the norm during those chaotic Symington years. Women who abandoned their husbands and stayed loyal to the church were known as 'widows for the truth'. They were stuck in marriage purgatory, forbidden from having contact with their former husbands but also from remarrying, because that would show a lack of faith in God's ability to work a miracle and bring their husband back to the fellowship. The theoretical gold standard was for a person to repent of their ways and come crawling back. When Symington came to meetings in

New Zealand, widows for the truth would queue up to see him, basking in their newfound heroism.

The devastating impact of having their families ripped apart was too much for some of the men, and in New Zealand alone, George later recalled, there were 'six or eight notable suicides'. In one terrible case in England in 1974, 41-year-old Roger Panes hacked his wife and three children to death with an axe and then hung himself three months after being withdrawn from.

The Exclusive Brethren began to draw the attention of both authorities and journalists. An investigation by the UK's Charity Commission found the practice of separation had become 'a harsh and harmful doctrine'. But the idea of stripping charitable status from a church proved too controversial for the Charity Commission, which said that any such decision needed to come from Parliament. British politicians, leery of being seen to restrict religious freedom, also backed away from taking action against the Brethren, who were allowed to continue with their cruel practices.

At the time, the publicity surrounding these deaths didn't raise any red flags for George, who accepted that external persecution was a badge of honour for the Brethren. Nevertheless, the public scrutiny was awkward, and Symington took a blunt approach when asked for advice at special meetings in Auckland during the last weekend of November 1977: 'Sue the bastards!' He was quoting Big Jim's advice for dealing with negative publicity in the UK more than a decade earlier, although George wasn't aware of that at the time.

It was a defining moment for my grandfather. He wasn't there when Symington issued his decree, but it was soon quoted all around New Zealand, and George had a strong internal reaction: 'That's not the spirit of Christ responding to an attack or persecution, that's not Godly at all. This man is wrong.'

*

When George eventually overcame his fear and spoke out against Symington four years later, the consequences were swift and severe. Lottie refused to continue sharing a bed with him, and he was shut up by the Brethren and then withdrawn from. It was school holidays at the time, and the kids were away. They never came home – George was never allowed to say goodbye to his children. When he tried to make contact with them in the weeks following his excommunication, three near-identical letters came back from the teens: 'To Dad, This is just to tell you that I feel my home is with those in fellowship with the Lord's Servant Mr Symington and that is the only place I think it is right to be. I would not be happy anywhere else.'

George pleaded with the Wellington Brethren to hear his concerns. He'd missed his chance to deliver a public address, so in the weeks following his excommunication he typed a letter explaining his position. The Brethren, George said, had gone astray from the noble ideals set out by John Nelson Darby in the 1820s and had lost sight of the fact that Jesus Christ was the only man who could speak directly on God's behalf: 'To claim it applies to some other (additional) man, supposed to be the representative of Christ on earth, is an arrogant presumption.' George was scorned and laughed at as the Brethren turned against him, just as I saw them turn against Lindy several decades later.

My grandfather couldn't quite believe what had happened. He began writing to other excommunicated men, asking whether they had attempted to fight for their children. Their responses were bleak. Trevor Waite, who had been excommunicated from the Hamilton assembly a few years earlier, told George it was a hellish road: 'I have since had ten major court cases and seven different judges and four years in all of court proceedings ... My wife and children never answer my letters though I constantly write to them.' Paul Allison, who had also lost his wife and children, wrote from Christchurch that 'any form of litigation is a complete waste of time and money'. Their letters helped persuade George to walk away. He decided he wasn't going to fight for custody of his children, as they would suffer like other Brethren children of separated marriages. Instead, he would move out of the family home so they would be able to continue their life with the least disruption.

Lottie had already sacrificed her two brothers and her mother out of loyalty to the Brethren. As George pleaded with her through those weeks, her stance never wavered: 'I have to be faithful to Mr Symington.' When her husband packed his bags and left Chelsea Street for the last time, she wouldn't even deign to bid him farewell, turning away in disgust. It was, he wrote in a letter to her, a final act of betrayal: 'The most recent memory

I will have of you is the symbolic significance of your turning away and closing the door.'

*

George was nervous about reconnecting with his relatives outside the Exclusive Brethren. It had been more than twenty years since they were abruptly shunned by Ruth and her children when the separation edict was introduced, and George – feeling guilty and diffident – apprehensively started writing letters. He wondered if his worldly relatives would want to talk to a cousin who had cut them off, ignored them and been scornful of them for so many years. But to George's surprise, his extended family reacted with open arms. His uncle Mick – Alf's brother, the same uncle who had been harshly turned away two decades earlier – wrote warmly to say there was 'no need for any apprehension or explaining': 'We harbour no ill-feeling whatever & will be pleased to see you at any time ... I think you have made a very big decision, but it's the right one, & I know it would not have been easy.'

News travelled fast, and soon my grandfather was getting letters from cousins who had heard the news: 'Word's going round that George is out!' He found it deeply emotional to reconnect with his non-Brethren family, and a visit to Uncle Mick particularly stood out. George was blown away by Mick's useful knick-knacks around the house, such as a hook strategically placed to hold the gate in position – they were exactly the sorts of things that George made at home. As he was leaving, Mick's wife pulled him aside and said, 'He's been quite emotional about your visit here, because you're so much like him.'

Happy as the reunions were, they were tinged with sadness. George's Aunt Phyllis hadn't seen her sister Ruth for more than twenty years and was still shocked by her abrupt disappearance, which had caused her so much sorrow. Even after two decades, Phyllis mourned losing her sister to the Exclusive Brethren: 'Oh, I wish Ruth could be here!'

Ruth cut her son George off just as sharply as she'd abandoned her sisters all those years earlier. But though she never said anything to George directly, 76-year-old Ruth's heartbreak seeped through in her journals; eclipsed only by shame that her son had caused such disrepute to the Wellington Brethren. She was humiliated when four senior leaders travelled from Auckland to take the assembly to task for George's 'attack upon the Elect Vessel', and she redoubled her efforts in prayer, pleading with God to 'keep me grateful & thankful & submissive'. She considered fasting again, just as her husband, Alf, had when he was dying of cancer thirty years earlier; long lists of her non-Exclusive relatives were offered to God for mercy. On one page, her prayer plea was simple: 'George, George, George.'

The fresh loss of her son was layered on top of her grief over the loss decades earlier of her brother and four sisters, and she was shocked to hear that her youngest sister, Eunice, was dying of a brain tumour – 'I feel it very much,' she wrote in her journal – but felt she couldn't reply to pleading letters. Ruth had clipped her siblings' death notices from the paper one by one, maintaining a stoic silence that astounded her sister Phyllis: 'I just can't understand the reasoning, not even a letter!'

On the weekend of Mother's Day 1989, nearly eight years after George was excommunicated, Ruth's brother-in-law Arthur Hayward turned up on the doorstep of her steep hillside home in Wellington, where she lived beside her daughter Aera. Arthur had returned to New Zealand after decades in South Africa and was astonished to learn that Ruth was still refusing to speak to the Hayward siblings. That autumn day, he angrily confronted her for her callousness. Later, not satisfied he had conveyed his message, he drafted a letter to Ruth invoking the memory of his brother, her late husband: 'I wonder what Alf would think about it? He was a good Christian man.'

Ruth, well into her eighties, was not moved by Arthur's plea. While it was sad that George was gone and that she had outlived all five of her siblings without saying a single farewell, she had a rapidly growing family within the Brethren: twenty grandchildren, who were themselves marrying and starting families, just as Ruth and Alf had all those years ago. In May 1989, a few days after Arthur's appeal, Ruth noted in her journal with shaky handwriting that her twelfth great-grandchild had been born in Hamilton at 8.50 pm: 'Craig Benjamin Hoyle.'

Four months after I was born, George received an unexpected phone call on a blustery Tuesday evening from his brother-in-law Graham, Aera's husband: 'I just wanted to let you know that we buried Ruth today.' In death, as in life, there was no chance to say goodbye; the family purposely excluded George from news of his mother's death until the funeral was over. This was standard practice for the Brethren, who had become accustomed to ugly graveside confrontations.

A week later, George – amid a wave of deep sadness – held a small service of his own beside his mother's grave at Karori Cemetery. Several dozen family and friends gathered that sunny spring Sunday to farewell Ruth: people to whom she had refused to speak for thirty years, there to pay their respects all the same. Just as they were singing their last song, what little wind there had been dropped completely to calm; the sun set, and George felt enveloped in a blanket of tangible peace – he was sure that God was present, even if the Brethren were staying away.

By the time of his mother's death, George had long since moved on, building himself a new life. It had been a financial blow to walk away from the family home and start again, but as a technical adviser for the Standards Association, his income wasn't controlled by the Brethren, and he was able to preserve his independence. His church life, meanwhile, became a journey of exploration; he knew the Exclusive Brethren had gone bad but wasn't sure how long ago it had happened: 'I've got to sort out which of the other Brethren lines is the true one.' After a short time exploring groups like the Open Brethren – just as his father Alf had – his mission widened: 'I've got to sort out whether it's one of the other church denominations that's the true one.' A few months after that, he gave up on trying to sort out which churches were right and wrong: 'That's a stupid quest, they're all following God to the best of their sincerity.'

George was convinced he needed to share his Christian faith with as many people as possible. Freed from the constraints of the Exclusive Brethren, he renewed his pilot's licence and embarked on nationwide prayer flights, praying for all New Zealanders as he crisscrossed the countryside in a small private aircraft.

As his beliefs evolved, he gravitated towards the Pentecostals – speaking in tongues, casting out demons – and became an enthusiastic supporter of missionary work. By 1992 he was ready to do it himself, joining a clandestine group of Pentecostals smuggling Bibles into mainland China, where religious literature was forbidden. George also applied his faith closer to home, becoming a regular volunteer at Wellington Prison, where once a week he would attend social events with inmates and listen to their stories. This, to George, was true Christianity: making a difference in the community.

It took my grandfather more than a decade to give up hope of being reunited with his wife and children. Through the 1980s and into the early 1990s he continued writing to Lottie several times a year, pleading with her to see sense and follow him out of the church: 'How much longer do you expect me to wait?' Many of his letters came back unopened, marked 'return to sender'. Lottie's replies, when she sent them, were brief and cold: 'We resent the way you have written. Your letters make it thoroughly clear that our feet are set in absolutely opposite directions.' In 1985, four years after the couple had separated, Lottie called in a lawyer to threaten George with a non-molestation order if he continued his letter-writing. The barrister Kevin Ryan – a prominent lawyer, popular with Exclusive Brethren, who had also advised my grandma Edith – plainly set out Lottie's position in a letter to George: 'She does not wish to engage in dialogue or even consider any reconciliation.'

The non-molestation order never eventuated, and George's sporadic letter-writing continued for another eight years. Eventually, in despair after twelve years of hoping and waiting, he set out his position to Lottie in a final series of letters: 'It is with great grief that I acknowledge the ultimate breakdown of our marriage.' Lottie, having refused to see her estranged husband for more than a decade, now refused to agree to a joint application for divorce; she wrote to tell him the only basis for dissolving their marriage was 'on the grounds of adultery' and sent the papers back unsigned: 'I have always stood faithful, hoping and praying that you would repent and get right and be recovered to the true assembly position.'

George was forced to file a solo application for divorce, and a hearing was set for 11 am on a Friday at the Family Court in Wellington. He spent five minutes in front of a judge – Lottie didn't show up – and the dissolution order was done on the spot. A friend who had come along in support took George to a nearby restaurant for lunch, and they reflected on the anticlimax. A few days later, George wrote to another friend describing what a relief it was to draw a line under his marriage to Lottie and begin the healing process: 'I have come right up out of the depression of uncertainty and wistful wishing, and a big load has just disappeared completely.'

While the divorce was a turning point, George was surprised over the following months by how difficult it was to move past his marriage, even though it had been twelve years since they'd lived together. He poured out his concerns in letters to friends: 'I find I still can't open up to the prospect of thinking seriously about looking for a new relationship. Several times I have started acting friendly towards a lady, but when she starts to show an interest in return, I suddenly get frightened and switch off, which doesn't do much for the friendship!'

George, in his fifties, fumbled around like a teenager as he tried to set a new romantic course. He reconnected with Norah, one of his former Brethren flames; they'd both gone on to marry other people, but now, thirty years later, they were both divorced and excommunicated, and it seemed like an opportunity for a fresh start. George asked her to join him for dinner: 'Let's go out, for old times' sake.'

Over a meal at a nice restaurant up the hill, he popped a wistful question to Norah: 'Can I hold your hand?' She agreed, but the hand-holding was more awkward than romantic; it was like they were kids again, and it was too much for poor George. In a subsequent letter to a friend, he reflected bleakly on the challenge of moving past his first love: 'Possibly I am still dreaming that Lottie might wake up and escape.'

Lottie, like her mother-in-law, Ruth, was far more affected by George's exit than she ever let him know. As she refused his letters and called in lawyers, she continued to wear his ring – a token of her status as a widow for the truth – even after they had spent more time apart than they had together.

I only saw her crack once when talking about George. We were sitting at the kitchen table during one of her visits to Invercargill. I was a rebellious teenager, she a jovial yet deeply religious grey-haired woman in a collared blue blouse. Tears welled as Grandma looked me in the eye and said, 'The devil took away my husband.'

11.

THE PHONE CALL FROM GEORGE'S SON, PATRICK, CAME OUT of the blue on a Wednesday evening in March 2003.

George hadn't heard from his family for years. He was happy in his small Karori apartment, catching the bus to and from his office job in town, and enjoying time with a new circle of friends and relatives. Greyer and rounder as he approached retirement age, he was still bounding up the steep concrete stairs to his unit.

Now, a decade after George and Lottie's divorce, Patrick wanted to know if he could visit with one of the Exclusive Brethren elders to talk over what had happened in the past. George was aware there had been a flurry of activity from the Brethren, who were suddenly contacting hundreds of former members in an apparent attempt to make amends – but he'd never expected to be on the receiving end of such a call, after being branded a traitor for speaking out against the Elect Vessel. He wasn't particularly interested in hearing from the Brethren, telling Patrick he was happy with his current circumstances; however, he agreed to a meeting out of curiosity. Over emails later that night, he asked friends for moral support: 'Your prayers would be valued.'

The Brethren had been shifting in the years since George's excommunication in 1981. On a spring Thursday in 1987, Jim Symington had died in hospital in Minneapolis – diabetic, blind and missing one leg, he'd had whisky smuggled to him in hospital by loyal Brethren right to the end – and the Brethren had been thrown into a new era as members anticipated the rise of the next Elect Vessel. My great-grandmother Ruth offered prayers in her journal for a list of contenders – waiting, like other Brethren, for a sign from God as to who would be anointed.

The man who came out on top was John Hales, the Sydney leader who had first risen to power after his younger brother Bruce Hales Snr married Big Jim Taylor's daughter in 1958. The Hales brothers had been treated like royalty because of their connection to the Elect Vessel, and members hung on to their every word; it seemed there was something special about them. However, while the Hales brothers knew how to turn on the charm, many Brethren were terrified of them.

Through the early 1960s, the brothers had demanded public confessions, with members urged to queue up and reveal their supposedly tawdry secrets in front of thousands of gathered Brethren. Some of these meetings went on for up to five hours, and girls as young as fifteen were pressured to confess – those who refused were made to feel as if they didn't belong. The confession marathons were one of the only occasions where females were permitted to speak publicly in church, aside from announcing hymns or reciting their wedding vows. Anything involving sex or sexuality drew particular attention, and Brethren elders milked these for all they were worth, reporting everything in graphic detail over the public address system; my own private priestly confessions decades later were bad enough, but this was humiliation en masse. It was all part of the Hales technique for bringing Brethren into line, as 42-year-old John Hales described at public church meetings in 1964: 'Hurt 'em, hurt 'em; hurt somebody, and then you'll be really effective. When you start to hurt people, you really know you're effective.' John and Bruce Hales were unsparing in their cruelty; their 53-year-old aunt Eva Hales gassed herself to death in 1965 following months of pressure to conform to Brethren teachings.

The Hales brothers were obsessed with money. John was an accountant, Bruce a time and motion studies expert who evaluated business efficiency, and through the 1960s they took it upon themselves to whip Brethren-owned businesses into shape – starting in Australia and New Zealand, and then spreading further afield. This network of financial control came to be known among Brethren as The System. Members were ordered to record every minute of their days, with weekly reports handed to church leaders who reviewed how efficiently time was being used. When John Hales visited Whangārei in 1964 – the city north of Auckland where, just a few years earlier, Big Jim had told the Brethren they must drink whisky – he made clear how far he believed his powers extended: 'Some men, we go in their offices when they're out on holidays, and one of their doors is locked. Well, he must have something in there that he doesn't want me to see, so I go looking for a key then. He's got no right to lock his doors, lock his cupboards.'

There was only one man with the power to stop the brothers: the Elect Vessel in New York, Big Jim. When he was hospitalised with alcoholism in 1965, his Sydney son-in-law launched what amounted to a Brethren power grab, travelling the world to stamp his authority on Brethren churches and businesses. John Hales, long considered the lesser of the siblings, aided Bruce's attempt to claim power, boasting to other Brethren in private that he considered his brother's spiritual ministering to be at least as valuable as the Elect Vessel's. He later admitted he'd given up on Big Jim's teachings – 'I had lost my taste for Mr Taylor's ministry' – and challenged his guidance.

When the Elect Vessel emerged from his extended hospital stay, he was taken aback to hear about this. He strongly disapproved of his son-in-law's attempts to control Brethren businesses, and the Sydney congregation was ordered to a special disciplinary meeting at the Ashfield hall. The Hales brothers faced a lengthy charge sheet: 'commerce in the assembly', 'dishonest ministry', 'injurious speaking' and, perhaps most damaging, the revelation that John Hales had lied to the Elect Vessel about financial matters. John, who was present at the meeting, acknowledged that the accusations against him were 'more than fair'. The Hales brothers, pulled up red-handed, fell on their swords and accepted the punishment of being withdrawn from. Bruce acknowledged he had been 'utterly cruel' in his treatment of the Brethren, while John wrote a series of grovelling letters apologising for the 'humiliation and anguish' he had caused: 'I am grieved at the pain and suffering I have inflicted on the saints.'

The brothers had been cut down to size. John spent four months out in the cold before being readmitted in February 1966, although the cloud of 'commerce in the assembly' hung over his head. After that, he hewed more closely to Big Jim and vigorously defended him when the Aberdeen allegations emerged.

Like many other Brethren, John Hales travelled a rocky road during the leadership of Symington, following Big Jim's death. Political power plays saw John excommunicated again in July 1976, when he was seen as getting too big for his boots and presenting a threat to the Elect Vessel. But he was readmitted in August 1978 – and then withdrawn from again just fifteen months later; this time, his wife was also excommunicated. Their son Bruce Hales Jnr later described how his father would kneel among the bushes in his garden so he could watch Brethren driving to and from church services, pining for the fellowship he was denied.

In February 1983, John and his wife were finally accepted back into the Brethren. He moved quickly to restore himself to favour with Symington, who was in poor health, and rapidly dispatched with a rival Australian leader, seeing him withdrawn from for threatening the Elect Vessel's power. His own experiences of being cast out seemed to have little impact on his willingness to inflict the same punishment.

Symington, apparently content that John had learnt his lesson, invited him to Winnipeg, Canada to attend the 1984 universal meetings – the annual leadership gathering at which Symington had stamped his authority in 1970. John's presence was a clear indication that he had been restored to favour. By 1985, Symington was too ill to host the universal meetings and delegated John to lead in his place. This level of rehabilitation was surprising for someone who had been withdrawn from three times and had recently been out of fellowship for three years. John went on to lead the universal meetings again in Winnipeg in 1986. It was clear he was angling for power, although some senior Brethren leaders were less than thrilled by the prospect of a Hales seizing control once more – memories of the System days in the 1960s were still fresh in their minds.

When Jim Symington died in April 1987, an American contingent attempted to have one of their own named to lead that year's universal meetings in Winnipeg. It was a bold power play: whoever led the first set of universal meetings following the death of an Elect Vessel was likely to be recognised as his successor.

Ultimately, Symington's son intervened to say his father had made it very clear that John Hales was to take the lead again in Winnipeg. It soon became apparent that the Sydney accountant would be the new Elect Vessel.

*

The Symington–Hales transition marked another continental shift, with global control of the Exclusive Brethren moving from North America to Australia. John Hales, older and wiser at sixty-five, trod carefully as he seized the power he and his brother had been denied two decades earlier.

First, his own ledger needed to be cleared. Six months after Symington's death, the Sydney assembly held a special meeting to acknowledge they had been wrong in excommunicating John three times – even though they had been acting on the orders of two different Elect Vessels – and collectively repented for the 'grievous personal pain, suffering and humiliation' they had inflicted on the ascendant world leader.

My childhood memories of John Hales are of a dull old man in woollen cardigans – I was too young to understand that many Brethren were still terrified of him, knowing what he'd been capable of in the 1960s. Under his leadership, excommunications eased somewhat, and there was much less of the heavy drinking to which the Brethren had become accustomed. In fact, speaking at public church meetings, he took a dim view of people who over-imbibed, having once said: 'It's a matter of self-control. You should know your measure. Just because somebody offers you a drink, that's no excuse for taking a drink.'

This Elect Vessel wielded his power in other ways. He reinforced the Brethren ban on technology, including computers, mobile phones and fax machines, and ruled on matters as inconsequential as whether the Brethren should eat Chinese food – he said they shouldn't. He ordered Brethren to withdraw their children from state high schools and colleges, and oversaw the launch of the first Brethren-run school in Sydney in 1994. He also had firm views on where it was appropriate for Brethren to live: during his tenure as Elect Vessel, members of the church were ordered to leave South Africa and India. Hundreds of African and Indian Brethren were scattered around the world, forced to move to other Brethren meetings as far afield as New Zealand and the Caribbean.

An accountant by training, John Hales employed a rigorous filing system at his modest brick bungalow in Meadowbank, a Sydney suburb on the northern bank of the Parramatta River. Records were sorted according to location and surname; if he was asked about a particular Brethren member, he could open the drawer that contained all files from their home city, then flip alphabetically to their surname to retrieve all correspondence he had sent and received about that person. He built up an impressive archive of Brethren leadership decisions and excommunications.

When the Elect Vessel visited my home city of Invercargill in 1999, he was a frail 77-year-old struggling with cancer. Nevertheless, he retained a keen interest in Brethren affairs; he inquired after my parents and told them that six was enough children. Mum didn't have the heart to tell the ailing Elect Vessel she was pregnant with another – there was no sense upsetting him with something that couldn't be changed.

I was told that he should be venerated, but I struggled to understand what my parents saw in him. After special church meetings in Dunedin, I was playing outside with other kids when a murmur went through the group that the car carrying the Elect Vessel was departing the grounds. My peers dutifully lined up to wave goodbye as though a royal tour was passing through, but this seemed weird to me. On the spur of the moment, shuffling my feet in embarrassment, I turned my back to the car as it slowly drove past. Mum was mortified that I had shown such disrespect.

As the new millennium ticked over, my parents fretted over the imminent death of the Elect Vessel. I lingered at the bathroom door, a curious eleven-year-old, and eavesdropped as they fretfully discussed what the death of John Hales would mean for our family. In their eyes there was no clear successor, and Mum feared the Brethren would face another period of turmoil as potential leaders jostled for the top spot.

My parents need not have worried. As the Elect Vessel declined in health, his youngest son Bruce Hales Jnr increasingly deputised for him, and the ambitious 48-year-old soon seized control of local administrative functions in Sydney. His father, too weak to exercise power, allowed his son free rein. Brash and extroverted, with six children of his own, Bruce was a very different man whose paunchy frame revealed a fondness for fine food and liquor. He'd experienced his father's rise to glory in the 1960s, then as a teenager lived through the shame of his excommunication in 1965. Bruce, a sharper political operator than his two elder brothers, knew which way the wind blew: he'd told Symington he supported the subsequent excommunications of his father in the 1970s and 1980s, then changed course to become one of his father's loudest cheerleaders once Symington was dead.

A few months after John died, in 2002, Bruce's moment came at special Brethren meetings in Timaru, the South Island town where he would later direct treatment for my sexuality. He'd had little experience leading Brethren conferences, and as the weekend approached, rank and file members watched intently to see whether senior leaders would offer Bruce the deference they had afforded his father. By the end of that weekend, it was clear: Bruce Hales Jnr was the new world leader, and we soon came to refer to him as the Man of God – a new title for a new era. It was the second time in fifty years that power had transferred from father to son, and Bruce was the fourth world leader to claim a personal connection to the Taylor dynasty.

Change was swift under Bruce. He declared a new era for the Brethren: a 'day of grace'. No longer would the church be ruled by fear and threat, we were told, but rather by love and compassion. Part of this new day of grace was making a break with the past.

In early 2002, Bruce's elder brother Daniel Hales was involved in erasing their father's archive: Daniel's sons oversaw the purging of their grandfather's paperwork by a document destruction company; they stood guard as fifteen years of Brethren records – two pallets' worth – were razed on-site by a large truck-mounted shredder. It was important, Daniel said, for family representatives to watch to ensure that not a single piece of paper survived.

A short time later, in mid-2002, Bruce ordered Brethren meetings worldwide to revisit all excommunications in living memory, and to reconsider them in light of the new teaching on grace and compassion. This sweeping undertaking came to be known as The Review. Invercargill, as a newly established meeting, escaped relatively unscathed, but the effects were more severe in larger, older Brethren assemblies such as Auckland and Wellington. In some cases, the people involved were now dead, or details had been forgotten. Many of the documents kept by his father that Bruce's nephews had seen destroyed had concerned cases that now were being reviewed – it seemed he wanted to rewrite history with an airbrushed version of events that put the Hales dynasty in a good light.

Families were wounded all over again as they were told their loved ones should not, in fact, have been thrown out of the Brethren. My grandma Edith had steadfastly refused to talk to her parents after they were excommunicated in the 1970s and had chosen the Brethren over her husband, Brian, in the early 1980s – decades later, she received the shattering news that neither her parents nor her former husband should have received such harsh treatment. Sacrificing all for the church was a heavy burden; it was many times worse to be told the sacrifice had been wrongly imposed. The retrospective forgiveness was cold comfort to Edith, as her parents were long since dead, and her former husband was happily remarried outside the church.

My parents' generation struggled to make sense of the new direction the Brethren had taken. They had come of age in the harsh Symington years, when even minor infractions resulted in excommunication. Now, those rules were tossed out the window, and there were completely different criteria for getting shut up or withdrawn from. I overheard a hushed conversation between my mum and another Brethren woman her age, quietly voicing the unthinkable: 'Was everything we were told a lie?'

*

When Grandpa George met his 38-year-old son, Patrick, on a Friday afternoon in March 2003, the two hours they spent together felt more like an interview than a reunion. A local priest turned up as well, and the encounter left George emotionally drained.

He was questioned closely on whether he accepted the legitimacy of the Man of God – 'In principle,' he said, 'I would object to all of them' – and was astonished to be told he had been cruel to divorce his wife, even though she had refused contact with him for twelve years. All in all, George was disappointed to learn that what he called the 'blinkers of ignorance' were still firmly in place.

As George once more rejected the Brethren, his sister Anna was again questioning her place among them. The Review saw her doubts return with a vengeance, and she was shocked to see decades of teachings overturned. If the Brethren had been wrong about so many of these excommunications, she wondered, who was to say they had been right about anything else? Many Brethren beliefs greatly troubled Anna.

The Review was a precious window of opportunity for Anna and George. Suddenly, Brethren men could reach out under priestly guidance to excommunicated relatives under the guise of putting things right and gauging whether they might be interested in returning to the fold. Anna, although a woman and not sanctioned to contact outsiders, seized the moment to start a clandestine correspondence with George and some of her non-Brethren cousins. She shared her fears and concerns, saying she felt like a 'prisoner of hope' and noting plaintively that she had 'felt trapped for most of my life'. George sent her a copy of his letter from 1981, in which he called out the Brethren for their devotion to a flawed man – and in January 2004 she told him she agreed with every word: 'Your letter ... which I have just seen for the first time, expresses my own feelings.'

For more than five years, well past the end of The Review, Anna poured out her troubles to George as her granddaughter Lindy and I prepared to leave the Brethren; we were both close to her but had no idea she was keeping up this secret contact with outsiders. She also kept him updated on what was happening in the Brethren and sent him photos of his children and grandchildren – knowing if she was ever discovered having unsanctioned contact, she risked being excommunicated herself. Anna's secret correspondence with George finally stopped after the priests reprimanded her for talking to Lindy and me, and she reluctantly decided it would be safer to cut off contact.

Anna, a sprightly great-grandmother in her sixties, wasn't the only person pushing boundaries during the chaos of The Review. Younger members began bending and breaking rules that had been in place for decades: going to the movies, listening to worldly music, and engaging in forbidden sexual dalliances.

At thirteen going on fourteen, I was too young and scared to get involved in any of those things, but it was dizzying to watch. For a brief time – from mid-2002 to mid-2003 – it seemed as though it was possible to get away with anything.

But that was too good to last. In May 2003, just a few days before my fourteenth birthday, Bruce Hales Jnr – furious that the Brethren had taken advantage of his 'day of grace' – cracked down on wayward followers with a scathing letter. It tore strips off members for their repeated rule-breaking and listed 'unacceptable features' that had crept in: 'Unsuitable hairstyles (e.g. sideburns and long hair – brothers / hair tinting). Attending venues of worldly entertainment including restaurants. Pre-recorded music, CDs, digital equipment, mobile phones.' The Man of God demanded public declarations of loyalty: 'Brethren in every locality should declare themselves in the Assembly in a conclusive manner that will leave no doubt that the regulation and control required will be respected and upheld without compromise.'

The letter was an explicit reprimand from the Man of God himself, with the implicit threat of excommunication for anyone who did not comply. It was read out repeatedly at meetings. At one tense gathering in Invercargill, every male householder had to make a public declaration: 'My household and I are in full support of our brother Mr Hales and the stand he is making.' After most had pledged their loyalty, we sat in awkward silence, waiting for the stragglers; it was clear nobody would be moving from their seats until every married man had sworn allegiance.

Eventually there was just one person left. It was excruciating: a hundred and fifty Brethren stared at him in silence, knowing his family's future hung in the balance. Finally, after a pregnant pause, he too swore fealty to Bruce Hales Jnr. We breathed a sigh of relief.

The May 2003 letter had slammed the door closed again. Young Brethren were once more punished for their transgressions, and there was a procession of members 'getting right' and apologising for their wayward behaviour, which usually took the form of extended confession sessions with elders. Once priests were satisfied that a follower was repentant, their case would be brought to the assembly with an announcement from a front-row elder: 'So-and-so needs to get clear about some matters.' All eyes would turn to the person being discussed – usually a young person sitting flushed with shame. The priests would tell us they had examined the guilty party's confessions and had established that they had 'made a break from sin'. There would be a murmuring of approval, then a chorus of 'amen' from the gathered Brethren.

Bruce Hales Jnr, obsessed with restoring his father's legacy, continued his mission of rewriting history. He told his followers that the Sydney Brethren had hated John Hales and that he had been withdrawn from three times only because the facts had been misrepresented to successive Elect Vessels. Bruce also proclaimed there had been nothing wrong with The System, and he soon started holding his own business conferences for Brethren in tandem with his religious conferences as the Man of

God. Advice and instructions flowed thick and fast. For example, he told unmarried men that they should be at work by 5 am each day. He said it wasn't necessary for workers to take meal breaks, describing how his own employees had lunch delivered to their desks. Such business instructions were compiled and printed as 'silver books', which were distributed to Brethren in the same manner as the Man of God's religious utterances. All members were expected to subscribe, with one memo describing his displeasure at their sluggish uptake: 'Mr Hales said only two thousand "silver" books have been sold ... He said there are four thousand Brethren businesses. He did not know his ministry was optional.' This conflating of monetary and moral matters was precisely what had seen the previous generation of Hales brothers excommunicated from the Exclusive Brethren, but few dared challenge the Man of God. When Brethren businesses were sent surveys requesting details of their revenues and profits, most complied.

In the 2000s, Brethren-owned companies found their profit-making endeavours hampered by the ban on technology. When I started working in the family business at the end of 2005, we weren't even allowed a fax machine; any faxes had to be sent and received via our non-Brethren neighbour, who charged a fee. Emails were unthinkable.

But by mid-2006, rumours circulated that the church's stance on technology was changing. Senior elders trialled car phones – a major departure from Brethren orthodoxy, especially considering the Man of God had reiterated the ban on mobile technology just three years earlier. But businesses were struggling to communicate with sales reps on the road, and the phones were also dressed up as a safety feature for young people. A few months later, they were rolled out to Brethren members more widely. We were forbidden from owning them, though: they were overseen by the Brethren-controlled Statcom Business Services, which was run by a group of senior elders, with subscribers paying a monthly rental charge. Fax machines were finally allowed, but like the phones they had to be rented from Statcom. This technology rollout became a significant revenue generator for the Brethren, with Statcom funds put towards church schools. The fees were extortionate: our family business paid a monthly charge of $50 for the use of a fax machine, when it would have cost only $125 to buy our own.

Bruce Hales Jnr may have been obsessed with restoring some aspects of his father's legacy, but he was happy to disregard others when it became clear that technology was essential for doing business in the twenty-first century. John had repeatedly told the church that computers were evil, but that rule went out the window in mid-2007 when Statcom began releasing brand-new Brethren-controlled computers that came pre-installed with tight restrictions. Known as the Wordex 1500, they were provided to members through a similar lease arrangement to those of fax machines and car phones. And they were highly restricted: emailing was permitted, while all other internet access was blocked. If a company required a particular program for the running of their business, a church representative had to temporarily unlock the system so the program could be installed once it was approved. Limited internet access – a whitelist of websites, mostly banks, airlines and government agencies – was allowed when Wordex 2000 machines with upgraded security protocols were rolled out a few months later. In October 2007, mobile phones were finally permitted, once again with extortionate rental fees.

Over the following year, Brethren businesses were able to pay a fee to have industry-specific websites added to their whitelist. By the beginning of 2009 – as I prepared to make my escape – they were launching their own websites. The Brethren explained away such shifts in doctrine by saying that times had changed: 'The Lord has turned a corner.' Between ourselves, we sometimes joked that the Lord must surely be dizzy from making so many turns.

12.

In mid-2009, I was leaving the Exclusive Brethren. My siblings had been removed from the family home, where I continued to live with my parents in deathly silence, waiting for the axe to fall. The house was as neat as a pin without nine people constantly passing through it: no banging doors, no piano playing, and no children's voices raised in argument or play. I would walk down the hallway past cold bedrooms that had been cleaned of my siblings' day-to-day belongings. Members of the church had flowers delivered to Mum with sympathetic notes: 'Feeling for you at this difficult time, and sending much love.' It was as though the flowers and silence were part of the funeral for what used to be my life, and the house was in mourning.

A week went by before my case was raised with the local Brethren congregation, who held their care meeting at six on a Saturday morning. When I woke that day I joked to Mum in the kitchen, trying to break the tension, about the deed that was surely now done: 'Well, I guess I've been shut up now?'

She looked at me with deep, sad eyes. 'No, you haven't been. I think you're underestimating how much the Brethren love you.'

I was stunned. It turned out the priests had, after all, avoided accusing me of 'defilement of young people' for telling my siblings I was gay, as they had threatened, instead opting for vague 'serious outstanding matters'. It seemed my own threat of marching into the hall to defend myself had had the desired effect. With the public charges watered down, a number of local householders spoke up in my defence instead of going along with the priestly plan to place me under discipline; they asked the priests to pass on a message of love to me and said they were looking forward to seeing me at meetings again soon.

Because I remained unsanctioned, my siblings were given permission to return home. It didn't seem to matter that my conversations with them a week earlier were the reason they'd been taken away. One by one, they came back through the door. My fifteen-year-old sister Megan handed me a random newspaper headline she had clipped out – 'Come back, be forgiven' – and threw her arms around me, crying. Although I hugged her back, I felt numb. I'd just been through the raw trauma of losing my brothers and sisters; it was as though a part of me had died. How could I let myself love them again, when sooner or later we'd be faced with the same heartbreaking separation?

My nine-year-old sister Bella was crying as she came running through the house and also threw her arms around me, saying, 'I love you, I love you, I always will, I promise.' Bella had no concept of excommunication, so she couldn't understand what was happening. Not long before, she had pleaded with me to promise I would never leave her; I'd told her I didn't want to but explained it could be forced by our parents and the church. She refused to believe that was possible: 'But they won't, they love you.' She was very upset when I tried to explain what it meant when Brethren members were shut up or withdrawn from, banned from seeing their family and friends. 'But if you're not a Brethren,' she said, 'you'll go to hell, and I'll never see you again, not even in heaven.'

That evening, Bella came to my room three times, pleading with me not to go. She cried as I told her I couldn't do anything about the Brethren rules, and she wasn't consoled when I said we could focus on enjoying the time we had left. 'If you leave,' she said, 'then I'll have to run away, because I won't be able to bear not being able to hug you.' On her final trip to my room, she asked if I would change my mind if she gave me all the cash from her pocket money savings. I was shocked and replied that it was her love that mattered most. She looked at me with tearful blue eyes: 'But if I give you a hundred dollars, will you stay?'

During those twilight weeks, as my membership hung in the balance, the Brethren doubled down on their efforts to persuade me to return to the fold. I was told repeatedly that I was loved. Church members would turn up unannounced at my family home and say they felt moved by the holy spirit to go for a walk with me, while I wished they would leave me alone. My brother Caleb kept a list of everyone who asked after me at church services: 'Ray Walton says the Lord is weary. Carl Currie sends his love. Shane Murray feels really sorry for you.' And the letters just kept coming. Uncle Rob, Anna's husband, wrote to say he'd been lying awake at night, thinking of my rebellion: 'Please accept some counsel from a friend ... You are really kicking against goads, and finding it hard.' I wrote back to him, and many others, to share the news I was gay – my list of people who knew now ran into the dozens. I told them, 'I fail to see the point of continuing to lead a life pretending to be something I am not.'

On a blustery Tuesday afternoon, I was picked up for lunch by a Brethren husband and wife who had children my age. Barrett and Lily had always been a bit outside the square, and I was intrigued when they took me to a local eatery – the Man of God had made clear a few years earlier that restaurant dining was forbidden, but Barrett and Lily were prepared to bend the rules. Over lunch, they asked what my 'problem' was; I said I was gay. They pleaded with me to change my mind – as if sexuality was a switch that could be flipped – and told me I should cut off my connections with other gay people. Then they said I should get down on my knees and beg for change. This went on for several hours.

The following evening, a waitress from the restaurant was killed in a car crash. She was nineteen, my age. Barrett triumphantly shared the news with me, saying it was surely a sign from God that I was meant to change my sexuality and stay in the Brethren. I was sickened. I wasn't sure what I believed about God anymore, but I knew one thing: God certainly wouldn't kill a stranger to send me a message. I told Barrett my mind was made up – this time in much stronger terms than I'd used over lunch.

My exchange with Barrett was reported back to the priests, and helped tip the scales. A few nights later, when the priests raised my matters once again with the local assembly, the decision was unanimous: I was to be shut up. One of the priests, Frank Moore, the same man I'd run away from outside the movies, later explained why I had been placed in the first stage of excommunication: 'The basis of the thing from our side was that scripture in 1 Corinthians, "evil communications corrupt good manners".' When I pressed for what exactly was meant by 'evil communications', he elaborated: 'Well, really, it was the conveying of defiling things to young people, especially your siblings and cousins.' He was at pains to say I had not been shut up for my sexuality: 'If we were going to shut you up for being gay, we would have done it a long time ago.' Instead, I had been shut up for telling my brothers and sisters I was gay. To me, the distinction was meaningless.

My mother broke the news early on a Wednesday morning, when I was alone with her in the kitchen as she ate breakfast. She was vague on details – neither she nor Dad had been at the meeting; Caleb had accepted the assembly discipline on their behalf. A few more questions back and forth didn't reveal much, so I got my breakfast and sat at the table across from her.

Mum promptly put her knife and fork down. 'Now that you're shut up, we're not prepared to eat with you.'

I felt sick, got up and tipped my breakfast cereal down the waste disposal unit in the sink, and walked out.

There was a marked shift in how the Brethren treated me after I was shut up. The unexpected visits, letters and phone calls stopped, a relief after the love-bombing I'd endured. Members were now forbidden from contacting me, but it was hard to avoid them in a city the size of Invercargill. Some local Brethren still smiled and said hello; others crossed the street, or pointed and sniggered. It was bewildering to try and make sense of each encounter, and I quickly learned to steel myself if I saw Brethren coming: what were they going to do or say this time? I ran into Grandma Edith at the bank – dear, sweet Grandma, who knew all too well what it was like to be under assembly discipline after her four years in the wilderness – and she allowed herself only the barest smile of acknowledgement as I walked past.

My Brethren relatives struggled, and some – like Anna, who kept in touch with secret phone calls, despite her priestly reprimand – clearly weren't happy with being told to cease contact. Other Brethren were much less accepting. As news travelled, I received a string of anonymous phone calls. I was called a 'faggot' and told that 'God created Adam and Eve, not Adam and Steve'. One prank call was from a group of young men saying they 'wanted dick'. I hung up, and they called straight back, hurling abuse down the phone line for five minutes, all kinds of insults about me and gay people in general. When they called a third time, I didn't bother answering; they left a voicemail saying I was a 'fat ginger bastard'. These calls were almost always from blocked numbers, but sometimes I was able to track where they were coming from. It was upsetting to realise cousins were among those shouting abuse.

One Tuesday morning, I hit a wall. My head was spinning when I got out of bed, and I felt like I was going to throw up. I couldn't go to work at the tyre shop. Mum came home from errands to find me weeping at the kitchen table. She put her arm around me, asked what was wrong, offered to cook me breakfast and made me lie down. Then she booked an urgent doctor's appointment and administered vitamins. At that moment, Brethren rules didn't mean a thing: she was still my mum.

Later that day, I saw a locum doctor at my usual GP clinic. Dr Pezaro was an older man, somewhat gruff but with a heart of gold. He listened to my lengthy explanation of the Brethren's claim I was mentally ill because I wanted to live as an openly gay man. He then looked down my throat and brusquely told me it was just the flu: 'No matter what the church says, this illness is not the wrath of God being visited upon you; it's a simple case of coming down with a contagious illness that is prevalent at the moment.' Dr Pezaro added there was no explaining the actions of a church like the Brethren, and he recommended I 'get out of there as soon as possible'. As I departed with a doctor's note for work, lest Dad question whether I was actually unwell, he had one final piece of advice: 'Remember that no matter what anyone else tries to tell you, you are a worthwhile person.'

*

I'd been warned the world was a cold, hard place, and that I'd only find love and acceptance among the Brethren. I found the opposite to be true. My new friends outside the church welcomed me with open arms, my friendship circle rapidly growing beyond the local rainbow support group. My non-Brethren mobile phone, now joined by an unsanctioned laptop with no internet restrictions, gave me access to a whole new world. Kiwi society was full of strangers who opened their hearts and homes to offer practical and emotional support; many were horrified by my ordeal, and news travelled quickly. Dozens of congregants from the queer-friendly Auckland Community Church signed a card sending support and prayers: 'God loves you as you are!'

All that support, though, couldn't mask the fact that I was being broken into pieces. I tried hard to convince people I was fine – 'I'm OK, I'm OK, I'm OK' – but, of course, I clearly wasn't. My siblings had all been sent away from the family home again after I was shut up, so it was back to just me and my parents. I was determined not to leave voluntarily and be accused of abandoning my family. My dad wanted me gone – he made no secret of that – but the Brethren knew it would be a bad look if he threw his son out of the house. So we reached a stalemate: I continued living under his roof and was treated with open hostility. I rejected the authority of the church, and my father's ability to enforce it, but suffered through emotional torture as I was told I was wicked and evil. I figured Dad was trying to make things as unpleasant as possible in the hopes I would leave, but I wasn't going to give him that pleasure. I told him I'd move out any time, so long as he put in writing why he wanted me gone.

Those months of purgatory were clouded by grief. The emotional torture went on and on and on, and it was as though the Brethren were trying to kill everything that made me who I was. My new friends watched helplessly, knowing there wasn't much they could do: this was my journey, and I had to keep going so I could come out the other side.

The back of my mind drummed with doubts and fears. Sometimes I contemplated pretending to be a good Brethren again so I could have my family back, then something awful would happen and I'd get a shock reminder: 'Hell no!' Like many young people who leave the Brethren, I was trying to overcome my fear with self-talk: *Oh, it'll be fine, I know people outside, I won't miss my parents anyway, and I'm sure they'll still be in touch.* There was a huge amount of fear, though, and my emotional scales seesawed between wanting to escape and being terrified of the consequences.

I found it helpful to talk to others who had left the Brethren and understood what I was going through. I discovered a whole network of former Brethren brought together by shared hope and grief – some were recent leavers, and others had been out for more than fifty years, but they all had similar stories of the agony of losing their families. I started finding excommunicated aunts, uncles and cousins who had walked a path similar to my own; it was an overwhelming relief to know I had relatives on the outside, although not all of them were welcoming. Grandpa Brian, my dad's dad – out of the Brethren for more than thirty years – wasn't interested in having regular contact with me. He and his second wife agreed to a single meeting on the condition I didn't reach out again, and for one strange afternoon we quizzed each other. It was bizarre to meet someone who looked exactly like my father yet felt like a stranger. 'You can ask any questions you like,' he said, 'but this will be your only chance.'

It took much longer for me to feel comfortable reaching out to my other grandpa, George Hayward. My whole life I'd heard about what a bad person he was, and I struggled to move past that. As a teen, when I'd asked Brethren about him, they'd warned me not to trust his friendly overtures; a priest had even quoted from the Book of Psalms: 'Smooth were the milky words of his mouth, but his heart was war.' I also knew that George was still deeply religious, which made me worried about how he would react to my sexuality. But after a few months I bit the bullet and searched the phone directory for his number. There was no need for an introduction – he knew exactly who I was. When I told him I was gay, I could almost hear him shrug over the phone. 'I can live with that,' he said. He added that life had taught him everybody had different viewpoints, and we'd all get on a whole lot better if we accepted that.

When I visited Wellington, Grandpa George and I headed to McDonald's for our first meal together. At the time, I didn't fully appreciate how significant this breakfast was to George: I was the first of his children or grandchildren he'd shared a meal with for twenty-eight years. An older man, almost seventy, he wore a thin woollen waistcoat vest and rimmed glasses, and he had a twinkle in his eyes that I recognised immediately – it was like looking into a mirror. His voice, too, sounded familiar, and those childhood comments – 'Isn't Craig just like George?' – clicked into place.

As we pushed our hash browns around at the fast-food joint on Wellington's Taranaki Street, Grandpa and I agreed we had no regrets in leaving the Brethren. Before we headed off, I gathered my rubbish and crammed it into the cup, as I always do, to make it as small as possible; I looked over at Grandpa and realised he was doing exactly the same thing. Our eyes met, and we laughed. It was eerie to have so much in common with a stranger.

Back in Invercargill, my strange double life continued. It must have been an intensely traumatic time for Mum and Dad, awakening memories of how they'd suffered family separation when their respective fathers were withdrawn from. Dad asked repeatedly if I'd found somewhere else to live, while Mum kept promising she would never kick me out and would do whatever she could to support me. She made all sorts of suggestions: maybe I could live in a caravan in the backyard; maybe they could build a separate cottage so that technically I wasn't living in their house; maybe I could move into a flat, where she would provide meals and do my laundry.

As the weeks stretched into three months, I would sit on the edge of my bed aching to be able to cry. I wanted nothing more than to sob and scream to release the tension, but the tears were nowhere to be found; it was as though my mind had passed its threshold for emotional pain and was numbing itself as a coping mechanism. I felt strangely detached from what was happening, as though I was watching an old black-and-white film from the opposite end of a long dark corridor. Would I ever be able to cry again?

Normally if I was feeling like this, I would pray to God – heaven remained a constant, even while earthly circumstances collapsed – but now even God felt dim and distant. It was a frightening feeling. Had I been abandoned in my hour of need? Or even worse: was it possible that God didn't exist, and my prayers were floating aimlessly into the dark void of space? That was too awful to contemplate. The Brethren might have had the power to strip everything else from me, but for now my belief in God was one thing they couldn't control. Following in Dad's footsteps, I threw myself on my knees and begged God to show me the path forward.

One day, I tried to explain to Mum that I still loved her very much. Later that night, she came and stood hesitantly near me in the kitchen. I asked her if she wanted something, and she burst into tears. I wasn't sure what to do, but eventually I awkwardly held her hand and asked what was wrong. 'With things the way they are,' she said through sobs, 'sometimes all I feel like doing is crying.' I was close to throwing my arms around her but pulled back at the last moment – I wasn't sure how she would react to my hug while I was under assembly discipline.

Eight weeks later, as the situation dragged on, I tried to explain my feelings in a letter to her: 'I know that you only want the best for me, and it devastates me that we are being driven apart. I feel as though there is a gaping hole in my heart where my family has been ripped out, and the contact that we have been reduced to feels like some kind of living death.'

*

In July, I appeared on the front page of a local paper, the *Invercargill Eye*, helping promote an upcoming social event for the local rainbow support group. The Brethren were disgusted by such a blatant public statement of homosexuality, and local priests Frank Moore and Peter Hickmott demanded a meeting at once.

In a letter to Frank, I outlined four conditions for our meeting. Firstly, they needed to agree they were speaking to me as representatives of the Exclusive Brethren; the Brethren often wriggled out of culpability by claiming that actions were taken by individual members, not the church itself. Secondly, they needed to provide me with a written agenda in advance. Thirdly, an independent witness of my choosing would need to attend. Finally, I needed a guarantee that my family would be left alone: 'You have stated in the past that the church will never bring pressure to bear on my parents, either to ask me to leave the family home, or to expel me from the family business. Your written assurance on this matter would be appreciated.'

We met at 7 pm on the dark winter's night of Sunday, 26 July. The two priests had begrudgingly agreed to my conditions, although their agenda was brief: 'Discussion regarding the publication in the "Invercargill Eye".' My friend Taniamaree, the former choir teacher, came as a witness, and the priests were taken aback to see someone they knew. She knew how the Brethren operated, and as we made our way upstairs to the boardroom at Tyremax, Frank's company, her strategy was to get them off keel. Her first question was, 'Have you prayed about this yet?' Frank admitted they hadn't, so Taniamaree suggested we pray as a group before getting underway. This was out of the question: Brethren were forbidden from praying with non-members. The priests shuffled awkwardly, then hurriedly left the room when Taniamaree prayed aloud for guidance.

Frank and Peter had prepared a written statement in response to the conditions I had stipulated for seeing them, but it was too vague. We debated a revised signed statement, confirming they were 'seeking to represent the feelings of the Brethren in Invercargill'. They agreed to leave my parents alone and not pressure them to have me 'expelled from the home or workplace'. They asked if I had any regrets about having my sexuality declared on the front page of the paper; I said I had no regrets. Then they asked if I was a member of the rainbow support group, a classic line of questioning for the Brethren as membership with other associations had been banned for many decades and was grounds for excommunication; I said that, yes, I was a member.

The meeting was a good opportunity for me to stand my ground. Frank and Peter tried to claim that because I'd already made my own decision to stop attending church meetings, the fact I had since been shut up was a moot point. I replied that, yes, I had voluntarily given up attendance, but I hadn't chosen to give up my family, my friends, my employment or my living circumstances – all aspects of my life, I said, that they seemed 'determined to force me into sacrificing'. I reminded them of how, in Brethren attempts to explain away my 'problems', I had been labelled as mentally unstable, depressed and not in my right mind, and how medical professionals had rejected that assessment.

Taniamaree fought in my corner: 'Instead of kicking Craig out, you should be embracing him.' It was, she told them, still possible to love me even if they disagreed with my new direction in life.

I had a Bible verse of my own as we argued back and forth: 'Judge not, that ye may not be judged.'

A few weeks later, with Invercargill still firmly in winter's grip, I left for a short holiday in Australia. Mum dropped me off at the airport around 6 am, and we joked and laughed as we waited for my final boarding call. It was just like the old days. She hugged and kissed me goodbye, seeming torn between conflicting loyalties. I poked my tongue out at her and laughed as I walked towards the aircraft. The look of indignation on Mum's face quickly turned to laughter, and she pulled a ferocious face back.

I was in Adelaide a few days later when my phone rang early on a Saturday morning. It was Dad. He was short and abrupt, and said I wouldn't be welcome in the family home when I returned to Invercargill. He repeated himself several times, making it quite clear they weren't prepared to go on with my 'gay lifestyle'.

In a daze, I stumbled out of bed and headed downstairs at the youth hostel where I was staying. As I passed through the main foyer, I noticed that someone had left a scribbled note on the noticeboard: Jesus, the note said, had not come to judge but to love the world and those in it.

When I posted on Facebook about what Dad had told me, there was an outpouring of love and support. My friends Courtney and Mel, a couple whom I'd met at a rainbow community event, got in touch immediately: 'We're really sorry. If you need somewhere to stay please, please don't hesitate to ask. We have a lovely spare room with a warm bed and would be happy to have you.' As I emotionally collapsed, I clung to the knowledge that the road ahead at least wouldn't be travelled alone.

I arranged to spend a couple of days with Grandpa George in Wellington. He met me at the airport with a beaming smile, then took me around town, out for afternoon tea, down to the laundromat – ordinary, mundane things that reassured me life would go on.

As Grandpa dropped me back at the airport, Dad called again. He said my belongings had been emptied out of the house into a storage unit, and that I had to contact him if I wanted the key. I took the connecting flight to Christchurch in silent, numb shock. But the final flight to Invercargill was worse – I felt like crawling under the seat when I saw one of my former Brethren peers coming down the aisle; I knew it meant a Brethren welcoming party would be at the airport. Sure enough, half his family was waiting at the gate. I walked past them with my head held high.

Beyond the Brethren group, Courtney was waving a name card with rainbows painted across it, a welcome sight. She took me home to drop off my bags, then we met Dad at Parklands Storage to collect the key. He was cold and distant, slamming his car door and accelerating hard as he left.

Later, as I unpacked my bags in Courtney and Mel's spare room, I realised some of my things were missing. My stomach flipped, and I felt sick as I ran through my options. What was I supposed to do? I wasn't sure if Mum and Dad had changed the locks yet – could I sneak back into their house while they were out at church? Or should I ask the police to help me retrieve my belongings? I realised that I needed to bite the bullet and confront my parents.

Courtney offered to drive me round to Mum and Dad's that evening. It was surreal to turn up back at the house that had been my home just a few weeks earlier, and I had no idea what to expect. My heart was in my mouth as I knocked at the front door, knowing my family was probably having dinner.

Mum's shoulders slumped when she saw me, and she refused to let me in. Then Dad arrived and told me, 'Our family can't go on with evil.' There was no emotion and no acknowledgement of the enormity of banishing their son from the family home.

I said I needed the rest of my things and also asked if I could say goodbye to my nine-year-old sister Bella. Dad said no; Mum said yes. They had a disagreement, and then – to my surprise – Dad walked off to fetch her.

When Bella saw me, she burst into tears. Dad was holding her arms behind her back to stop her from running to me. We stood there, sobbing. I told her over and over that I loved her, and reminded her of the promise we'd made – that we'd always love each other, no matter what.

I asked Dad if I could hug her goodbye, but he said, 'Definitely not.' He tightened his grip on her arms.

We both sobbed out a goodbye, then Dad marched her off again before returning with my things.

Courtney and I were speechless as we drove to her and Mel's place.

*

As I scrambled to adjust to life outside the Brethren, I felt like Alice tumbling down the rabbit hole. I'd lost my family, my home and my job in one fell swoop. Courtney, Mel and other friends stepped up to help me integrate, although it was difficult to know where to start, and for a while I withdrew into myself and took stock as I dealt with the huge shock. How was I supposed to make this work? I had no idea how to tune a radio dial, go to a worldly party or watch TV. Now, I could go to the movies without fear of being seen.

The first shows I watched were *The Simpsons* and *Family Guy*. Most of the jokes went over my head, and I peppered Courtney and Mel with questions. They were very willing to teach me although also very surprised at what I'd missed out on. I watched the TV news in wonder and laughed as TV3's *60 Minutes* reporter Sarah Hall challenged a scam artist – he claimed to be calling from England but couldn't name any of Queen Elizabeth II's four children.

Over time, friends introduced me to movies, shows and music they thought were important. After missing out on a lifetime of lyrics and famous people and pop culture references, I was keen to catch up. My friend Anastazia was taken aback by my almost complete lack of cultural reference points. I was baffled one day when she made an offhand remark: 'It's like we're caught in a glitch in the Matrix.' What on earth was she talking about? She laughed and later returned with a DVD that had a strange man on the cover, wearing sunglasses and a long trench coat. That evening we watched *The Matrix*, and her joke about déjà vu clicked into place – now I, too, could make *Matrix* references and sound like I was in the know.

Radio stations were another new experience. I started listening not long after buying my first car, a silver Subaru Legacy – I'd previously driven a company vehicle, which had disappeared along with my job on my return from Australia – and learned how to twiddle the dials to find the music I wanted. Not long after that, I first heard the song 'Burning Bridges' by the Mike Curb Congregation. As I played the plaintive lament on repeat, I kicked the tyres. I'd dubbed my car The Brucester in dishonour of Bruce Hales; there was no doubt in my mind that he was ultimately responsible for overseeing the Brethren's cruel system of excommunication.

The Brethren were never far away. On a Friday at 9.14 pm, I received an anonymous call warning me I was 'under observation'. Courtney and Mel freaked out when a black sedan with tinted windows became a regular presence on the street outside: 'Jeepers, what have we got ourselves in for here?' The car hung around for weeks; the occupants never revealed themselves – monitoring us, we assumed – as we carried on with our lives. While this was frightening for my friends, I shrugged it off as typical Brethren behaviour; I'd spent years being stalked and chased by them.

Mum tried hard to hold on to me, even after I'd been shut up and kicked out of the family home. I was still technically a member of the Brethren – the second and final stage of excommunication, being withdrawn from, hadn't yet happened – and she used that to justify keeping up contact, calling me several times a week over the following few months. She said she'd tried to organise a flat for me to live in when I came back from Australia and bawled her eyes out when it fell through. In a later conversation, when I said that Courtney and Mel didn't have an ironing board, Mum told me to come over while Dad was out so she could press my shirts. I didn't take her up on the offer; it felt strange and I was worried about Dad finding out. I challenged her during another exchange on how she could go along with his plan to get rid of me; she bleakly replied, 'What choice did I have?' The only way she was able to get her other six children back was by disowning me.

A few weeks after that conversation with Mum, Anastazia and I walked along a local beach, Ōreti, as we talked about our grand plans for travelling the world. I was nearly free of the Brethren, and she'd just gone through a bad breakup – together, we dreamed of heading to Europe and escaping the dark memories that hung over Invercargill. 'Imagine how good it would be to get away from this place!' Her bulldog Stu panted along beside us, slobbering excitedly while seagulls swooped and screeched. The sun was low in the sky as we headed back through the dunes to where Anastazia had parked her car; I hopped around on one foot, brushing off sand, as she emptied a water bottle into Stu's travel bowl.

To start with, I didn't notice the van approaching behind us. Although we were on a reasonably quiet country lane, there was still the odd car passing as people made their way to and from the beach, and I tuned out the engine noise. The vehicle sped up as it drew closer, needing momentum to get through a patch of soft sand, and I glanced across to see if the van would make it.

It was my family. There's no way they didn't know it was me – as they drove past I was standing right there, impossible to miss. My entire family saw me, then kept staring straight ahead as though I didn't exist. They might as well have been strangers.

Later that evening, I broke down and sobbed on Taniamaree's couch. We didn't talk a lot about it – what can you say when something like that happens? – but there was lots of crying, lots of mourning as the crushing reality hit home. Was Mum really so cold to me that she could pretend I was invisible? Had Bella forgotten our promise that we would always love each other? I was now an 'out', one of those wicked people I'd been warned about my whole life, just like Grandpa George. Although I'd known this day would come, the reality of it crushed me.

The final blow landed on Halloween. It was a sunny spring morning, and I was with friends debating how best to load a refrigerator onto a trailer, when my phone rang. Frank Moore was calling to tell me I had been withdrawn from, the final excommunication. This meant the Brethren had formally given up all hope of me seeing the error of my ways. But Frank refused to say 'withdrawn from', instead giving a lengthy explanation of how 'the assembly has sorrowfully decided that it has to accept your decision not to continue in the light of the fellowship'.

I was past caring about Brethren technicalities. Just as Grandpa George had all those years earlier, I felt a heavy weight come off me. It was as though my life had been a block of stone that had crumbled into sand in my hands; I'd been furiously trying to stop it from slipping through the cracks, but now I forced open my clenched fists and watched as the last few grains were carried away. I was finally free.

13.

FIVE WEEKS AFTER BEING WITHDRAWN FROM, I WAS SURPRISED to get a call from reporter Sarah Hall, one of the first people I'd seen on TV. She was investigating the Exclusive Brethren and proposed that I share my journey with *60 Minutes*. 'To have the courage to stand up and be heard is no mean feat,' she said. 'I also think your story will be just an incredible gift for young gay people.' She told me that her producer and the camera operator were lesbians: 'These girls are my best friends, and I promise we will take you out for a drink in Invercargill and tell you all about how much more fun it is being an evil outsider or whatever the heck those loonies call us (although I'm guessing you already know!)'. After some initial hesitation, I agreed. Those burning bridges were already burnt, and having come this far I figured I might as well go a bit further.

When the day of the big interview arrived, I overcame a bad attack of nerves. TV3 had flown me to Auckland, and I switched from shirt to shirt in the hotel room that Sunday morning. I settled on a blue-and-white pattern, then checked my hair repeatedly. I spiked it up as high as it would go – silly in retrospect, but that style was forbidden by the Brethren, so it was a statement that I was free to make my own choices.

The filming – at producer Charlotte's Ponsonby villa – was a bewildering flurry of activity and I struggled to keep track of everything that was going on. Chairs were arranged, lights and screens were set up, and there was five minutes of shuffling before the camera operator was happy with our positions. I had a microphone rigged to my lapel, with a cable running under my shirt to connect to a battery pack. Once it was all set up and the interview was underway, I relaxed and quickly forgot the camera was there.

Sarah, a no-nonsense woman in her early forties, looked at me intently as we sat opposite each other on kitchen chairs. 'You lost everything by coming out ... How did you find the courage to do it, do you think?'

To me, the answer seemed straightforward. 'It wasn't so much the courage to do anything as sheer desperation.'

A few days later, we flew to Invercargill together to show TV3's audience the magnitude of what I'd lost. My stomach turned into knots on the plane, and I wanted to shut myself in the bathroom so I could throw up. I was stuck in a window seat, though, and didn't want anyone to know how I felt, so I spent the flight gazing down blankly at the South Island as I shook in quiet grief. I found it hard to return to Invercargill, which stirred a thousand memories I'd rather have kept buried. Although I composed myself in time for landing, I fantasised about running away, screaming my lungs out and curling up in a corner.

I found it even harder to film at the Brethren hall in Invercargill. The gate wasn't locked, so we let ourselves in. As Sarah and I passed between two brick pillars to enter the main yard, she asked when I had last attended a service. It had been six months.

Then she asked, 'How does it feel being back?'

'Really weird,' I said. 'It's bringing back a lot of memories.' How could I condense a lifetime of vivid experiences into one short sentence? Memories flooded my mind as I stared down at the tiles. I remembered playing on them as a small child, running down them when I knew I was late for the service, standing on them being quizzed by Bruce Hales, walking down them happy, walking down them sad, angry, upset, confused – my life was flashing before my eyes.

That afternoon, Sarah sat with me in a rental car across the road from my former family home, watching as my siblings arrived back from school. She wanted to know how it felt to be within calling distance. 'It feels really weird,' I said. 'I know they're quite close physically, but emotionally they might as well be a thousand miles away.' I was philosophical; Sarah was indignant: 'It seems so strange that if you went and knocked on the door, you wouldn't be welcome.'

Later that day, with Sarah's encouragement, we did just that. It wasn't part of the *60 Minutes* story, and there were no cameras; she moved beyond her role as a journalist, saying she felt compelled to try and speak with my mum, one mother to another.

Walking up the driveway was almost as hard as walking back over the tiles at the meeting room. My stomach churned as I knocked at Mum and Dad's front door – the memory of retrieving my belongings was still fresh. How was Mum going to react when I turned up with a TV reporter? Then again, what did I have to lose? My parents had made it very clear they wanted nothing more to do with me, so if there was even the slightest chance that Sarah could get through to Mum, then it was worth trying.

Mum looked perplexed when she opened the door to find me with a strange woman, then frightened when Sarah introduced herself as a journalist. Poor Mum was like a deer caught in headlights. Sarah hastened to reassure her that while we were in town filming a story about my experiences in the Brethren, we weren't at the house to try and get an interview, and wouldn't be quoting anything she said to us. 'Craig loves you very much,' Sarah went on, 'and has spoken of you very highly all the way through this process.' She tried to reassure Mum that although she could no longer care for me, there were plenty of others who would step up: 'Craig will be OK on the outside, and there are people, including me, who will do everything they can to look after him.'

Mum shuffled awkwardly. 'I appreciate you saying that.'

For me, too, it was hard to know what to say. 'Love you, Mum.' After a strained goodbye we walked off around the corner out of sight. I let out a deep breath and Sarah gave me a big hug. 'I'm very proud of you,' she told me.

Sarah may have been baffled by the Brethren, but Grandpa George understood them all too well. He was reflective when he sat for an interview with Sarah, struggling to find the words to explain how it felt to reconnect properly with someone from his immediate family for the first time in twenty-eight years. 'I have seen photos of them, so that's been a … I have a photo of them on my wall, so …' Grandpa kept trailing off. He paused, looking down as he gathered his thoughts. 'I feel connected more now than I did for many years.'

Grandpa hadn't chosen this heartbreak, and neither had I. From a motel room landline, I dialled local priest Frank Moore for a recorded conversation; Frank had been the one to deliver the news that I was withdrawn from, and I was determined to show viewers that Brethren practices were the only thing preventing contact with my family and friends. When Frank tried to claim I had been excommunicated for my 'associations', I reminded him that I'd been shut up for 'evil communications' – 'and then you clarified "evil communications" as having been telling my brothers and sisters that I was gay'.

Frank conceded the point. 'You're right … Evil communications.' But he was unapologetic. 'You know, you've chosen the way you're going, we're going the way we've always gone.'

I reminded him: 'The only thing I chose was to stop going to meetings. I didn't choose to lose my family, or my job, or my living circumstances.'

He doubled down: 'You chose your company and your associations.'

I kept on with my questions, and after a few minutes the line went dead. I was indignant – 'He's cut me off!' – and called straight back. He didn't pick up.

Sarah later managed to reach Frank by calling from a blocked number. She explained she was a TV reporter covering my story and requested an interview. He declined, although he later sent through a lengthy statement in response to her questions. 'The Brethren are fundamentalist Christians who believe the Bible is the Holy Word of God and seek to live their lives according to it,' it read. Frank went on to describe homosexuality as 'immoral and contrary to the teachings of the Bible'. He said I had come from a 'loving family' who had cared for and nurtured me for many years, adding, 'It was his choice to leave his parents' house and the church to go his own way and that choice is accepted.'

When I read the statement, I was incensed. Dad had explicitly told me I was no longer welcome and dumped my belongings in a storage unit so I would never darken his door again. This twisted version of events felt like a betrayal after I had worked so hard to make clear that I wasn't losing my family by choice. The weight of the Brethren spin machine had turned against me, just as I had seen happen with my cousin Lindy. Frank's statement that I had chosen to leave the family home wasn't true.

*

Three months later, I agreed to film a segment in Sydney with another reporter, Jackie Quist, for Australia's Channel Seven.

This was my first time back in Sydney since my invitation from the Man of God, and it was strange to return as an outsider, free to look at other queer people on the street without fear of being reported to the priests.

It was a grey and overcast Tuesday when I caught the train from Central Station to Circular Quay. A half-hour ferry ride took me to Manly, where Jackie was waiting with the filming crew, then we drove through Sydney's northern suburbs and up the Pacific Highway through Ku-ring-gai Chase National Park, towards the coastal city of Gosford.

We were on a mission to find evidence that the Brethren doctor Mark Craddock had prescribed me a libido-suppressant drug in a bid to treat my sexuality. I no longer had a copy of the script but remembered it had been filled at a Gosford pharmacy while I was staying with relatives of the Man of God – that was our only lead. With my permission, Jackie had called dozens of pharmacies to inquire after my records but come up empty-handed. Our Plan B was a stab in the dark: combing the streets of Gosford until I saw something I recognised. It was like playing hide the thimble; I narrowed it down to the suburb of Wyoming, then drew a blank. After some joint head-scratching, I had a vague memory of stopping at the pharmacy on a drive between my host's home and business, and suggested we retrace that route. We'd only driven a couple of blocks when a shopping centre leaped out: 'I think that's it!'

Memories assailed me as I went through the sliding doors. I would never forget the humiliation of standing at that diagonal counter, handing over the piece of paper that said I needed a sexual suppressant and seeing the look on the pharmacist's face. But as I approached the counter once more, I wondered whether this was a long shot. A few minutes passed as an assistant with a furrowed brow pondered her computer screen. Eventually she told me she'd found the record but couldn't see the original prescription details, and she offered to write down the name of the drug for my current doctor. That wouldn't do – I politely insisted I needed a printed copy of the original prescription. Another staff member got involved, and eventually a piece of paper shot out of the printer. They smiled as they placed it on the counter. It was a full record: my name, Dr Craddock's name, the name of the drug and directions for taking it. Five repeats.

Jackie was waiting around the corner when I walked out and said, 'I got it!' We laughed with relief and delight.

Back in Sydney the following day, we waited for Dr Craddock. Dogged research had located the clinic where he practised as a radiologist, and we sat in the car all afternoon, waiting for him to emerge. I read a magazine and sipped soft drinks, and we placed bets on what time he would appear. Shortly after 5 pm, the clinic's 'open' sign flipped to 'closed', and a handful of nurses trickled through the door. And then, there he was: a man in his seventies with combed white hair, rimless glasses, a white shirt and a red tie. The boredom of the wait gave way to action as the TV crew headed briskly in the doctor's direction.

Craddock, caught unawares, blustered his way through while Jackie introduced herself and started a relentless interrogation:

'You prescribed Cyprostat to a healthy young eighteen-year-old male ... not a sex offender.'

'It was at his own request!'

'He's not a sex offender!'

'No, I know he isn't ...'

'And he doesn't have prostate cancer!'

'He didn't have to take it!'

'Why would you prescribe this for a healthy young man?'

'Well, he wanted ... he wanted to be helped with his problem.'

'What was his problem?'

'I'm sorry, I cannot speak to you further.'

The doctor claimed he couldn't remember what he'd prescribed; Jackie flourished the patient record. Then he claimed the drug had only been a trial; Jackie pointed out he had given five repeats. He tried to claim he couldn't discuss it because of doctor–patient confidentiality; she gestured at me: 'Why not? He's right here, he gives his permission.' Craddock said he'd only been trying to help; she flourished the Cyprostat pill bottle: 'This is what you call help? Giving drugs to a young man who's not ill?'

I had a question for the doctor: 'I was being helped with a "problem" ... What was the problem? I'd like you to say what it was.'

He dodged the question. 'Well, you... You... You came to me voluntarily.'

That wasn't true: I'd seen him under church guidance. Craddock was the second Brethren doctor I'd been told to see, and as a teenager I would never have dared to disobey such a directive.

Craddock shoved past us and got into his car. As he was fastening his seatbelt, the cameraman, Mitch, pushed the lens right up against the window, and fired one last question: 'Would you put your own son on this drug?' The doctor glared balefully back at us as he turned his key in the ignition. He didn't answer the question.

We were left standing in the middle of the street. As I became aware of my surroundings for the first time since the interrogation began, I realised I was shaking from head to foot. My heart felt like it was thumping out of my chest, and bile rose in my throat as hot tears spilled from the corners of my eyes; no amount of blinking could stop them from rolling down my cheeks. I was vaguely aware of a camera pointing at my face as Jackie patted my arm and asked if I was OK.

A crowd had gathered to watch from the shopfronts and car park opposite the clinic. Later, when Jackie crossed the road to buy a Coke, the deli shopkeeper wanted to know who Channel Seven had been chasing. 'Did he do something to that young man?' He waved her wallet away as she reached across to pay, insisting she take the drink for free. 'I love it when you catch the bad guys.'

*

A few hours later, I arrived with the film crew at the main Brethren hall in Ermington. We discovered a meeting was in progress. Hundreds of vehicles were parked across the yard in neat rows, and a security guard patrolled the gates. He spoke into his lapel microphone as Mitch began unloading his camera. When Jackie asked the guard if we could join the service, he said he would need to check with internal security. There was no reply when I buzzed the intercom.

Ten minutes later, the doors of the hall swung open. Crowds of Brethren emerged through them, and I began pointing out which ones I knew. When Dr Craddock walked out, Mitch zoomed in. The main gates slid open almost immediately, and marshals were stationed at each entrance to direct traffic. It was just as I remembered. A stream of vehicles poured through, face after familiar face flashing past. A few glanced at me briefly, then looked away as though I was a stranger. Could these really be the same people I remembered so fondly from just a year earlier?

One of the traffic marshals caught my eye, and I realised he was a cousin of mine. Pain, betrayal and anger flashed across his face.

My phone rang, and I scrambled to fish it out of my pocket. It was Dad, calling from New Zealand. He was furious with me, having heard I was 'attacking the holy fellowship' in Sydney. My reply was caught on camera: 'So I'm playing into the hands of the devil and doing the devil's work? All I'm doing is telling the truth, to show exactly what it's like.' Dad berated me and demanded I come back under his authority as the head of the household.

When he realised I was still with the TV crew, he began dictating a message to them. I told him he may as well speak to the reporter directly and handed the phone to Jackie. Dad told her that I needed to 'find the holy spirit and let God work in me to bring about a change'. She disagreed and took a different tack: she acknowledged how hard the situation must be for the family, then asked Dad whether he still loved me as his son and could find it in his heart to accept me as I was. Dad broke down in tears.

Overcome with emotion, and weeping again myself, I felt a flash of pity. I knew this must be torturing him and how the Brethren would condemn him for failing as a father. Before hanging up, I once again reminded Dad: 'You've done what you believe is right regardless of the cost, and now I'm doing the same.'

Filming outside the Brethren's Sydney epicentre was a provocative move. I knew it would anger Bruce Hales and his heavies, although we had no idea how far they'd go to try and shut us down. What we did know was that this was one of the more serious threats they'd had in recent years, in terms of public exposure, and they were probably holding crisis talks at the highest level as we stood there on the street in Ermington.

One of the compound neighbours accosted us, insisting the Brethren were 'good people'. He demanded that we leave and threatened violence if we did not comply.

We were pretty much done by then, so to avoid escalating the situation we packed up and left. I was in the passenger seat beside the sound recordist, Geoff, with Jackie in the back. We looped around the block and waited for a gap in traffic to turn back onto the main road.

Geoff's phone rang as we idled at the intersection; it was Mitch, who had left in a separate vehicle. When Geoff hung up and said that we were being tailed and that Mitch was too, I thought it was a joke. Jackie leaned forward, telling us to lock our doors, and I laughed. Geoff's voice became urgent: 'No, seriously.'

I squinted into the side rear-view mirror and did a double take. A black Mazda four-wheel drive was right behind us, but it was following us so closely that only its edge was visible. I was surprised they weren't scraping our bumper.

Geoff stepped on the accelerator as we took off down Victoria Road, and I didn't dare check our speed. The black Mazda stayed hard on our tail, weaving in and out of traffic with bulldog tenacity. When it became obvious that we weren't going to shake our pursuers, Geoff slowed down. A service station appeared to the left, and on the spur of the moment he pulled in under the bright lights. The black Mazda pulled in right behind us and waited in an alley that ran alongside the station. Geoff jumped out, ignoring Jackie's pleas to be careful, and ran towards them with his camera. The Mazda roared off down the alley, and Geoff laughed jubilantly as he got back in the car.

Sweet with the success of having shaken them off, Jackie checked in with Mitch. He was faring much worse: driving alone, he had four people on his tail in two vehicles. When he tried to do a U-turn, one of the pursuers veered across the road to block him.

He and Jackie were discussing what to do when Geoff checked his mirrors: 'Oh shit! They're back!' He hunkered down behind the wheel, and at one of the next intersections he made a sudden left. The black Mazda flipped the same sharp turn and stayed bumper to bumper as we flew through deserted back streets.

It was dark by then, and there was no-one else in sight. At least there had been witnesses on the main road. We were all panicking – Jackie feared there could be an accident, while Geoff was afraid we'd be run off the road or even killed. At that point, it didn't seem unthinkable that we could all end up dead and dumped in the harbour.

We were relieved when the bright lights of Victoria Road reappeared. As we stopped for a red light, Geoff leaped out again to film our pursuers' vehicle and number plate. As he filmed through the windscreen, the Brethren inside covered their faces with their hands so they couldn't be identified.

Undeterred by the cameras, they continued their chase as we drove towards central Sydney. They were running red lights and cutting off traffic, doing whatever it took to stay on our tail.

Channel Seven management, alerted to our predicament, put through an urgent request for police assistance. We were told we'd be safe at the city's Central Police Station. Meanwhile, Channel Seven stepped in to save Mitch as he managed to get to the main studio building and sought refuge in its secure underground car park, with Brethren still in hot pursuit. A guard had to get between the vehicles, then the security gates came down behind Mitch. He had finally escaped.

Across town, we still had the Brethren hard on our tail. They'd been chasing us for more than twenty kilometres, often at a distance of less than a metre. I wondered what would happen if we needed to brake suddenly. As we approached the police station at speed, we were thrown around when we bumped over judder bars, literally flying through the air. It was like being in a movie, one of those surreal moments where everything moves in slow-motion.

At the station, we ran for safety and were met with raised eyebrows as we burst into the lobby. Jackie explained we were from Channel Seven, we were being chased, and Sergeant Greg Cooper was expecting us. People stared in surprise when we were ushered through to the back offices.

A short time later, a team of plainclothes officers fanned onto the Sydney streets to track down our pursuers. I was surprised to see they were armed – one lifted his shirt, and the handle of a firearm poked from his hidden holster.

Sergeant Cooper listened intently as we told our story. Two female investigators joined us, and I was asked detailed questions about my experiences with the Exclusive Brethren. One of the women told me that allegations of Dr Craddock's malpractice would need to be investigated by a medical board.

Half an hour later, the police told us that one of our pursuers had been arrested. At least one other had made off on foot. He was still at large when Jackie needed to catch her return flight to Melbourne, so she was taken to the airport in a patrol car. Officers escorted her through the terminal and onto the aircraft; they believed we might still be in danger and didn't want to take any chances. Jackie just wanted to get out of Sydney as quickly as possible. There was no guessing what the Brethren might try next.

Back at the station, Geoff and I thought we were in the clear, and he offered to drop me back to the youth hostel where I was staying. As we approached our destination, chatting about the day's events, he said he'd just make a quick pass around the block to make sure we weren't being followed again. We were astounded to realise we had another Brethren vehicle in pursuit – I couldn't believe they'd have the audacity to chase someone directly from the police station.

This time, there was no beating around the bush: Geoff pulled over to park as I called the sergeant, and a patrol car was dispatched. We locked our doors when the blue ute pulled into a no parking zone right behind us. Within ten minutes, police arrived and pointedly questioned the vehicle's occupants before taking them into custody.

Sergeant Cooper was waiting for us at the station, shaking his head in disbelief. The events of the evening had been surreal, and the sergeant asked if we could talk about it outside because he needed a cigarette.

As we stood talking under the trees, he questioned me about the Brethren. He was perplexed by the men who had been taken into custody and felt police were getting nowhere with their questioning. The Brethren were insisting they'd done nothing wrong and demanding to speak to their lawyers; they claimed they hadn't been following us, didn't know about Channel Seven and didn't even know who I was. I later discovered one of them was a relative.

Cooper nodded as I explained how Brethren often thought they were above the law. He said that duty officers would track me on the city's security cameras to make sure I was safe, and if anything further happened I would be given a police escort.

*

Lionel Laming, the passenger in the black Mazda, was much less intimidating when he appeared at the Downing Centre Local Court six months later. Slightly paunchy, with balding blond hair, the 32-year-old Brethren man was wearing a navy suit with a striped white-and-blue shirt and a pink tie. Brethren don't usually wear suits, but Laming was out to make a good impression on the worldlies. He took the fall for his accomplice and refused to give them up, instead pleading guilty to a charge of failing to disclose a driver's identity. He pleaded not guilty to a charge of intimidation.

His case was argued by a top Sydney QC, which spooked police prosecutors. When they rang Jackie at the hotel the night before the hearing, they urged her to reconsider taking the witness stand. She was indignant: 'No way, I will not give in to their intimidation. No way, I don't care. He can shred me on the witness stand if he wants to, but I'm not going to let them win like that. Forget it.'

Her persistence paid off when Laming was convicted of intimidation, then placed on a twelve-month good behaviour bond. Facing a criminal conviction would often have resulted in excommunication for Brethren members, but there was no such punishment for Laming, who had taken the fall to protect his fellow goons. Instead, the Brethren issued a mealy-mouthed statement saying his conviction was a 'private matter', and he would remain 'a valued, loved and active member of the Exclusive Brethren community'. All the same, I was quietly satisfied that a public conviction had been lodged over that frightening car chase – maybe, I hoped, it would send a message to Bruce Hales that Brethren henchmen couldn't get away with whatever they liked.

I had another win when Dr Mark Craddock was banned from practising as a GP. Following the advice of the police investigators, I'd laid a complaint with the NSW Health Care Complaints Commission, and a Professional Standards Committee Inquiry had found him guilty of unsatisfactory professional misconduct. The committee drew attention to Craddock's failings in relation to 'basic patient examination and care, his irregular prescribing practice' and 'boundary violation'. He was severely reprimanded, and the resulting GP ban meant he would no longer be able to prescribe drugs to fellow Brethren. This would stop him from doing to anyone else what he'd done to me. And it was a significant blow for the Brethren: Craddock was their last remaining medical doctor in New South Wales.

I also alerted Queensland authorities to the practices of Dr Roger Kirkpatrick. However, the state's independent health watchdog said it was unable to take any action because my interaction with Kirkpatrick had happened in New Zealand, beyond its jurisdiction. Kirkpatrick, one of the few remaining Brethren doctors worldwide, continued consulting with and prescribing to other members; I wondered how many young people were still being grilled in graphic detail under the guise of 'medical treatment'.

Taking the fight to the Brethren was a surreal experience, and I wasn't sure where I'd found the strength to stand up to the church. It had all been so strange – the TV interviews, the confrontations, the car chases – and I wondered what might come next. Would the Brethren leave me alone? One thing I knew for sure: I was outraged by the audacity of their behaviour and would continue speaking out against them.

14.

ON A WARM MONDAY EVENING IN THE LATE 1970S, BENJI and Wilson crept up the driveway and round the back of a small cottage in rural Waikato. The brothers, who had just come from a prayer meeting in nearby Cambridge, were on a Brethren spying mission; they were convinced that Gladys Kissane, the resident of the cottage, was having an affair with Hubert Hoyle. Hubert had been excommunicated several years earlier, but his wife, Jocelyn, had stayed with the Exclusive Brethren, and the sect was convinced of his suspected infidelity.

Gladys's dark brown cottage sat nestled beneath a thick shelterbelt of trees behind a white picket fence. Benji and Wilson, who had been dropped off some distance up the road to avoid detection, slunk through the bushes to her yard; they were careful not to make any noise as they crept across to her bedroom window. Hubert's car was parked in the driveway. The two Brethren believed if they could just get a glimpse through the window, then they were sure to find Gladys and Hubert in a compromising position.

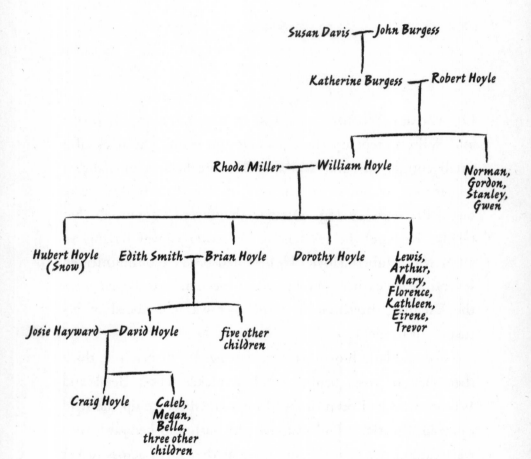

The curtains were drawn, but there was a thin gap above the fabric. Benji and Wilson surreptitiously dragged over the nearby cellar door, loose from its hinges, and positioned it beneath the window. Certain that Hubert's adultery was about to be exposed, the brothers prepared to ascend for their righteous voyeurism.

At that moment, a voice interjected behind them: 'Can I help you?'

Startled, they turned around to be confronted by Hubert's son Wayne, himself freshly excommunicated in his early twenties. Two more young men materialised from the trees and stopped the Brethren peeping Toms from making a run for it.

*

Hubert – the older brother of my grandfather Brian – had tried to stay out of trouble with the Brethren during the Symington heydays of the mid-1970s. He thought the way the church was going was crazy, although he kept quiet because he had a wife and six children, knowing he might lose them if he rocked the boat. He told himself it was the only option and figured if he kept a low profile he'd be spared the cruel treatment meted out to rulebreakers. He knew you were either in the church with everyone and everything, or you were out of the church and possibly split up.

Hubert was working as a farming contractor, and it was his construction of a grain store that ran him afoul of the local Cambridge leaders. Hubert, pressed for time, had started digging the foundations before driving twenty minutes to nearby Hamilton to seek the necessary permits, a move that raised the ire of the local building inspector when he happened to drive past. Hubert was rapped over the knuckles, and a stop order was put on construction. This news quickly made its way to the local Brethren leaders, who convened an assembly meeting to address Hubert's sins. He was astonished when the priests told him he was being withdrawn from: 'You broke the law, therefore you're a lawless man, and we don't have fellowship with lawless people.'

The impact on Hubert's life was catastrophic. His two sons promptly quit working for him, at the busiest time of year as grain was being harvested. His four eldest children were taken out of the family home and sent to live in other Brethren households, leaving only the two youngest with Hubert and Jocelyn. From that day on, the couple, who had been married for twenty-odd years, didn't sleep or eat together. As the weeks passed, even their two youngest daughters demanded to be allowed to stay with other Brethren. After several months of torment, Hubert decided to move out so that at least his children could be reunited with their mother; the alternative was a ghostly existence with a woman who had been stripped of her children and was absolutely beside herself.

Hubert's loss of everything at once – his wife, children, extended family, social network, home, employees – almost finished him off. To him, it was like the sky was falling in.

One day, he drove aimlessly in his ute and ended up parked on the bank of the Waikato River near the Carter's Flat industrial zone in Cambridge. Hubert stared at the swift current as it rolled past and asked himself, *What am I doing here?* It would have been so easy to release the handbrake and let gravity do the rest. But something pulled him back. There was still a chance he could be forgiven by the Brethren and reunited with his family, so he slowly reversed his ute away from the river.

*

Hubert stood out from the crowd when I met him for the first time at Melbourne's Flinders Street railway station in 2009, the year I left the Brethren myself. He had a full head of snowy white hair, so striking that his family and friends called him Snow. We'd never seen each other before, but there was no mistaking the family likeness, and Uncle Snow beamed as he stepped forward to shake my hand. 'You must be a Hoyle!'

Conversation came easily as we caught the tram to the suburb of Camberwell, where his younger sister Dorothy lived. Snow and Dorothy were my grandfather's siblings, but until my recent excommunication I'd only been vaguely aware of their existence. They were both, in the Brethren telling of things, bad people: Snow had 'abandoned' his family when he was excommunicated, we were told, while Dorothy had brought deep sorrow to my great-grandparents when she ran away as a wayward teen. I quickly discovered the truth was rather different.

Dorothy and Snow's stories of their upbringing in the 1940s and 1950s sounded familiar: dancing was forbidden, school sports were banned, and the Hoyle children weren't even allowed to take library books home. Dorothy kept a stash of secret books in a tin at the bus stop, three miles from the family home; if a book was particularly good, she'd sneak it home and read it with a torch under the bed covers, hoping she wouldn't be discovered by her religious mother. Dorothy, freckled with whitish blonde hair and piercing blue eyes, knew she faced a life of drudgery if she stayed in the Exclusive Brethren. Forced to leave school at a young age, she would be consigned to help her mother with the housework until she was married off to be a dutiful wife – an agonising prospect for a girl who regularly came top of the class.

Dorothy carefully planned her escape as a teenager, just as I would two generations later. She saved up £14, took a few things from home, gave notice at her job, cycled into town one Friday morning for work, then packed her bag and bike onto a bus leaving Cambridge that evening. When the bus got to Hamilton, she sent a short telegram to her parents: 'I've left home.' They were distraught. Later, when Dorothy was tracked down at a hostel in Auckland, police officers were sent to check on her wellbeing. The Brethren seemed to expect the officers would escort the wayward teen back home to Cambridge; instead, she was told she was free to set her own path.

Although she had fled the family home, Dorothy wasn't quite ready to abandon the church of her upbringing. She started attending services in Auckland, putting on a nominal show of being a good Brethren woman. The harsh doctrine of separation was yet to be introduced, and in 1957 it was still tolerated, although frowned upon, for a young woman to strike out on her own.

Behind closed doors, though, Dorothy took an irreverent view of Brethren doctrine. She was soon flatting in the central suburb of Parnell with Marion Bacon, another young Brethren woman, and the pair took great delight in seeing how many transgressions could be committed simultaneously: 'You could swear, put your feet on furniture, not go to church, wear lipstick ... about twenty or thirty things at once!'

When Dorothy had fled the small Waikato town, she wasn't only escaping her family and their restrictive church; she was also escaping abuse. Dorothy's voice fills with disgust when she remembers Roy Brewer, the Brethren man who sexually abused her: her friend's dad. It started during a beach trip to the coastal town of Thames, where she found herself sunbathing on the beach beside Roy, a respected elder in his mid-forties, whose wife lay to his right. 'I'm lying on my tummy, and he slides his hand under my breast. I didn't do anything. Didn't move, didn't say anything, just froze.' It was the beginning of a months-long pattern of sexual abuse. Roy would 'tickle' Dorothy in the pool, fondle her with his feet under the table at family meals – 'he was fairly practised' – and watch for her on the streets of Cambridge.

To add insult to injury, her abuser was one of the elders sent to Auckland to appeal for her return. Roy Brewer – 'probably terrified out of his head, thinking that it might be something to do with him' – showed up with his wife to tell Dorothy she was missed by their daughter, 'and tried to talk me into going back'. Dorothy intended to take Roy's secret to her grave.

A year after she made her escape, Dorothy unexpectedly found herself back in Cambridge. Driving from Whangārei, she'd been involved in a car crash and had a minor head wound, and authorities sent the teen to stay with her parents while she recovered from her injuries. Her highly religious mother, Rhoda, sat on the bed as she lay in the spare room, looking concerned and touching her injured head – before launching into a very personal line of questioning about whether she'd been involved in 'improper' behaviour. Rhoda's questioning was so oblique that Dorothy assumed she must be referring to what had happened with Roy Brewer. Nothing was asked about the details, just indirect questions about whether Dorothy had acted improperly. Vulnerable and ashamed, she proffered a simple confession: 'Yes.'

Upon Dorothy's return to Auckland, she was invited to dinner at the home of Cyril Bennett, Roy's brother-in-law. Cyril cornered her after the meal and led her into his office, where she was ordered to name her sin and depart from it. Dorothy didn't know what on earth Cyril was talking about, so he helped her out: 'It's adultery.' Baffled, and not having any idea what 'adultery' meant, Dorothy went along with his suggestion: 'OK.'

Her matters were soon addressed at an assembly meeting in Cambridge, where members packed in to hear about her sins. Dorothy, sitting in the back rows with her mother and sisters, clung to a young niece as though the toddler could shield her from judgemental stares. It was surreal – she'd become a branded person, withdrawn from and completely humiliated, and still had no idea what the accusation even meant.

Dorothy's family refused to talk to her after she was excommunicated, and she was abandoned to live her supposedly wicked life. Nobody ever questioned her about what exactly had happened; as she left the Brethren hall that day, condemned for adultery, she'd never had sex. The only sexual acts she'd been involved in were done to her without her consent by one of the elders sitting at the front of the congregation; he went scot-free, while the teen girl he'd abused was sent packing in shame.

*

Dorothy was the first member of the extended Hoyle family to be excommunicated from the Exclusive Brethren, but she was far from the last. Over the following decades, as rules tightened and shifted, a steady stream of Hoyles fell afoul of the church's leadership. Dorothy was reunited with her brother Snow when he was thrown out; another brother followed, then another. Two uncles and an aunt were also thrown to the kerb. By the 1970s, Dorothy's nephews and nieces were old enough to be getting in trouble, and a wave of them swelled the ranks of banished Hoyles. By the 1990s, there were so many of them that they held a family reunion.

When I had escaped from the sect in 2009, a large, well-established network of rebel Hoyles had welcomed me with open arms. Everyone had a story of heartbreak and grief, some of which would be comical if the impact hadn't been so severe. A cousin was tossed out after challenging the ban on men wearing shorts. A niece was excommunicated after falling in love with a Catholic boy. A nephew was withdrawn from for having sexual contact with his fiancée before their wedding night. And there were dozens more stories like this, of Hoyles who had their lives upended as punishment for their 'sins', with the family ripped apart across five generations.

Dorothy and Snow's uncle Norman had been withdrawn from in his late sixties for refusing to drink alcohol. A gentle farmer who worked as a security guard at the bank in semi-retirement, Norman Hoyle had witnessed the havoc of alcoholism. It had torn apart his grandparents' marriage; when he was a young boy his grandfather John Burgess – my great-great-great-grandfather – lived away from the family home in a small shack where he could drink to his heart's content. Norman would be sent to deliver meals to his booze-ridden grandfather, a task that left a lasting impression. For the rest of Norman's life, he referred to alcohol as 'the devil's firewater'.

Norman kept his head down as the Brethren started drinking heavily through the 1960s and into the 1970s. He loved his wife of more than thirty-five years and didn't want to rock the boat. As drinking alcohol went from being encouraged to being enforced, however, abstinence became evidence that you didn't fully agree with the church's teachings and must be suffering from some moral defect.

Determined to flush out Norman's allegiances, and under pressure from the priests, his wife, Josie, placed an alcoholic drink beside his dinner one evening in the 1970s. Norman recoiled: 'Take it away!' Dismayed, Josie reported to the elders that her husband would not drink alcohol, and Norman was promptly excommunicated. More than three decades of happy marriage weren't enough to keep Josie by her husband's side; one day while he was out, she packed up her things and disappeared. Nearly seventy years of loyal Brethren life counted for nothing: he'd been kicked out like so many others – all because he refused to drink whisky.

Norman had recurring nightmares about his excommunication. In one vivid dream, his judgement day at the Peachgrove Road meeting room ended with the priests proclaiming he must die before the firing squad. He watched helplessly as his first cousin retrieved rifles from the hall and handed them out to other elders. When Norman woke, very much alive, he reflected that the Brethren had indeed passed judgement and ripped away the only life he knew.

A few years after Norman was excommunicated, his sister Gwen Hoyle, who never married, was working in a doctor's surgery in Auckland. At the nightly church services she would often regale other Brethren women with stories of patients the doctor had seen that day. One evening after church in 1979, Gwen described a particularly difficult patient to her cousin June Scarlett and jokingly added an aside: 'If it had been up to me, I would've prescribed arsenic!'

Gwen should have known better than to make such a flippant joke to June, whose husband was Don Scarlett, one of the New

Zealand leaders who would later thunder at the Wellington congregation about the sins of my grandpa George. It never occurred to Gwen that she might be out of line, until to her shock she discovered that June had reported her comment to Don; it was even more of a shock to be told that the Brethren were excommunicating her for having 'murderous thoughts'. With no warning, she found herself on the outside at the age of seventy.

When I was a child, her story was often repeated as a cautionary tale. Sometimes when my siblings and I made petty remarks along the lines of 'I wish you were dead', a warning would come from older Brethren: 'Remember what happened to Gwen Hoyle.'

The Auckland Brethren assumed Gwen would be another case who came crawling back for forgiveness. After a few weeks of isolation, during which every Brethren member refused to talk to her, the elders visited her home in the southern suburb of Papatoetoe to see if she had repented. They knocked at the door, then knocked again. Nobody answered. Gwen was gone.

For years she had sat at the back of Brethren services in Auckland – remaining silent, as was expected of all women – daydreaming as she saw member after member excommunicated for their sins. *If they ever do that to me*, she thought, *I think I'll go to Norfolk Island*. A remote subtropical outpost between Australia and New Zealand, the island was the kind of holiday destination that was forbidden for Brethren. Gwen had never been on an aeroplane before, but that wasn't going to stop her; when the elders knocked on her door that evening, she was already on Norfolk Island.

For Gwen, going back to the Exclusive Brethren was out of the question, even though it was the only life she'd known for seventy years. She forged ahead and reconnected with the other excommunicated Hoyles. Her Exclusive brothers cut her off, but she reunited with Norman, writing to him about how overjoyed she was with her freedom: 'Like the good old days. I'm so pleased.' She also reconnected with her niece Dorothy, and they travelled the world together, taking a mountain train up the Jungfraujoch in Switzerland, visiting the former home of Anne Frank in Amsterdam and road-tripping across the English countryside – always with a trusty thermos for Gwen's fifteen cups of tea a day.

I met Aunty Gwen for the first time at her one hundredth birthday party, just a few weeks after my excommunication. She had spent thirty years as the matriarch aunt of the excommunicated Hoyles – loved by her brothers' children, their grandchildren and then their great-grandchildren – and had enjoyed life to the full. Her story is proof that no matter how old you are, it's never too late to escape and start again.

*

None of the Hoyles I speak to regret leaving the Brethren, but as with my grandpa George, there's a deep collective sadness. Dorothy still feels grief and anger more than sixty years after being publicly humiliated and withdrawn from as a teen, and her life on the outside – while happy and fulfilling – has shadowy edges. 'It's a loss,' she tells me, when I ask what it's like to reflect on her journey. Her hair is now the same snowy shade as her brother's, framing those same piercing blue eyes. Being excommunicated robs you of your background, she says, and removes stability from a person when they need it most.

She pauses reflectively when I ask what damage has been done, then says, 'It's probably made me cautious. It deprived me of early social formation skills. It deprived me of conversational things that you never catch up on like the music you listen to, the dances you go to and the books you read.' There's also the ongoing grief of being rejected by family. She has endured more than six decades of judgement, first from her Brethren parents and then her siblings, and the letters she's received over sixty years make for grim reading.

As the clock ticks towards midnight, Dorothy turns the tables on me with her own question. 'Do you think you will ever feel like a fully normal "in-the-world" person?'

After taking my turn to pause, I tell her, 'It's a difficult thing. In many ways I feel it's very easy to create the perception of someone who's fully adjusted.'

But perceptions aren't necessarily reality: when I listen back to a recording of our conversation, I realise I never directly answered Dorothy's question.

Uncle Snow chuckles with delight when I ask about how the Brethren tried to spy on him and his neighbour Gladys. He tells me he'd had his suspicions after seeing familiar vehicles driving past while he enjoyed dinner at Gladys's home. Then, one night, she heard someone scrabbling around beneath her bedroom window, which gave her a terrible fright. On a subsequent Monday evening, Snow and his son Wayne – by then also excommunicated – laid a careful trap: Snow parked his car outside Gladys's house and walked home, so it looked like he was still there; Wayne hid in the cellar, and two of his friends lay in wait in the bushes.

Snow claps his hands together as he describes how Benji and Wilson took the bait. The brothers, caught in the act, tried to bluster their way through: 'We're here to see Mrs Kissane.' But there was no explanation for why they were trying to see Mrs Kissane through her bedroom window. The brothers were marched to the front door and told if they wanted to see Gladys, they should knock and do it properly. When Gladys, in on the plan, emerged in her dressing-gown, she stared at the two peeping Toms and said, 'I don't know them!'

She decided not to press charges, but it was the final nail in the coffin for Snow. For three years, he'd held out hope that he might find a path back to his Brethren wife and children: 'I tried to get back in for so long!' Now he gave up hope and filed for divorce.

More than twenty-five years after his excommunication, during the infamous Review, the Brethren contacted him and apologised for how he had been treated. The elders laid an offer on the table: 'You can come back and marry Jocelyn.' It was an enticing thought, and Snow had a simple message for his ex-wife: 'I would love to marry you again.' But for Snow, the offer of a second chance at marriage to his first love came decades too late. He had built a life for himself outside the sect and was blunt when his brother Lewis got in touch for the first time in many years: 'I couldn't come back to a system that breaks up families.' Lewis trotted out a familiar retort: 'The Brethren don't break up families, it's the devil!' Snow was so disgusted he didn't reply.

For a few years, though, he took advantage of the loosened rules to re-establish contact with his four Brethren adult children. They welcomed him into their homes, but he found it difficult to have any sort of conversation with them. About the only thing they'd say was, 'Dad, would you like a cup of tea?' He'd reply, 'Yes, thank you,' and get his cup of tea, but nobody else would have one. He would sit awkwardly sipping while his estranged children watched on in silence. After decades of no contact, he didn't feel a connection to them: they were 'strangers, really'.

Snow, by then living in Melbourne, decided to cease contacting his Brethren children. He paid a special visit back to New Zealand to tell them so in person, explaining to each of them, married with grown-up kids of their own, that he felt they were being disrespectful and leading him on with their arms-length contact: 'I'm only encouraging you to do what I consider wrong, by calling and seeing you.' His children seemed shocked, and they cried. There was one important caveat to Snow's announcement: he was happy to see his children at any time, he told them, but they had to take the initiative and make first contact. He was done with constantly trying to build bridges: 'My door is wide open, my love for each of you is unconditional, you can contact me if ever you want to.' Then Snow went on with his life. None of his Brethren children made an effort to stay in touch; they were happy, it seemed, to drift back to being strangers, despite their tearful remonstrations.

Uncle Snow's experiences resonate with me, just as Grandpa George's do. 'It's exactly the same but different,' Snow tells me, reflecting on our shared trauma. The pain, he says, never goes away. Even as happier memories are layered on top, 'you've always got it there ... you can't get away from that'. Snow shakes his head. 'Look, it's absolutely crazy. You're one of the few persons that I could talk to about this sort of stuff, and not just shake your head and say, "Goodness, you must be making this up, Snow."' He prefers not to dwell on the pain of the past, instead being quietly supportive of others who have been through terrible things.

'Do you have any regrets?' I ask him.

'No, not from my side. I wish the Brethren hadn't lost my family for me, but I would never have met you like this if they hadn't done that. And there's a lot of other beautiful people that I would never have met. My glass is always half-full.'

15.

WHEN I RETURNED TO INVERCARGILL FOR A VISIT TWO YEARS
after my excommunication, Dad threatened to call the police
on me.

It wasn't like I wanted to be back in town – I'd rather have
been anywhere else, in fact – but I still had bits and pieces stuck
in storage, so I reluctantly hired a van to drive it all up to my new
home in Auckland. I knew full well that my family didn't want
to see me, yet in some forlorn recess of my mind I hoped they
might have a change of heart. Dad was abrupt when I phoned
to ask if I could see them – 'No' – but I figured he couldn't do
much if I just showed up on the doorstep.

That Saturday afternoon, I regretted my decision almost
immediately. Mum wasn't home, and Dad stood coldly at the
front door, arms crossed, as he refused to let me come inside.
Was this really where I used to live, and was this really the man
who had raised me?

My parents were clearly a lost cause, but maybe Grandma
Edith would be more welcoming. Her final letters had been full
of beseeching love, and I couldn't wrap my head around the idea

284

that she might turn against me after our heartbreaking farewell. My throat tightened as I drove the short distance to her house. Everything looked just as I remembered: the newly mown lawn, the neatly trimmed hedge, the tidy white bungalow with pale blue trim. The curtains were drawn, but I could see her Toyota Corolla in the driveway. I took a moment to steel my nerves before knocking on the door. What was she going to say?

There was no reply to my persistent taps, no twitching of curtains nor signs of life, yet I knew she must be there. Why wasn't she coming to the door? Even if she didn't want to see me, the least she could do was tell me so to my face.

I hadn't been wondering for long when a diesel engine roared around the corner, and Dad pulled up in his work truck. He was seething with righteous anger as he marched across Grandma Edith's front lawn, telling me, 'Get off the property right now.'

I wasn't going anywhere – especially now that Dad was trying to order me around. Who did he think he was, still trying to wield that bullying Brethren authority? Had he forgotten that I no longer believed in his supposedly divine position as the head of the household? Determined not to let him win, I sat down on the front doorstep. 'I'm not going anywhere until I see Grandma.'

As Dad ranted at me from the front lawn, threatening to call the police, out the corner of my eye I saw the passenger door of his truck quietly open. Had he brought along priestly backup? Two gangly legs emerged, then a white T-shirt and a freckled face surrounded by coppery ginger hair.

It was my youngest sister, Bella. Two years had passed since that evening when she'd offered to give me her savings if I agreed to stay, and I was surprised to see how much she'd grown. Dad didn't see her emerge; his view was obscured by the bushes in Grandma's front garden – and besides, he was too busy berating me for my wickedness. I was torn: I wanted to run to Bella, offer a warm hug and tell her how much I loved her, but if Dad realised she was out of the truck, he'd quickly intervene. I couldn't give her away.

While his tirade continued, and I pretended to listen, Bella quietly closed the truck door and crept into position between two bushes – away from Dad's eyes, but in my direct line of sight. What was she trying to do? Was she just a curious eleven-year-old, wanting to know what all the fuss was about? She waved to make sure I was looking; I couldn't wave back without drawing Dad's attention, but we locked eyes for a moment, and she mouthed, 'I still love you.'

It took everything I had not to break down and cry. This was proof that at least one person in my immediate family still loved me – and how could I possibly have believed their feelings were completely gone? When Dad paused for a brief moment and looked away, wearing himself down with his religious anger, I flashed the briefest of smiles at Bella and mouthed back: 'I love you too.'

That encounter with my little sister was the merest of olive branches, but it held me back from giving up on my family. I tried to keep in touch with Mum, occasionally sending letters to tell her I was OK. Letters were easier than phone calls: I didn't have to endure being hung up on. She never wrote back, but one day my baby book arrived in the mail, filled with her notes from the months after my birth. There was no letter or card, but wrapped around the book were the recipes for twelve of my favourite childhood dishes. My hot tears dripped onto the list of ingredients for chocolate silk pie.

A year later, I tried to explain my feelings in another letter to Mum: 'I still miss you terribly, but it's more of a dull ache as opposed to the sharp stab it used to be. I look at pictures of you and the family occasionally and sometimes it feels as though I'm staring at strangers.' Mum was disgusted when I called to tell her I had a boyfriend: 'It actually just sickens me, Craig, so please don't. It's an abomination for man to be with mankind.' She cut the conversation short: 'Please hang up now, I want to go. I don't want to listen.' It took me three years to send another letter: 'I don't hold out much hope that we'll ever have a meaningful relationship in the future, but please know at least that I think of you with fondness and love.'

*

As I'd made my first halting steps in the outside world, Sarah Hall – true to her word – had stepped in to replace the mother I'd lost. My first flat in Auckland was just around the corner from where she lived with her husband, Grant, and they took part in all the occasions when my parents were absent: birthdays,

Christmases, graduation. Knowing what was lost, they went out of their way to make sure I wasn't alone.

Meeting Mum had made a deep impression on Sarah: she could see that what had happened to me was horrific but felt that what had happened to my mother was too. Knowing she must wonder what had happened to me, Sarah wrote to her – 'one mother to another' – to reassure her I would not be alone in life. 'Craig and I have become extremely close,' Sarah explained, going on to tell Mum I was 'happy and content': 'I realise your religious beliefs prevent you from seeing Craig, so I want you to know that here, on the outside, he has a family. Our three children treat Craig as a brother and my husband and I will continue to watch over him as he goes through life. He will spend Christmases and birthdays with us – he will not be alone ... Please rest assured that Craig is loved, accepted and supported and surrounded by people who care for him.'

One evening at Sarah's house, a casual reference to 'Mr Tambourine Man' revealed that I didn't know who Bob Dylan was. Discovering the extent of my pop culture ignorance was astonishing for Sarah, and then exciting: 'What do you mean, you've never heard of Bob Dylan?' We were tucked up on armchairs beside an open fire, and Sarah reached for her laptop. The opportunity to introduce someone to her favourite music was too good to pass up, and she lined up song after song after song.

Many more evenings passed like that, hours of laughter as we listened our way through decades of back catalogues. We were far beyond anything I was used to from the Brethren, and it was remarkable to think that so many songs had passed me by. Sometimes the laughter faded away as we hit a familiar song that triggered memories; Sarah hugged me and poured another glass of wine as I wept and talked about Mum and everything else I'd lost. We'd sit quietly for a while as the enormity of what had happened came sweeping back up. What do you say to someone who's lost everything – that it's going to be OK? Sarah knew better than to talk like that.

Through it all, she remained indignant about how the Exclusive Brethren were treating young queer people. She and Grant offered their spare bedroom to several gay boys who left after me. One arrival was particularly dramatic: the Brethren had chased him from a neighbouring region, and church members skulked around outside the couple's home. After Grant confronted them on the street, they agreed to sit down at the kitchen table for a proper conversation. Grant and Sarah made it very clear where they stood: 'The boys are safe here, and they'll be looked after, and you're not to threaten our family. Don't come round to our door and threaten us with your standover tactics.'

For Sarah, each gay boy she helped rescue from the Brethren was a personal victory, and she let us all know about it as she walked around the house: 'Sarah three, Brethren zero!' We laughed, but a serious message lay behind her celebrations: 'These poor kids in the Brethren are being told that they're evil, and that they're going to hell, when all they need is some love and affection, and to be accepted for who they are.'

Sarah and Grant stood beside me as I learned about nightclubs, dating, and how not to be hurt by one-night stands. Those early attempts at meeting guys were awkward; I carried a lot of emotional baggage and had to learn a whole new language of love and lust – and how to try and distinguish between the two, sometimes easier said than done. It was tough, too, to address the guilt and shame the Brethren had layered onto sexual encounters, and get to a place where sex was a positive experience.

Through it all, Sarah gave me the space to make my own mistakes and was there to help pick up the pieces whenever it all went wrong. Inspired by her example, I enrolled at university to become a journalist myself, landing a transcribing job with *60 Minutes* as a first-year student and then rising through the broadcasting ranks with various producing and reporting roles.

Grant, too, had a huge influence on me in those early post-Brethren years. A gruff former nurse now working in the education sector, he was one of the first well-rounded male role models I'd had in my life. He challenged my ingrained Brethren ideas of what it meant to be a man, and I realised that gender boundaries were more blurred than I'd thought: it was OK to spend the day chopping firewood and going fishing, then come home and shed a few tears while watching a fashion show on TV.

Stonewall and *RuPaul's Drag Race* formed part of a new cultural tapestry as I began to fully understand what it meant to be gay. Now I was free to sing as many Elton John songs as I liked. I had my first boyfriend. Life was good.

*

About eight years had passed when I heard through the grapevine that Grandma Edith had cancer. Steeling myself, I called Mum and said I wanted to see Grandma one last time to say goodbye. Mum retorted, 'She's not interested in seeing you.' But I refused to believe that Grandma would say such a thing. I didn't blame her for not coming to the door on my visit to Invercargill – I was sure Dad had ordered her to stay inside. 'If that's truly how she feels,' I said to Mum, 'put her on the phone and she can tell me so herself. Otherwise, I'm coming to see her whether you like it or not.' I knew this kind of tactic was par for the course from the Brethren, but now that I'd spent a few years on the outside and seen how normal people interacted with their families, it seemed outrageous that my parents would try and prevent access to my dying grandmother.

While Mum never put Grandma on the phone, she and Dad agreed to have a conversation with her. Eventually Mum called me back with a compromise: Grandma would see me to say goodbye if I agreed to stay away from her Brethren funeral. She didn't want a repeat of the scenes that had unfolded at the funeral of her mother-in-law – my great-grandmother Rhoda Hoyle – when my excommunicated uncle Snow got in a physical altercation with church members as he tried to reach his mother's graveside. I figured I wouldn't lose anything by agreeing to avoid the funeral; it was a long way from Auckland to Invercargill, and if I was going to make the trip I'd rather see Grandma while she was alive. Besides, I didn't think I had the strength for a graveside confrontation with all those Invercargill Brethren. The memories were still too raw.

My stomach was in knots when I finally made it to the hospice. This wasn't just about seeing Grandma: I was also about to see Mum for the first time since leaving Invercargill. When she met me in the car park, I noticed her hair was much greyer, but her voice hadn't changed. 'Hello, Craig.' There was no hug – I was an evil outsider – just a brisk greeting, then I followed her through the front doors, wondering if she still loved me but not daring to ask. So many unspoken questions: *What's life been like for you since I left? Have you had any doubts about the Brethren, or are you still convinced that Bruce Hales has a direct phone line to heaven? Do you hate me for speaking out against the church? Are you curious about what my life is like now?*

Grandma, asleep in bed, looked frail, her wispy white hair tucked neatly away from her forehead. An uncle and aunt stood guard in the corner of the room – there was no hello, my arrival met with stony silence. They watched on as Mum gently woke Grandma: 'Craig's here to say goodbye.'

Grandma half stirred. There was a hazy moment of eye contact – 'Goodbye, Craig' – and then she drifted off again.

I kissed her on the forehead. The other family members didn't say a word as I quietly wept beside the bed. They didn't care how I felt: I was no longer Brethren, therefore undeserving of their sympathy.

Strangely, though, although I was upset, the wrenching grief of that earlier farewell – the day Grandma and I sobbed in each other's arms – was gone. As I walked out of the hospice, I realised she had been dead to me for years. Other relatives in my life felt much more like real family: Grandpa George, Uncle Charles and Uncle Alan in Christchurch, Aunty Dorothy and Uncle Snow in Melbourne, and my cousin Lindy, who initially also lived in Auckland and then moved to Wellington with her husband. These people understood my pain, and wouldn't stand by in cold silence.

Grandma Edith's death emphasised it wouldn't ever be possible for me to fully escape my Brethren upbringing. Sure, I could build a new life, with new friends and family and a partner and career, but moments like this would always drag me back to the agony of what I'd lost. Perhaps I could have avoided that deathbed farewell with Edith, but then it would have sat with me as an unanswered question. Was I truly ambivalent about seeing her again, or had my trauma been buried so deeply I couldn't recognise it? The only way to find out for sure was to dive back in.

And it's not just deaths that prompt these reflections in people like me who have left. As the years pass, you hear that one of your siblings is married, but you weren't invited to the wedding and only found out months after the fact. People send you photos when they see your family on the street. Your nephews and nieces are born, but you'll likely never meet them; they're just names added to the family tree. They'll barely know you exist, and the few stories they hear will be about how wicked you are.

People who have never been in the Brethren often expect former members to be delighted when a loved one leaves the church. They ask questions like, 'Wouldn't it be great if your parents came to your wedding?' There's an element of celebration, for sure, but while in principle we all want our families back, it can be traumatic to re-engage with people who have wounded us so badly. Lindy and I had a long conversation about this during a walk around Auckland's waterfront, grappling with the difficulty of missing people while also being hesitant about seeing them again. Realistically, my biological parents are the last people I'd want showing up at my wedding. Destroyed family relationships can't be rebuilt overnight; the grief and shock of being rejected by a Brethren family member doesn't suddenly disappear if they, too, make an escape.

I couldn't quite believe it when my brother Caleb was excommunicated eight years after me. He'd always been a loyal member, and I vividly remembered how he'd clutched my suitcase in a bid to stop my attempt at running away. We had an awkward first meeting in TV3's Newshub broadcasting centre, where I was working as a senior radio reporter; he was passing through Auckland, but I was on shift and couldn't get away, so I suggested he drop past for a quick cup of tea.

Caleb was on edge: this was as big a step for him as reaching out to Grandpa George had been for me. He wasn't ready to share a cup of tea and suspiciously demanded to know whether I was wearing a wire to record our conversation.

I laughed and said, 'You're not that interesting.'

He was insistent. 'Can you unbutton the top of your shirt to prove it?'

During those first halting attempts at reconnection, I was ambivalent about whether I wanted my brother back in my life, even though we'd been close growing up. Here, again, there was a shared connection with Lindy, when her younger brother Braden was also excommunicated. We'd been through the grief of losing our siblings – was opening our heart to them again worth the risk? I'd built a new life and wasn't sure if I wanted to make space in it for Caleb, but my boyfriend insisted: 'He's your family, so you need to make an effort.' Still, every conversation with my brother felt like a grind. Although he was no longer walking the Brethren path, he was defensive of the church and wouldn't hear a bad word said about the Man of God. I struggled to make sense of Caleb's beliefs; he clearly accepted he didn't fit with the Brethren lifestyle, yet still believed Bruce Hales was a 'very special man' and even had a picture of him on his bedroom wall.

Caleb and I were distrustful of each other. I hadn't forgotten his part in my rejection, and he was angry for the pain my leaving had caused the family. It was traumatic to hear his stories of how they'd suffered; I'd always known I'd hurt my parents and siblings, a cost I accepted as part of leaving, but now it was no longer abstract. As I drove Caleb to job interviews, and we had long difficult conversations over drinks – whisky, of course – I heard how he felt I'd tarnished our family's standing in the Brethren. For years, he'd been embarrassed to tell people his surname when he travelled to church meetings outside

Invercargill. And Mum – poor Mum. Behind the cold rejection, she'd been devastated to lose her eldest son; she had wept at the assembly meeting where my excommunication was discussed and walked out because it was too much to bear. This knowledge was crushing.

I squirmed with embarrassment as I observed Caleb's fresh inexperience in the outside world – and realised I must have seemed equally wet behind the ears when I first left the Brethren. I remembered those early forays into dating and applying for my first worldly jobs ... Had I really stuck out as such a strange outsider?

When I asked friends, they laughed fondly. 'Yes,' they said, 'but it wasn't surprising considering your background, and it was obvious you wanted to learn as fast as possible.'

Then there was the inflated ego that came with growing up in the Brethren, which I only recognised in myself with hindsight. When you've been told your whole life that you're one of the privileged few, with special access to power and intellect, it's easy to carry that arrogance into the outside world. It can be a hard landing when you collide with the realisation that you're no better than anyone else.

Rebuilding my relationship with Caleb was a long, slow task. We agreed that if we weren't siblings, we wouldn't bother putting in the effort to keep in touch – there were just too many things we disagreed on, and he didn't fit naturally into any part of my life. I was also agonising over letting myself have feelings for my brother, after so many years of telling myself I'd never see him again.

The evening before I left New Zealand to move overseas, following my then boyfriend on a years-long work relocation, we were at a cousin's house for dinner. It was a farewell party with people I loved – and I choked up when Caleb arrived. How could I leave my brother behind for a second time, when he'd only just come back into my life?

After the meal, we had a quiet moment to ourselves beside the bookshelf, but I struggled to find the words for how I was feeling. He asked me, 'Would you like to go outside for some fresh air?'

I'd been keeping it together, but as soon as we got past the front door – away from watchful eyes – my heart crumbled. There were no words. Caleb and I burst into tears, and I threw my arms around him. I would never have admitted it, but it turned out I still loved my brother very much.

*

Mum and Dad seemed dejected when I met with them in Invercargill a year after Grandma Edith's death. My boyfriend and I were passing through en route to a ski holiday in Queenstown, and as a courtesy I let Mum know we'd be in town. I was ambivalent about catching up: the grief and pain of not seeing my parents had faded over nine years into a strange flatness, and we had nothing in common. Mum hadn't replied to my past four messages, so her text came as a surprise: 'Hello Craig, Dad has agreed to see you.' They didn't want me in their house, so we met back at the hospice, up a secluded driveway out of sight from any Brethren who might happen to be driving past. I wondered if they'd told the priests about our meeting. They were very clear that they didn't want to meet my boyfriend: 'Just you … Please.' He waited in the car.

My parents, looking pinched and worn, told me they saw themselves as failures. Losing one Brethren child was a tragedy, but losing two was a reflection on how they'd raised all of us. Mum and Dad awkwardly apologised for the difficulties of my childhood and reflected on how as the eldest I'd borne the brunt of their youthful parenting. They said they were sorry for the harsh and unforgiving way they had treated me. They refused to hug me, but Mum clasped my arm for just long enough that I knew she still cared.

My anger towards them collapsed into pity for the sadness of their broken, restricted lives. Filled with regret, my parents told me they wished they could have another chance at raising children. This took the wind out of my sails. I found myself reassuring them – 'You weren't that bad!' – and offering thanks for all they'd done.

They were particularly distraught at my lack of religion; they'd heard that I no longer believed in God, which was a thought more distressing to them than their knowledge of my sexuality. Casting around for a diplomatic solution, I told them I wasn't comfortable saying I believed in God: 'But the Bible says that "God is love", and I'm happy to say that I believe in love.' A look of relief crossed Dad's face, as though I'd granted him a faint ray of hope.

As we left the hospice, I again asked Mum and Dad if they'd like to meet my boyfriend. 'No,' they said, 'it would just add to our sorrow.' But then, a strange pause before a question from Dad: 'Would he like to meet us?'

I fetched him from the car, and for a few surreal minutes my parents stood chatting with my boyfriend, asking where he was from, talking about our travel plans and making general small talk. Their breath rose in clouds through the frosty morning air. I had to pinch myself – not a dream.

Ultimately, though, this exchange was meaningless. Mum and Dad still wouldn't have regular contact with me, wouldn't eat with me and wouldn't let me see my siblings, and I wasn't welcome in their home.

As my boyfriend and I drove to Queenstown for our skiing holiday, I told him I was no longer interested in the exhausting emotional work of trying to stay in touch with my parents. They felt like strangers to me now.

16.

GRANDPA GEORGE WAS A SHADOW OF HIMSELF WHEN I arrived at Wellington ICU two days after his heart attack in March 2019. His niece Kate – Anna's daughter – had rushed there from Nelson as soon as she heard the news, and we looked over Lindy's scribbled grim notes from conversations with doctors: 'Major artery blockages. 12 mins of no heartbeat. After 4 mins will have brain damage. Not moving right side (possible stroke).' The three of us joined George at his bedside.

Grandpa, the doctors told us that Sunday morning, had suffered massive organ damage and was essentially brain-dead. It was unlikely he knew we were there.

At first I was too shocked to be upset. We found it hard to comprehend that this unconscious wreck in a green hospital gown was the George we knew and loved; that in the click of a finger he'd been reduced from someone living independently – still working part-time at seventy-eight, strolling around town with his brown vest and twinkling eyes – to a shell who couldn't open his eyes. It was confronting to see such a strong, gentle giant in a place of total vulnerability, and there wasn't much we could do besides trusting the ICU doctors to make him comfortable as they ran their tests.

I tucked Grandpa's dog-eared pocket Bible into his left hand.

It had been hard for Grandpa George to build a relationship with me, his apostate gay grandson. He'd remained very conservative in some of his views and spent years believing that queer people were possessed by demons. A handwritten list from a few years after he left the Brethren reveals all those receiving his prayers for deliverance: 'cursers, drug pushers, nightclub owners, homosexuals, transvestites, prostitutes, street kids, glue sniffers, alcoholics'. He hadn't moved far from Brethren beliefs when it came to his opinions on the queer community, so a gay grandson was a challenge indeed.

Grandpa, to his credit, kept an open mind. He'd spent twenty-eight years praying for his lost children and grandchildren, and now there I was – an answer to prayer. Such a message from God could not be ignored. During our long phone calls, as we slowly came to understand each other, Grandpa listened as I described my first tentative forays into the rainbow community. On my visits to Wellington, he invited me to his home prayer groups. We agreed to tell our story together on *60 Minutes*, and when my mum – in a brief, tense conversation – criticised how we'd appeared on the show he was pleased to think that our Brethren family might have been shown a recording of the programme, because that way they would have heard his comments.

Grandpa was frank in acknowledging what he called the 'gulf between our lifestyles and associates'. When I invited him to my twenty-first birthday party – held at a gay bar on Auckland's Karangahape Road – it was a bridge too far. 'I'm sorry, even for you I can't face the prospect,' he wrote in an email, telling me that attending would 'personally be quite uncomfortable ... So I will wish you well, and happy birthday, from a distance, and look forward to catching up again in other circumstances.'

Our religious differences were a side note – we had so much else in common and shared all sorts of quirky traits. I was frequently amused by how much Grandpa reminded me of myself.

The third time we met, we headed out to Petone Working Men's Club for ham steaks, and he brushed off my objections when he paid for the meal: 'After twenty-eight years of no contact with my children or grandchildren, the least I can do is shout you dinner!' He valiantly rose to see me off for a 2.25 am ferry sailing, and we sat in my car for half an hour in the middle of the night, talking about all sorts of things – family memories, work problems, favourite desserts – while I waited to board.

On a later visit, I asked Grandpa what he'd like to do while we ate our ice-creams at the mall. A mischievous grin: 'Well, let's just ride up and down the escalators.'

Beyond the humour, Grandpa and I connected over our shared sadness and loss of family. He emailed me after seeing copies of the official Brethren photo books: 'I note the usual form, that you and I are both stricken from the record, as though we don't exist anymore.' We'd learnt to live with the possibility that old wounds might be opened unexpectedly, and – like Uncle Snow on the other side of my family – neither of us wanted to beat around the bush with one-sided communication. But it wasn't that we didn't still love those we'd lost.

In his own way, Grandpa quietly celebrated being able to build a relationship again with someone from his family. 'I'm not an emotional, demonstrative personality,' he told me. 'I don't jump up and down and say, "At last, I've found my long-lost grandson."' His reaction, as he arched an eyebrow, was much more understated: 'Well, this is a development that's worthwhile. I'm very pleased about this.'

*

As Grandpa lay dying, Kate, Lindy and I agonised over how and when to tell the Brethren side of the family. There was no predicting how they'd react; we'd heard horror stories about Brethren relatives swooping on deathbeds to assert control one last time. On the other hand, it was respectful to let them know. And how could we demand they tell us about our Brethren loved ones if we didn't afford them the same courtesy? 'I'm feeling it's important to let them know soon,' wrote Lindy in an email suggesting we break the news to Grandpa's son. 'Shall I call Patrick?' And then, a short time later: 'I've called Patrick. He was good about it really.'

When I later called Mum to ask if she'd like to pay final respects to her dad, she wasn't interested. Grandpa's Brethren family had been absent in life for thirty-eight years, and now they were absent in death – all except Patrick.

George's son was the only Brethren family member who came to pay his respects. I found it bizarre to see Patrick at the hospital almost daily, after he'd effectively ignored his father for almost four decades. Lindy, Kate and I had to awkwardly explain to ICU staff why George's son was showing up but avoiding family conferences about end-of-life care that fell instead to a grandson and two nieces. Patrick – a bachelor in his fifties, somewhat of an anomaly in the Brethren – was polite yet distant. After their encounter during The Review, Grandpa had called him from time to time but had become fed up by the one-sided communication:

'Why am I always the one calling you? How come you never call me?'

'We'd call if we were worried about you.'

'How long would that take?'

'Oh, probably about five years.'

Grandpa, in a fit of frustration, had sat back to put Patrick to the test. Months had passed, and then a year, then two. The five-year threshold came and went. There was no call. Now, here was Patrick at Grandpa's deathbed, acting as though he cared about his dad. It left a bad taste in my mouth.

*

Grandpa George's apartment laid bare a life interrupted. There was food in the fridge, paperwork on his desk, and laundry waiting to be washed. He could have walked through the door at any moment and put the kettle on, digging through the cupboard for his famous chocolate biscuits.

Lindy, Kate and I felt like voyeurs as we spent two weeks dipping into the unsanitised pool of his life. There was barely room to move in his small man cave, dust flying as we dislodged boxes that hadn't moved for decades. Lindy's months-old son went in the bath because there was nowhere else for the baby carrier.

We were astonished to discover that Grandpa had meticulously recorded his entire life. He'd kept a carbon copy of every letter, printed every important email and even made notes of important telephone conversations; all were methodically dated, sometimes with additional reflective notes. The past came alive through yellowed diaries, press clippings and photographs. It was all there: George's troubled childhood with a widowed mother, his whirlwind courtship with Lottie and his brutal excommunication. There, too, were his parents' life records: Alf and Ruth's courtship letters, journals, scribblings, and the agony of Alf's death when George was a child.

Even earlier letters told stories of George's own grandfather's excommunication and the chaos it had wrought; stories of family members who had joined a fledgling religious movement back in England two hundred years ago, believing in it so strongly that they travelled as missionaries and ended up in New Zealand. A cacophonous ghostly chorus shouted from the pages with grief, pain and joy.

EPILOGUE

BRUCE HALES JNR HAS CONTINUED TO REWRITE EXCLUSIVE Brethren history. The Brethren have returned to The System launched by his father and uncle in the 1960s, with a strong focus on business strategy. Members are told that Big Jim Taylor was lied to about the Hales brothers in 1965 and that 'all those deep convictions at the time were wrong'. These days, the Brethren run their own retirement-saving schemes and have launched members-only supermarkets. They'll eat with outsiders in a business context if it's required, although eating with them socially is still strictly forbidden. Generally, the church seems to put profit over principle. In an interview, a recent leaver tells me how poorer members are looked down on: 'There is a definite caste system in the Exclusive Brethren.'

Like many other religious groups, the Brethren were forced onto Zoom when Covid lockdowns meant they couldn't gather in their meeting rooms, which this recent leaver says 'gave rise to more control': 'Previously anyone could pick up the microphone and say something, but you can't really do that on Zoom – you have to notify the host and wait for someone to unmute you.

And of course the people hosting the Zoom meetings are Hales loyalists.' During the pandemic, virtual appearances by Bruce Hales were tightly controlled, with the Brethren 'paranoid in the extreme' about the Man of God's utterances being leaked to the outside world.

One unexpected twist of the Covid Zoom era was that members could return to Big Jim's 1960s practice of drinking whisky during services. When I asked the recent leaver what alcohol consumption was like in the Brethren these days, their response was blunt: 'Pretty horrific, if I'm honest.' One member in the UK was shamed for serving Johnnie Walker Red Label Scotch whisky to Hales instead of the top-shelf Blue Label: 'It went around the community as one of the stories of "you don't do this". Bruce had to have only the most gold-plated alcohol.' Back in New Zealand, a current member tells me about the rise of a Brethren social phenomenon known as The Guzzle, where dozens of young members meet up 'to get drunk' between Sunday afternoon church services: 'Heavy drinking runs rampant in the Brethren.'

There's been a steady stream of contact from Brethren members since I made my escape. Some want advice about leaving, some share information that helps expose the sect's practices, and others just need a sympathetic ear. 'I feel so trapped and lonely in here,' writes one member, who feels they can't leave because they're caring for an elderly parent. Another member describes their discomfort at hearing Bruce Hales 'ridicule' someone for their native accent, while a great-grandmother in her eighties looks back with grief and regret on a life lived within Brethren confines: 'What could have been a pleasant life, I can only dream and imagine. Instead, I have felt very lonely and insecure.' She reminds me of Aunty Anna. There's a deep sadness to some of these messages from people who know their lives could have been so much happier.

*

The Exclusive Brethren aggressively attack those who cross them. In April 2022, at a special church meeting in London, Bruce Hales spoke at length about how the Brethren 'live with resistance' and described the many letters he received criticising Brethren practices: 'They're probably thinking of that saying that said the pen is mightier than the sword, or something. Well, I'd rather them come across and have a sword fight, as long as I had about a month's practice.'

In 2021, investigative reporter Nicky Hager revealed the Brethren had been using a controversial private spy agency to keep tabs on former members in New Zealand. He detailed how the agency 'built dossiers on at least 20 ex-members', combining information from social media with public records and on-the-ground monitoring: 'The private investigators have watched ex-Brethren from cars and parked surveillance vans and have taken photographs of people entering and leaving their homes.'

In Australia, the Brethren have turned to other means to try and shut down critical reporting. In a report for Melbourne's *The Age* newspaper in 2017, investigations editor Michael Bachelard described how the Brethren's former spokesman, Tony

McCorkell, made him an offer to stop his reporting, including an all-expenses-paid trip to New Caledonia. Bachelard has been a persistent critic of the sect; his 2008 book, *Behind the Exclusive Brethren*, is a comprehensive review of their business and political activities. McCorkell was also instrumental in a scheme to pay Bachelard a 'six-figure sum' to stop him from writing about the group but ultimately decided that such a strategy would likely 'achieve the exact opposite' of what was intended.

Bruce Hales has learnt the hard way that scrutiny can't be avoided. In June 2012, the Charity Commission for England and Wales declined to grant charitable status to the Preston Down Trust, an Exclusive Brethren charity running church meeting rooms, finding that the sect's doctrine and practices contained elements of 'detriment and harm' – in an echo of the commission's 1970s inquiry into the Brethren, which had concluded that the doctrine of separation was 'harsh and harmful'.

In their attempt to retain charitable status in the UK, the Brethren published a new 'Faith in Practice' charter. Trust deeds were updated to reflect this document, which outlines how the Brethren will supposedly care for the welfare of excommunicated members: 'Where persons seek to leave the community, reasonable assistance should be afforded to them in terms of support and/ or financial assistance relating to employment or other matters, where they have been dependent on the community for that support.'

The Faith in Practice document also states that the Brethren principle of separation 'permits inter-personal communication and social interaction with non-Brethren (including former Brethren)'. Members and recent leavers I speak with dismiss this as a 'legal fiction' and 'not accurate'. One person still in the church tells me, 'Anyone who was found to be associating with outsiders with any friendliness or familiarity would be quickly alienated from the social lives of other Brethren.'

But the lofty promises were enough for the commission: charitable status was restored to the Preston Down Trust in January 2014.

Later that year, in October 2014, the Brethren launched a charitable arm called the Rapid Relief Team, with international branches soon popping up around the world. Brethren volunteers now distribute food parcels to disaster victims, raise funds for homeless shelters and provide free catering to emergency services. 'A good amount of it is political, basically,' says a recent leaver, who tells me that the Rapid Relief Team is little more than a publicity stunt. They now describe themselves worldwide as the Plymouth Brethren Christian Church, and a member laughs when I ask why: 'They needed the rebrand.'

Behind closed doors, Brethren members know that what is promised to outside investigators and what is practised within the church are two different things. In leaked notes from a March 2022 meeting in Sydney, Bruce Hales explicitly forbids his followers from interacting with 'persons that are opposing the truth', despite the assurances given to British charity commission investigators. 'We can't have anything to do with them,' Hales is quoted as saying at that meeting. 'You don't greet them, don't even greet them; don't have to, there's no obligation to do it.'

*

My shared experience with my cousin Lindy had deepened when her own younger brother was excommunicated in 2019. Braden had faced intense pressure for having sporadic contact with her while he was still in the church, and Bruce Hales said publicly that Braden would be better off killing himself than continuing with the 'rotten poison' of having contact with 'someone who's under discipline and opposed ... He'd be better to take arsenic, or go and get some rat poison or something, take a bottle of it.' Aunty Gwen, excommunicated for her careless arsenic joke, must have turned in her grave. But this, to Hales, was the logical extension of his public advice when I was a teen: 'Better to die than to go on sinning.' It was, the Man of God added, speaking to hundreds of Brethren gathered in the UK city of Sutton in June 2015, 'Better to finish yourself off that way than having to do with the opponents of the truth.' He didn't seem concerned that Braden could follow in the footsteps of Martin Lawson, Roger Panes and the many others – including Bruce's own great-aunt Eva Hales – who had been driven to suicide by the cruelty of Exclusive Brethren doctrine. The advice was printed and distributed to tens of thousands of members worldwide.

Lindy and I often talk about whether it's possible for us to overcome the trauma of our Brethren background. We don't know what the future holds or how we'll react to inevitable events like the death of a parent. Lindy says that becoming a mother dramatically shifted how she felt about her Brethren experience, making it much harder for her to understand how anyone could cut off their own child. But, she adds, there are no regrets: 'Living in the Brethren was like being forced to live in monochrome, and then when you leave it's like being able to live in colour. Sure, there is ugliness and hard things out here, but there's also creativity and beauty, and you're free to engage and live according to what you believe is right. And that's an incredible feeling.'

Most casual observers would say I've moved on. I've travelled the world, built a career, fallen in and out of love, and run the gamut of life. I'm happy and independent, and loving it. Yet the memories of my Brethren experience hover in my periphery. The smell of fresh baking reminds me of Mum in the kitchen, cooking dinner while juggling seven children and still getting us to church on time. Old gospel songs trigger something deep inside, even though I've long since stopped believing the words. Memories rush back of Mum singing 'The Blackboard of My Heart' to us kids. Hot, silent tears seem to come from nowhere – grief, yes, but it's hard to pinpoint. Tears, so many, many tears, stream over blackboards and permanent ink.

Jill Mytton, a British psychologist and fellow former Brethren member, tells me it's probably not possible to fully forget loved ones, 'but we can perhaps learn to bracket off the pain and longing'. To illustrate the lifelong impact, Jill draws on the writings of the nineteenth-century poet and author Edmund Gosse, who himself had a Brethren upbringing. In his book *Father and Son*, Gosse describes his ordeal with a deeply religious father as being like a plant in a pot struggling to grow around a large rock placed upon it. 'It really struck me,' says Jill, who swaps out the rock for a pile of pebbles in therapy sessions, 'because you can never take a rock off in one go, you take it off in bits ... One by one new shoots start to grow, but even as you take all the pebbles off, if that's possible, in the centre of that plant there's always going to be damage. You can't get rid of the scarring, but you don't actually need to, because the plant can still grow strong and tall and powerful and colourful.'

Jill is in her seventies and has become a good friend of mine. She listens patiently as I pepper her with questions about what this means for my future: 'Do you think it's ever really possible to move past that Brethren trauma, or is it something that we're stuck with for life?' Jill remarks on a beautiful sunset from her English cottage, and I look out my own window to see the sun rising over Auckland's misty volcanic cones. We're at opposite ends, both literally and metaphorically. Jill's decades of training and experience mean she's quite sure of her answer: 'We're stuck with it for life, I think.'

*

Mum and Dad's fervent faith feels like an alien world now, a dim reminder of strange beliefs I once shared. They don't feel like my parents anymore. When I called Mum on another visit to Invercargill five years after our hospice meeting, she no longer recognised my voice. I told her I was in town if she and Dad would like to catch up. 'Probably not,' she said. She promised to let me know either way, but never called back. On the same trip, I took a long shot and messaged my youngest sister, Bella, on LinkedIn; she blocked me without replying.

It's been more than sixty years since Grandma Lottie threatened to return George's ring. She's alive, although I haven't seen her for nearly fifteen years. Her grey hair has faded to white, but I hear she's still a commanding presence, not taking any nonsense from her children. Pictures show her beaming with that broad Irish smile of her father's, belying the great sadness that she too has experienced. Lottie stayed loyal to the Brethren, but in the process she lost her husband – the charming, cheeky student she'd fallen in love with as a teen, when they promised to spend the rest of their lives together. A 'widow for the truth', she kept wearing George's ring for decades after his excommunication, not giving up hope that one day they might be reunited. Now George is gone, and Lottie has finally taken off his ring.

George's sister Anna has broken free in her own sad way. After years of emotional torture, her once-brilliant mind has succumbed to dementia, and she's living in a care facility in Auckland.

For the first time in many years, I'm able to visit Aunty Anna without the Brethren getting in the way. To my surprise she remembers who I am – even though she's a shell of her former self – and her brown eyes sparkle with joy as she sets about making introductions to a fellow resident: 'It's Craig! Come and meet Craig Hoyle!'

Anna remembers I've left the Brethren and listens avidly as I tell her about trekking through the Amazon, seeing the Queen and reporting from protests in Hong Kong. Her short-term memory has disintegrated, and I tell the same stories over and over; she's equally fascinated by each telling: 'You've had such an interesting life!' She tells me she's struggling to remember things. Picture boards across the wall display dozens of Brethren children, grandchildren and great-grandchildren. Anna's vague on who they all are but remembers her granddaughter Lindy, even though her picture's missing: 'Oh Lindy, I loved her dearly, please give her my love.'

Poor Anna spent her life between a rock and a hard place: she never agreed with Brethren teachings yet felt powerless to break free. But there were silver linings, as I'm reminded when I notice a picture from her sixtieth wedding anniversary. Tongue in cheek, I ask if she's still in love with Uncle Rob, and she beams and says, 'Even more so than ever.' Anna tells me she's still a Brethren member and wrinkles her forehead when I ask if that's what she wants to be. She replies, 'Well, I do what my husband says, and he's with the Brethren, so that's where I am too.' I nod in understanding, quietly pleased that Anna still doesn't have a good word to say about the Brethren.

Two centuries have passed since Sam Childs was first attracted to a fledgling religious movement in England. I wonder what my great-great-great-great-grandfather would make of it all: the missionaries, the excommunications, the demands for blind loyalty – two hundred years of a family divided, with both sides convinced of their truth. Now, Lindy's children will likely grow up not knowing their grandparents, an eighth generation affected by Brethren dogma. When Lindy and I reflect on that intergenerational trauma – eight generations of grief and loss – she takes a long pause and stares into the distance before she says, 'It makes me deeply sad that the fingers of this group have been able to reach across so many generations, and leave such huge claw marks and disfigurement across families. I'm still confused at how intelligent people can remain so deeply enmeshed within such an abusive system.'

I nod and reply, 'It's so complicated as well. It's not just one arc. Like our great-grandparents Alf and Ruth deciding to go back, after having spent most of their lives criticising the Exclusive Brethren, and the cognitive dissonance that has run through the generations.'

Alf and Ruth's grave lies in an unkempt corner of Wellington's Karori Cemetery, tucked into a non-aligned hillside between the Anglicans and Catholics. Weeds grow through cracks in the concrete, and a ten-foot pittosporum clings to its vantage point inside a neighbouring grave. I sit and ponder on a sunny summer afternoon. How would Alf feel about the Brethren's strict separation doctrine? Did Ruth ever regret cutting off all her siblings? Would they even recognise what the Brethren have become? How would they feel about the secret correspondence between Anna, their bright-eyed daughter, and George, their excommunicated son? Ruth's decisions still ripple across much earlier decisions from her parents, grandparents and great-grandparents.

My journey of family discovery has lasted years. Using Grandpa George's meticulous records as a springboard, I've collected documents and photographs, pieced together conflicting accounts, and interviewed dozens of relatives and former Brethren members, trying to make sense of it all. There's poignant grief among those I speak with, but also joy. Hundreds of pages of transcripts contain more laughter than tears. 'You could actually write quite an interesting book on it,' says my great-uncle Alan, Lottie's younger brother, when we reflect on how generations of Brethren stories weave together in a complex tapestry. 'Maybe you will one day!'

*

It's summer when Lindy and I trek up Te Ahūmairangi Hill to pay our respects to George eighteen months after the blustery winter's day when we scattered his ashes. The dirt track is dry, and a tree canopy muffles the noise of the city below. The wind blasts through up here, just as it did when George's dad Alf was a radio operator on this hill all those years ago.

Lindy's young son, named in George's honour, is a cheeky two-year-old in a blue sunhat and George-style brown woollen vest. Unimpressed by this impromptu outing, he makes his feelings known – he has no idea yet that he's been named after the man whose former apartment stands on a hillside opposite.

The radio station where Alf worked has long since gone, but a towering sentinel pine keeps silent watch and casts dappled shade as we stand in the shadows of our family history. These are the same hills where Alf and Ruth walked together and agonised over whether to return to the church of their upbringing. Now this is their son George's final resting place, and he's finally beyond reach of the Exclusive Brethren.

Our family's roots have continued to sprawl. I've become a sperm donor, sending tendrils tumbling in directions that would have been unthinkable to our forebears. A counsellor at the clinic asked if I was prepared for children to emerge unexpectedly in coming decades, and I laughed, thinking of the parallels with how I'd gone searching for Grandpa: 'Family complications are something I've lived with my whole life.'

Two centuries of grief and loss fade into the background on Te Ahūmairangi Hill. We're here because we've broken the cycle; the next generation will grow up free of Exclusive Brethren dogma.

Grandpa's young namesake twinkles with curiosity as he looks across the valley, pointing at something that's caught his attention.

'Isn't he just like George?'

ENDNOTES

Chapter 2.
'a modest length': Handbook, Aurora School, 2003.
They couldn't deviate from the rules in the handbook: Ibid.
a London elder called Mr Giles attempted to raise the alarm: J.S. Giles,
    'Recent Teaching and its Effects', 1 October 1920.

Chapter 4.
'In you, Lord my God, I put my trust': Bible, New International Version,
    Psalm 25:1.

Chapter 6.
'Yet the firm foundation of God stands, having this seal …': Bible, Darby
    Translation, 2 Timothy 2:19–21.
'We knocked. Ruth opened the door …': E. Amosa, *Emmeline: The First
    80 Years*, Copy Press, 2007.

Chapter 7.
*Elders shouted at Elsie and Winifred … leaving them 'crying and shaking
    with fear'*: D. Burgess, *The People* newspaper, March 1968.
'Without are the dogs, and the sorcerers …': Bible, Darby Translation,
    Revelation 22:15.
'You bum, you. You big bum …': J. Taylor Jr, reading at Aberdeen,
    25 July 1970.
'At the ministry meeting, Mr Taylor …': W.T. Petersen, letter to Robert
    Stott, 5 October 1970.

Chapter 8.
'Never accept yourself for who you are': Craig Hoyle, 'Leaving the
Exclusive Brethren: 10 years on', *Sunday* magazine, 9 February
2020.

Chapter 9.
'For thy sake we are put to death …': Bible, Darby Translation, Romans
8:35–39.
'Again therefore Jesus spoke to them …': Bible, Darby Translation, John
8:12.

Chapter 10.
'Why should you drink a gallon of wine …': J.H. Symington, 3-day
meetings at Redbridge, 23 November 1973.
'a harsh and harmful doctrine': Charity Commission, Statement to
Members of Parliament, 11 May 1976.
'Sue the bastards': J.H. Symington, 3-day meetings at Auckland,
26 November 1977.

Chapter 11.
'Hurt 'em, hurt 'em; hurt somebody …': J.S. Hales, address at Adelaide,
19 February 1964.
'Some men, we go in their offices …': J.S. Hales, reading at Whangārei,
27 March 1964.
'It's a matter of self-control …': J.S. Hales, 3-day meetings at Wagga
Wagga, 8 September 1973.
It tore strips off members for their repeated rule-breaking …: B.D. Hales,
letter 'To The Beloved Brethren', 5 May 2003.
'Mr Hales said only two thousand "silver" books have been sold …': Notes
from business meeting at Oasis, 5 January 2009.

Chapter 12.
'evil communications corrupt good manners': Bible, Darby Translation,
1 Corinthians 15:33.

'Smooth were the milky words of his mouth ...': Bible, Darby Translation, Psalm 55:21.

'Judge not, that ye may not be judged': Bible, Darby Translation, Matthew 7:1.

Chapter 13.

'You lost everything by coming out ...': 'Exclusive', *60 Minutes*, TV3, 7 December 2009.

'How does it feel being back?': Ibid.

I dialled local priest Frank Moore for a recorded conversation ...: Ibid.

'You prescribed Cyprostat to a healthy ...': 'Biggest Cult', *Today Tonight*, Channel Seven, 7 March 2010.

'So I'm playing into the hands of the devil ...': Ibid.

'basic patient examination and care ...': Professional Standards Committee, Findings of inquiry into Dr Mark Christopher James Craddock, 23 August 2012.

Epilogue

Bruce Hales spoke at length about how the Brethren 'live with resistance ...': B.D. Hales, fellowship meeting at London, 24 April 2022.

In 2021, investigative reporter Nicky Hager revealed ...: N. Hager, '"We had vehicles outside the house": Exclusive Brethren used Thompson and Clark to spy on ex-members', RNZ, 20 April 2021.

Michael Bachelard described how the Brethren's former spokesman, Tony McCorkell ...: M. Bachelard, 'Potential witness in Exclusive Brethren sex abuse case paid to remain silent', Stuff.co.nz, 29 October 2017.

'six-figure sum' ... *'achieve the exact opposite'*: Ibid.

'detriment and harm': Charity Commission for England and Wales, 'Preston Down Trust: Application for registration of the Preston Down Trust – Decision of the Commission', 3 January 2014.

'harsh and harmful': Charity Commission, Statement to Members of Parliament, 11 May 1976.

'Where persons seek to leave the community ...': Charity Commission
for England and Wales, 'Preston Down Trust: Application
for registration of the Preston Down Trust – Decision of the
Commission', 3 January 2014.
Bruce Hales explicitly forbids his followers ...: B.D. Hales, reading in
Sydney, 19 March 2022.
Bruce Hales said publicly that Braden would be better off ...: B.D. Hales,
fellowship meeting at Sutton, 9 June 2015.
'Better to finish yourself off that way ...': Ibid.

BIBLIOGRAPHY

Adams, N. *Goodbye, Beloved Brethren.* Impulse Publications Ltd, 1972.

Aebi-Mytton, J. *A narrative exploration of the lived experience of being born, raised in, and leaving a cultic group: the case of the Exclusive Brethren.* DPsych thesis, Middlesex University / Metanoia Institute, 2018.

Amosa, E. *Emmeline: The First 80 Years.* Copy Press, 2007.

Bachelard, M. *Behind the Exclusive Brethren.* Scribe Publications Pty Ltd, 2008.

Bachelard, M. 'Potential witness in Exclusive Brethren sex abuse case paid to remain silent', Stuff.co.nz, 29 October 2017.

Charity Commission, Statement to Members of Parliament, 11 May 1976.

Charity Commission for England and Wales. 'Preston Down Trust: Application for registration of the Preston Down Trust – Decision of the Commission'. 3 January 2014.

Childs, S. Personal collection.

Darby, J. N. *The Collected Writings of John Nelson Darby.* G. Morrish, 1879–1883.

Gosse, E. *Father and Son: A study of two temperaments.* Heinemann, 1907.

Hager, N. *The Hollow Men.* Craig Potton Publishing, 2006.

Hager, N. '"We had vehicles outside the house": Exclusive Brethren used Thompson and Clark to spy on ex-members'. RNZ, 20 April 2021.

Hayward, A.E. & R.A. Personal collection.

Hayward, G.B. Personal collection.

Hoyle, C.B. Personal collection.
Hurley, B. 'Exclusive Brethren: Sect's secretive leader tells followers to drink rat poison'. *Stuff*, 10 April 2016.
Jacomb, B.R. Personal collection.
Lineham, P.J. *The 1956 Auckland Crisis in the Exclusive Brethren and the Shaping of Taylorism*. Brethren Historical Review 11:61–75.
Lineham, P.J. *The Significance of J.G. Deck 1807–1884*. Christian Brethren Research Fellowship Journal, 1986.
Lineham, P.J. *There We Found Brethren*. GPH Society Ltd, 1977.
Nason, J. *Joy and Sorrow*. Port Campbell Press, 2016.
Peebs.net. *Memorial Project*. Web archive, 2009.

ACKNOWLEDGEMENTS

When commissioning editor Holly Hunter first approached me about writing a book, I was hesitant. Holly's vision and encouragement helped get me over the line, and her support over the past few years has been greatly appreciated. Editor Kate Goldsworthy did a fantastic job of tightening and improving the manuscript. Likewise, senior inhouse editor Madeleine James, who brought a fresh pair of eyes on the home stretch. Holly, Kate and Madeleine were crucial in turning a sprawling idea into something understandable.

My cousin Lindy Jacomb was a huge support. Lindy checked everything chapter by chapter, providing detailed input on how to represent our family through this deeply personal project. I'm also grateful to Deb Ghinn, Ian McKay and Ginette Whitten-Day, who read through the manuscript and provided feedback and fact-checking.

Writing this book while working full-time at the *Sunday Star-Times* came with challenges, and I'm grateful to my colleagues for their support. Editor Tracy Watkins, one of the best bosses I've had, allowed as much time and flexibility as was needed, which made things so much easier. I'd also like to thank my colleague and fellow author Kelly Dennett for her advice and reassurance.

To my friends and family: I'm looking forward to spending more time with you again! This has been a massive undertaking, and I've spent holidays with documents sprawled over the table, doing interviews, and tapping away on a seemingly never-ending collection of notes. I'm grateful to Sarah Hall and her husband, Grant, who always believed I would write a book, and offered a rural writing retreat when I needed to get away from the city. And I'm especially grateful to my partner, Ryan, who has graciously never complained about my disappearance down the rabbit hole.

Dozens of fellow former Brethren contributed to this book; it wouldn't have been possible without them. These people generously shared their records and memories and allowed me to explore what was often a deeply painful past. They brought a richness for which I am grateful. I'd like to honour Aunty Gwen, Uncle Snow and Uncle Charles, who have died since the events described in these chapters – and also Uncle Alan, who knew I was writing a book but did not live to see it published.

Special tribute goes to those still in the Brethren who helped with my research. These people provided corroboration and background, often at danger to themselves, knowing they risked excommunication as traitors if found to be in contact with an 'evil opposer' like me. Some of these people have since escaped; others remain trapped in the sect by circumstances beyond their control. I think of you often.

This book is dedicated to Grandpa George, whose meticulous records helped launch my exploration. Grandpa paid the ultimate price, losing his family for holding true to his convictions. We remember you with admiration and love.